ROMAN
BODY
ARMOUR

ROMAN BODY ARMOUR

HILARY & JOHN TRAVIS

AMBERLEY

This edition first published 2012

Amberley Publishing
The Hill, Stroud
Gloucestershire, GL5 4EP

www.amberleybooks.com

British Library Cataloguing in Publication Data.
A catalogue record for this book is available from the British Library.

ISBN 978-1-4456-0803-7

Typeset in 10pt on 12pt Sabon.
Typesetting and Origination by Amberley Publishing.
Printed in Great Britain.

CONTENTS

LIST OF TABLES

LIST OF ILLUSTRATIONS

LIST OF COLOUR PLATES

ACKNOWLEDGEMENTS

This book has been the result of a team effort with my husband, J. R. Travis, who has not only provided most of the photography and illustrations, but who has also modelled the reconstructed Kalkriese *lorica segmentata*.

I should like to acknowledge the assistance of Dr Philip Freeman, of the University of Liverpool, for his encouragement and ceaseless editing and re-editing of the following text. I should also like to thank Georgina Plowright (Corbridge Museum) and Lindsay Allason-Jones (Newcastle University Museum), for allowing full access to the finds from the Corbridge Hoard and facilities for their examination and reassessment. Similarly, I should like to thank Robin Birley for his advice and time, and for access to material from Vindolanda. I should like to thank Susanna Wilbers-Rost of the Kalkriese Museum, Germany, for supplying literature, information and scaled photographic images of the finds from the Kalkriese excavations.

I should also like to thank the members of the Deva V. Victrix (Chester Guard) Roman Living History Group who agreed to be photographed in their various first-century AD personas, and some of whom may also recognise themselves depicted within the following artist's representations.

Mostly, I should like to dedicate this book to the late J. R. Travis Snr ('Lord of the Rings') for both his assistance in winding and cutting mail links, and for his knowledge and experience as a retired member of the Life Guard cavalry.

I

INTRODUCTION

BACKGROUND TO THE RESEARCH

This book arose out of a perceived weakness in current studies of Roman military equipment. Although the study of the Roman military is not a new subject (the earliest work, dating back to the sixteenth century, being based on surviving Greek and Roman literary works and the descriptions of events and lives of individuals), the study of Roman military equipment only really commenced from the eighteenth century. However, this was still desk-bound study, based on sculptural rather than artefactual evidence (for the most part using imagery from Trajan's Column) to produce two-dimensional graphical reconstructions, with no attempt at testing the designs for materials, methods of manufacture, or field-testing the practicalities of use (for example, von Groller, 1901a; 1901b).

By the mid-twentieth century, reconstruction was based on archaeological evidence, although these were in many cases based on illustrations rather than first-hand examination. The new phenomenon of living history re-enactment initially arose out of groups of individuals with a passing interest in history for amusement at village fêtes. Although dressing up in historical costumes at village fêtes was a popular Victorian pastime, the current trend for Roman re-enactment can be seen to originate with the Ermine Street Guard. The group was founded in 1971 to make a one-off appearance at a historical pageant organised by the local vicar to promote the history of the village of Witcombe, Gloucestershire, and with the hope of raising funds for a new village hall (the founder members reconstructing their first eight suits of Roman armour, including plastic helmets, based on the early work of H. Russell-Robinson). The popularity of the event then led to further appearances, with the Ermine Street Guard now being the oldest Roman re-enactment group, with some of its earliest founder members still actively participating (Bill Mayes, founder member ESG, personal communication [pers. comm. hereafter], Stoneleigh Festival of History, 2003).

With public appreciation of this bit of fun, there was a desire to improve costumes for future performances, which developed into passionate study by many amateur enthusiasts (which continues to this day). Subsequent copies of academic replicas by some re-enactors have 'field-tested' reconstruction equipment, although using modern rather than authentic materials. However, the equipment produced by others is often over-engineered, to minimise maintenance or to maximise commercial profit (using modern factory mass-production machinery), their copies perpetuating inaccuracies of earlier copies. Now, by the twenty-first century, academic reconstructions have come almost full circle, with their reconstructions, although now three-dimensional, being desk-top based, executed on computer (CGI), and not tested by actual reconstruction (Bishop, 2002). Unfortunately, this approach to reconstruction does not test the feasibility of designs for the human factor (whether these designs are actually wearable or practicable in general use).

Modern research is currently segregated into two factions: academic and 'amateur' (mostly re-enactors). Unfortunately, there is little crossover between the two groups. They rarely combine their efforts, mostly through mutual mistrust, with the academic view of re-enactors being that they are the 'nutty fringe'. They do not see them as a wealth of untapped enthusiasm, skills and resources (many having connections in commercial/industrial sectors with access to materials, machinery and skilled craftsmen, where most academics are generally unskilled and only have access to books) and as an opportunity to field-test theories. Furthermore, recent changes in legislation have given specific exemptions to re-enactors (but not to academics) to permit the manufacture and use of armour and weaponry (for example Criminal Justice Act 1988, Section 141–11E; Statutory Instruments 2008 – CJA 1988 (Offensive Weapons) (Amendment) Order 2008). This then makes it all the more important that academics should review their relationships with re-enactors in order to legitimise their future research, grasping the opportunity to maximise their efforts, by sharing resources and findings.

The purpose of this study was therefore to address these issues by returning to basics, reviewing wherever possible the available original archaeological evidence (to identify those features not appearing in published photographs and illustrations). Where access to artefacts was not possible, the original illustrations and publications were critically reviewed, to consider any possible anomalies. This research was then used to physically reconstruct replicas, with methods and material as close as possible to that used in antiquity (the reconstruction of several of these replica items are featured in the following chapters). These were then tested 'in the field', with the co-operation of members of the re-enactment community, to identify any problems with design and areas of weakness in everyday use or combat situations.

As the Roman army existed for over a millennium, the basic components of its defensive armour assemblage would have been subject to continal improvement and adaptation to its current conditions and requirements. As the Romans did not exclusively invent and develop armour, each piece of equipment would have had a history beyond that of the Roman army, and consequently it was necessary to view the pre-Roman origins as part of the bigger picture.

By establishing therefore the basic chronology of the origins of the Roman army and of its equipment, following this through time to view developments and innovations in equipment design, in comparison to contemporary events and the changing political and organizational climate, it is possible to theorise on possible reasons for the introduction of many design changes. The term 'changes' here is perhaps more appropriate than 'innovation', as not all 'changes' were necessarily improvements. The chronological changes noted in the panoply are then also echoed in the changing social structure of the army, with expansion of the boundaries of eligibility for military service and the transition from independently funded volunteers to a modern, paid professional army.

THE STUDY OF ROMAN MILITARY EQUIPMENT

The study of the past is as old as the past itself, with the Roman historians of our classical literature reflecting on their own ancient origins. As our literary sources exist now as written reflections, this gives the appearance that their primary interest had been the political and social interactions of individuals, rather than visual imagery. However, even in the Roman period, imagery was used on wall paintings (as seen at Pompeii) depicting images from mythology, and presumably also from more ancient histories. This imagery would, however, have been based on contemporary styles of buildings, clothing and weaponry, with the exception of some classical Greek-style idealised armour for representations of deities. This tendency to make use of contemporary styles of dress for subjects from the distant past can be seen still to exist in more recent periods, where the artists (or their intended audience) were perhaps unable to comprehend the passage of time.

Up to the seventeenth century, therefore, figures in the past, including those of the Roman period, were portrayed artistically dressed in a style contemporary with the artist. An example of this is the portrait of William the Conqueror, commissioned by the Vatican in 1522 on the reopening of his tomb, where he is depicted in a sixteenth-century costume (half a millennium after his death), a copy of which still exists at St Etienne (Wood, 1981, 243, plate 29). Similarly, from the sixteenth century, engravings by Andreas Alciati (*Emblemata*, 1581) depict Roman soldiers dressed in costumes of that period, but in a style which suggests a time of culture and grace, in much the same way that the Romans themselves appear to have viewed the culture of classical Greece in their own artistic representations (Feugère, 2002, 19).

However, during the eighteenth and nineteenth centuries, following the discoveries in Herculaneum and Pompeii and the introduction of neoclassicism, artists began to portray the Roman soldier in more authentic dress, basing their views on images from ceremonial sculptures such as Trajan's Column. This can be seen in the engravings by Saint Sauveur in 1787, by Rich in his *Dictionary of Roman Antiquities* in 1861 (Feugère, 2002, 20), and even into the twentieth century by Couissin (1926), although these still depict an image of artificially genteel culture and not one of battle-hardened professional soldiers who had in their time conquered half of the known world.

A more enlightened attempt at authenticity, using both sculptural and archaeological evidence, can be credited to Jacques Louis David (1748–1825) who painted a series of scenes with a Roman theme, including *The Oath of the Horatii*, the latter inspired by Corneille's tragedy *Horace*. As an example of neoclassicism, his painting depicts a frozen dramatic instant within a setting of Roman-style architecture. The clothing was based on imagery from wall paintings, as found at Pompeii, and the armour on sculptural representations, such as seen on Trajan's Column, so that, in his way, his depictions were as close as he felt possible to current (for his time) archaeological and sculptural evidence, although in a somewhat theatrical style. Other paintings in the series include *The Lictors Bring to Brutus the Bodies of his Sons* (1789), and *The Rape of the Sabines* (1799), painted from Livy's *Early History of Rome*, although these are of limited use in depicting military equipment, the former containing no armour and the latter depicting naked warriors armed with just helmets and weapons. Based on a study of available archaeological evidence, their purpose was not to depict historical events, but rather to echo contemporary events of the French Revolution, the artist himself being a member of the Convention which voted for the death of the French king (Lucie-Smith, 1971, 175–6).

Despite the work being carried out at Herculaneum and Pompeii, and at the forts along Hadrian's Wall, the early historians and antiquarians continued to use, as their main source of references for their image of the Roman soldier, images from gravestones, coins, small bronze and terracotta figurines, the Column of Marcus Aurelius and Trajan's Column. Of these, Trajan's Column was seen as the definitive image of the Roman army.

The development of what we would recognise today as 'real' archaeology commenced in the later nineteenth century (as opposed to the work of early antiquarian 'collectors'), with systematic and organised excavation of sites (such as those along the German *limes* from 1892 onwards). The publication of these excavations has then led to a greater knowledge-base upon which to build increasingly more plausible reconstructions.

Our current knowledge of the Roman military and its equipment is still nevertheless of an organic nature, constantly changing and updating with new finds, developing an expanding bank of available information, particularly over the past century. There have been many merit-worthy and pioneering works attempting to draw together the information current at the time, such as the work of Couissin. With the benefit of hindsight, building on the work of numerous subsequent individuals, we may raise a knowledgeable smile at the (now) 'quaintness' of his illustrations, but can we be sure that in future decades others may find our reconstructions equally risible.

With the discovery of a large quantity of military equipment at Carnuntum in 1899 (von Groller, 1901a; 1901b) and still more remains from Newstead in 1905–9 (Curle, 1911), it was possible to compare actual finds to the sculptural representations on Trajan's Column, and it was von Groller's conjectural reconstruction of this material which then formed the basis for Couisson's artwork. However, von Groller's interpretation was purely desk-based, untested in practical terms, as have been many subsequent reassessments by historians. It was not for another half century that this material would eventually be studied by someone with an extensive knowledge of the manufacture of armour, H. Russell-Robinson, Keeper of Arms at the Tower of London. In 1953 he was able to apply his knowledge of medieval and oriental armour to the Newstead and Carnuntum material to produce an initial and plausible reconstruction, which was on display for many years at the Grosvenor Museum at Chester. With the discovery of the Corbridge Hoard in 1964, comprising the well-preserved remains of up to sixteen different cuirasses, some partially assembled, we gained a sizeable and significant level of the necessary information. This then allowed Russell-Robinson in

1975 to build a credible and complete reconstruction of the *lorica segmentata* which is difficult to improve upon (Russell-Robinson, 1975), assisted by pre-reconstruction concept drawings by the historical artist/illustrator, Peter Connolly (1975).

The actual artefacts themselves, while solid, tactile and tangible, are often in fragile and fragmentary condition. With this as the only source of information it would be a similar situation to attempting to complete a jigsaw with half of the pieces missing and with the edges of all of the pieces frayed for added challenge. What is needed is a 'blueprint' of how all of the component parts interacted. The Corbridge Hoard, to a certain extent, provided Russell-Robinson with this blueprint, with sufficient recognisable components for him to be able to identify their interrelationships.

However, despite his evident experience in armour manufacture, his reconstruction was still limited in its scope by his lack of access to the actual finds, being confined to working with 2-D illustrations, and so falling victim to any inaccuracies within the published work. Similarly, Connolly, in his own published works (1975, 1977, 1978, 1981), graphically represents a vast range of equipment (used by not only Roman, but also Greek, Celtic, Carthaginian and early pan-Italic peoples, such as Samnite, Lucanian, Apulian, Etruscan/ Villanovan). With many items he attempts to show their current archaeological state, their component construction, and visualises their original use in combat context (pictorially bringing the subject to life in a format appealing to younger readers). In the case of the Corbridge material at least, however, this imagery was flawed by factors outside of his control, by reliance on published illustrations and lack of access to the original material.

The study of Roman military equipment, however, was not the sole reserve of Russell-Robinson, nor did it end with him. Neither was it confined to the study of material found in Britain, nor to English-speaking scholars. There has been a great deal of valuable work completed by historians and archaeologists worldwide before and since the 1970s. Major contributions include Bishop and Coulston (in addition to their invaluable individual works), whose *Roman Military Equipment from the Punic Wars to the Fall of Rome* (1993, and updated 2006) draws together information from across all time periods, from the Republic to Late Empire. Similarly significant are the works of Feugère, again spanning all time periods (2002); Junkelmann, for time and motion studies with reconstructed material (1986); Stephenson and Dixon, dealing with later Empire and cavalry equipment (2001 and 2003); James, for the study of military equipment remains from Dura-Europos (2004); and Stiebel and Magness, for the study of artifacts from Masada (2007).

Invaluable in the promotion of this field of study since the mid-1980s have been the annual Roman Military Equipment Conferences (ROMECs). These have provided a forum for sharing current information and ideas between scholars worldwide, cutting through the linguistic and cultural barriers which would otherwise distance their work. Their contributions are then disseminated to an even wider audience by publication of the ROMEC proceedings. This work then continues on a daily basis, through instant interchanges of ideas on internet chat forums such as RAT (Roman Army Talk), where questions can be raised and contributions made by both academics and amateurs alike.

However, as discussed, the work of many of these authors, while undoubtedly invaluable, is for the most part desktop-based, including some 3-D CGI imagery, with little or no interaction with the more 'amateur' manufacturers of reconstructed equipment, whereas the re-enactment contingent, through unquestioning reliance on the published material, continue to perpetuate and even exacerbate inaccuracies through copying other copies. Similarly, a demarcation can be seen between the works of the archaeologists and the historians, whose interest lies in the literal interpretation of the classical sources. This can then lead to differences of opinion between the solid evidence and the written descriptions, based on what is the current 'accepted' correct interpretation. These interpretations then vary through the decades, dependent on the current political climate, social biases and aspirations to political correctness, and even between the cultural backgrounds and personal biases of contemporary writers, so that the accepted 'history' of Rome of even a decade ago can merit avid disagreement today.

RECONSTRUCTION – THE ACADEMIC APPROACH *V.* THE RE-ENACTOR

With the possible exception of the body of men known as *Symmachiarii* (who fought with the absolute minimum of equipment, barefoot and stripped to the waist), almost all would use some form of body armour, perhaps *segmentata* (articulated plates), *hamata* (mail) or *squamata* (scale). Other items of basic 'kit' would include helmets, shields and a variety of fittings, utilities and accessories, and these will be discussed in subsequent publications.

This book, therefore, will consider the various types of body armour used by the Roman military, testing the processes of assembly through actual reconstructions, using materials as similar as possible to those of the originals. It is believed that this will aid in the identification of the component parts archaeologically as well as the identification of their assembly and/ or repair locations. In the case of the *lorica segmentata*, it was decided that the intended reconstruction would focus primarily on the earliest 'prototype' Kalkriese variant, this being the form least represented among current reconstructions and in need of greater discussion.

I have attempted to redress inconsistencies identified in the core publications by examination of the full range of material, from actual archaeological remains where possible, along with illustrations and photographic records of similar material and sculptural representations. The remains from Corbridge provide an example of every component part to be found in this *lorica* type, although not all from the same piece of armour. In view of the deteriorating condition of the Corbridge material, after over forty years in storage (which also gives rise to fears for the condition of the Carnuntum material if similarly stored now for over 100 years), it was hoped that further examination could still identify features not previously appreciated, polishing and improving on Russell-Robinson's original design.

The remains from Kalkriese, however, as with those from the later period 'Newstead' type, are fragmentary and do not include the full set of component parts. Any reconstruction therefore of either type (Kalkriese or Newstead) will always be to a certain extent conjectural. With close study of the construction methods employed in the Corbridge armour, it is feasible, however, to produce as closely as possible a speculative image. In the case of the Newstead-type *lorica*, a great deal of work has already been completed, as seen in the works of Russell-Robinson (Russell-Robinson, 1975, 179, fig. 181) and later by Bishop (2002, 54, fig. 6.6), although the latter version was only tested using computer simulation and not by actual reconstruction.

Prior to this study however, the Kalkriese *lorica* had never been reconstructed in any form, although more recently (and since the first appearance of my reconstruction detailed within this book on a now-redundant internet webpage), some conjectural images have again been produced by Bishop (2002, 28, fig. 4.7). With the apparent need for a closer study of the Kalkriese 'prototype' form of *lorica*, it was decided to attempt a full reconstruction, drawing on all of the available evidence. This therefore required a comprehensive examination of the Corbridge material to avoid the perpetuation of any possible inconsistencies in the published material. With the information derived from the physical remains, it was hoped to build more accurate reconstructions, using material matched as closely as possible to the originals (although in the case of the *lorica segmentata*, to extend those methods and features to the earliest prototype form, the Kalkriese).

Chapter II, therefore, will consider the sculptural and archaeological evidence for Roman segmental body armour (*lorica segmentata*), with Chapter III discussing methods of its construction, in particular reassessing the most significant finds from Corbridge, and the resulting reconstruction. It is also intended to discuss the evidence for its earliest prototype form, as found at Kalkriese, Germany, and to present my suggested reconstruction based on the results of the Corbridge reassessment (see plate section).

In addition to most common types of body armour, plate and mail (*lorica segmentata* and *hamata*), other types are also known, some of which date back to the early Republican period or even before, and could be seen as more 'traditional' than these later, more common forms. The different types in use include the muscle cuirass, scale (*lorica squamata*), and lamellar armour, along with variants on the ubiquitous mail (*hamata*): for example, mail

Fig. 1 Early reconstruction of Newstead-style *lorica segmentata* by H. Russell-Robinson. (*Grosvenor Museum, Chester*)

with *phalerae* and mail with scale (*lorica plumbata*). Although these less common forms in the later periods may appear to be exclusively used by higher-ranking soldiers (officer classes), historically (particularly at a time when the individual soldier supplied his own equipment) they could have been used by any rank.

This definition of officer is not just restricted to meaning high-ranking officers, but also lesser-ranking officers, including centurions, standard bearers, cornicenes and cavalry (for combat and sports/parade use), all of whom may have had resources to possess separate ceremonial armour. It is not absolutely clear whether purely ceremonial armour existed at all, with all armour potentially being used for combat purposes. The only known exception to this may be the late Roman ceremonial/parade armour (helmet and cuirass) from Egypt made from the skin of a crocodile, radio-carbon dated to the third or fourth century AD, from Manfalout, Egypt, now in the British Museum (EA5473). However, where potentially 'ceremonial' armour is used, it often exhibits archaic features possibly derived from Greco-Etruscan influences. Subsequent chapters, therefore, will discuss these various additional types of body protection, their origins, developmental progression and possible identity of user.

It is hoped through reconstruction, replicating as closely as possible the end product, to consider different possible methods of manufacture and construction, and through study of simulated wear determine the implications for the need for field repairs and possible reasons for developmental changes in armour types. As with the *lorica segmentata*, reconstructions were also made of mail (*hamata*) to test the methodology of construction, 'time and motion' of the processes involved, and the quantities of materials necessary. Although both of the words 'mail' and 'chainmail' are commonly used for this type of armour, purists prefer the former as being the correct terminology. For the sake of consistency, therefore, the term 'mail' has been used throughout the book. All reconstructions were then field-tested for durability and to identify areas of potential wear damage (although only in 'living history' re-enactment situations – never in true, full-on, life-threatening battle combat conditions for obvious health and safety reasons, and lack of volunteers willing to fight to the death for the purposes of academic research).

Although further examination can still identify additional features not previously discovered, polishing and improving on Russell-Robinson's original design, we still have to recognise the limitations. The reconstruction of one item of equipment is not the whole picture, no matter how accurate. We also need to view that piece in relation to who owned it, how it co-ordinated and accessorised with other equipment, its intended use, the status and function of the owner and how he came to possess it. This book therefore not only attempts to draw together the streams of available evidence, but also to consider the limitations to the quality of this evidence. The artefact, and the context of its discovery, can aid in some way, but ideally we need expert, first-hand contemporary evidence. In the absence of a living, breathing Roman, the closest we can find to this is provided by literary sources and sculptural representations, these being primary evidence from first-hand living witnesses.

THE SOURCES OF EVIDENCE

Although this study will primarily focus on the body armour of the Roman army of the Imperial period, it is also necessary to consider events and equipment of earlier periods in order to understand its origins, developmental sequences and the reasons for change. The literary sources therefore, despite any minor variation in interpretation of events, provide us with the basis for this study, with historical writings that build a basic chronology of events which can help to explain the social and organisational structure of the army of the Republic, and later of the Imperial period. This then helps us to view the epigraphic, sculptural and archaeological evidence in clearer context.

LITERARY SOURCES

Covering the wide period of Roman history, 'ancient', Republican and through the Imperial period to the later stages, we have access to a number of classical literary sources. Not all of these authors were living at the same time, so their own personal views and political, social and military experiences varied. Furthermore, not all are primary sources, many writing about events from their own recent past, previous generations or 'ancient history'/mythology, drawing their information from other authors whose work no longer survives. When using the works of these sources, therefore, we have to keep regard for potential problems and limitations in their accuracy, whether through deliberate or unconscious bias, through lack of personal experience, or through their own misunderstanding of the sources of information available to themselves (or even through any of the above weaknesses within those earlier sources no longer extant).

It is apparent that the earliest periods of Roman history are somewhat shady, based on legends, mythology and folklore, carried down initially through verbal histories, with no known written recording of events until after the foundation of the Republic (traditionally in 509 BC), from which time events were recorded by the Pontifex Maximus (Rich, 2007, 7). Many modern historians now believe these early ancient histories to be more of an attempt by later classical historians to create order out of the unknown (Forsythe, 2007, 26; Le Glay et al., 2005, 17–22), where others less kindly view them as 'literary confections' and 'imaginative reconstructions' (Rich, 2007, 7).

The Romans, originally one of the many simple, pastoral, indigenous peoples of the Italic peninsula, had little use for written histories. Their written language appears to have been adopted from the neighbouring Etruscans. They were a more technologically and politically advanced civilisation, who influenced many of their Italic neighbours socially, militarily and linguistically, either through trade associations, expansionist policy or a combination of both, their alphabet eventually becoming a model for all Italic peoples. It is perhaps no coincidence, therefore, that Roman written histories only commence after a period of Etruscanisation, following the rule of its last three 'Etruscan' kings (traditionally identified as Tarquin the Elder, Servius Tullius and Tarquin the Proud; Le Glay et al., 2005, 22).

Other than in fragments or quotes within the works of later authors, the works of most of these early authors no longer exist. For example, the earliest Roman historian whose work only survives in quotations is Quintus Fabius Pictor. He wrote in Greek, describing events of the Second Punic War from his personal experiences as a survivor of the Roman defeat at Cannae. He provided a surviving list of magistrates dating from the earliest Republic, which he used to set the chronology of the history (Le Glay et al., 2005, 21; Rich, 2007, 8).

The first Roman historian to write in Latin was Marcus Porcius Cato (234–149 BC), also known as 'The Elder' or 'The Censor', who fought in the Second Punic War as a military tribune. His only surviving work is on the subject of agriculture (*De Re Rustica*), so its relevance to military equipment would be limited, but is notable as the earliest surviving Latin text. However, quotations of his work are also used in the histories by other authors as fragments, one of the most famous of these being his deliberate ending of every speech, regardless of subject, with the words 'Carthage must be destroyed', to emphasise his views on the matter.

The literary works of numerous ancient authors have survived to present day. These then form our primary sources of information concerning the Roman world, civilian and military, mostly from a near-contemporary viewpoint (although, as outlined, some are not primary but very much secondary sources, describing events in their own 'ancient' history). As individuals, their writing styles and subject matter varied immensely, as did the level of their military knowledge. Some authors clearly had only the most rudimentary knowledge of military affairs and military equipment, in common with many of us today. Others, in contrast, came from military backgrounds, with first-hand experience of Roman army life, tactics, organisational structure and equipment.

The writings of the ancient authors cover a myriad of subjects, with only occasional glimpses of relevant information, but may describe the materials, technology and industrial/trade infrastructure available. Some sources help by building the historical context, describing the early inter-Italic wars, expansionist activities, later wider-reaching international wars (such as the Punic or Hannibalic Wars) and the inevitable home-grown Social War, allowing us glimpses of the adoption of new battle formations (from phalanx, to manipular, and to cohort formations) and associated development of new armour and weaponry. They also describe political events, to show the emergence of the embryonic Republic, the development of its political assemblies, and their links to military organisation. They show how these changed over time, through necessity, to encompass the inclusion of non-Roman, Italic allies, and extending military recruitment to the lower classes. This then allows us an insight into the changing nature of the Roman army, with the changing aims and aspirations of the soldiers, and their reasons for fighting.

Some of the events described may therefore have driven later changes in the organisational structures of the armies, or may have been instrumental in developmental changes in armour, weapon types or battle formation, perhaps following less than successful military conflicts (or conversely, successful use of innovations), or possibly in answer to changing enemy weapons and fighting styles, as with Tacitus' description of the invasion of Moesia by heavily armoured Sarmatian cataphract horsemen (*Hist.* I.79).

Polybius (*c.* 200–118 BC), is one of the primary sources for the early to mid-Republican period, and is generally considered to be a reliable and knowledgeable source for the period from the First Punic War with Carthage in 264 BC, through the Hannibalic War (218–202 BC) down to 146 BC. Polybius provides details of the level of available manpower raised by the annual levy at the Campus Martius, describing the methods of recruitment. He also describes the desired physical qualities of those eligible (able-bodied, aged 17–46 years) and their personal attributes (Polybius, 6.19–42; 31.29.1). From his own experience Polybius described the manipular battle formation (6.19–26), and his close association with Scipio in Spain during the Hannibalic War permitted him first-hand opportunity to witness the latter's first use of the new cohort formation (11.23.1; 11.33.1). He also recorded the equipment used by legionary forces at that time, describing the rich members of the military alone as having access to mail (*hamata*), with the poorer *assidui* using the older-style pectoral plates (*cardiophylax*), the state providing equipment where necessary, for which the individual would make reimbursement from their paid allowance or *stipendium* (6.39.15).

Some of the same information was also provided by Livy (59 BC–AD 17), although as Livy was writing a century after the events, Polybius is in all probability the more reliable source of the two. Livy had no political or military experience, Rich (2007, 18) describing his details of military equipment as 'questionable', although accepting the probability of some testimony being acceptable, possibly where these do not diverge too greatly from those of other sources. As a secondary source, therefore, one must be cautious when using him as an accurate source for specific dates, calculations and quantities. On the other hand, as a primary source who lived through the majority of Caesar's campaigns, the rule of Augustus and transition in to the early Empire, he can provide first-hand accounts of events affecting the population of Rome, what they saw and felt, and any personal repercussions (although from his own potentially biased viewpoint).

This divergence is highlighted in the two authors' descriptions of the 'Spanish' short sword, or *gladius*, adopted by the Roman legionary (Polybius, 6.23.6). Livy describes its use by the Roman cavalry in the slaughter of Macedonians in 200 BC, producing beheadings and 'hideous other wounds' (31.34.4). However, the gladius being a short, stabbing sword suited to close-formation fighting (as in legionary manipular or cohortal battle line-up), it would be an unlikely choice for horsemen. Cavalry would more usually prefer a longer-bladed weapon, producing slashing injuries. The wounds described by Livy above would be more consistant with those produced by another 'Spanish' sword in use at that time, the *falcatta*, which has a long, heavy, curved blade. From experiments carried out by the author using a reproduction weapon, the blade was found to become almost weightless at the apex of its swing, its weight gaining momentum on the downward sweep, producing sufficient power to remove heads or limbs. The possible misunderstanding of the 'Spanish' sword by Livy therefore highlights his lack of familiarity with military equipment, compared to Polybius' more extensive first-hand experience.

Unlike Livy, some sources had substantial first-hand military experience. As with Polybius, Sallust (who wrote works describing the Catiline conspiracy in Rome in 63 BC, and the Jugurthine War in Numidia in 112 to 105 BC) and Julius Caesar (in describing his Gallic Wars) were able not only to accurately describe the equipment used, but also its manner of use. For example, Caesar (*Bell. Gall.* II.21.5), Tacitus (*Histories*, II.22, II.42, IV.29), and later Ammianus (VI.12.44; XX.11.8; XXVI.6.16), all describe the use of shields, both defensively and offensively, specifically in how to use them to stop arrows, and working co-operatively with fellow combatants; how to build a testudo; and how to build a shield wall. Other authors wrote military manuals and pamphlets, some of which have survived, even if in fragmentary form, the most notable of these being Xenophon, a serving cavalry officer who wrote a book (*Cavalry Commander*, c. 357 BC) describing the duties of a cavalryman, horsemanship and tactics. Other notable authors include Sextus Julius Frontinus (AD 30–104), who held the office of governor, writing a booklet, *Strategemata* (in four books), and Hyginus Gromaticus (of the third century AD) who wrote a manual on the fortification of camps, and on the participation of *nationes* (ethnic troop units).

Sallust (86–35 BC) is not only a valuable source for the historical events of the Jugurthine War and the involvement of Gaius Marius, but had also served as one of Caesar's officers during the Civil War (Sallust, *Jug.* 85.11–12; Rosenstein, 2007, 139). As an officer and supporter of Caesar, his reports of the latter's ancestor Marius' part in the Jugurthine War show his personal bias towards the *populares* movement, depicting Marius as the plebeian saviour of Rome (an exaggerated view which is not supported by many modern classical scholars).

Plutarch (AD 45–120) lived during the reigns of Trajan and Hadrian, but wrote of historical rather than current events, describing many similar events to those found in the writings of Sallust, Caesar and Livy. Although focusing his works on the lives of famous statesmen and heroes, particularly their personal attributes and motivations, he also documented events that may have been instrumental in developmental changes to military organisation, armour and weaponry. For example, he described the life not only of Marius, and his 'reforms' to the army and its weaponry (Plutarch, *Marius*, 1–46), but also the lives of subsequent influential persons, including Sulla, Crassus, Pompey and Caesar, who collectively contributed to and participated in the fall of the Republic.

As a valuable supplement to Livy, Dionysius of Halicarnassus, in his *Roman Antiquities*, wrote a detailed history starting with the foundation of Rome, covering the period down to *c*. 443 BC, using as his main source the official Roman Annals, which no longer survive (Rich, 2007, 7; Howartson, 1997, 192).

Although the writings of some authors focused on important events and personas from their past, others wrote of more contemporary events and military campaigns. For example, Josephus reported on the Jewish Revolt of AD 66 from the viewpoint of the non-Roman, losing side, providing valuable first-hand descriptions of military organisation, battle formation and siege warfare, as well as the armour and weapons used by those involved (although by the time of writing he had transferred his allegiance and was perhaps also writing from a more Roman viewpoint).

While we can find much in the writings of authors such as Josephus that is plausible and relatively reliable, others were perhaps not as accurate as one would have hoped. For example, the author Vegetius (writing around AD 430–435) wrote on military methods (*Epitoma Rei Militaris*). However, although these read as though describing actual practices, often the author was portraying an ideal situation which he would have wished for, possibly reflecting his imagined view of past glorious times. Therefore, when he describes each fort striving for self-sufficiency, the reality perhaps may have been less efficiently performed.

Similarly, the collective works known as the *Scriptores Historiae Augusta* are not what they would at first appear. They purport to have been written in the late third or early fourth centuries by a single author, describing events during the period AD 117–284, but with a gap around AD 244–253. However, they are now believed to be the work of a single author writing in the fourth century, who, for some reason, chose to conceal his true identity, perhaps for the purposes of making veiled political or religious comments (possibly anti-Christian). Much of the work, particularly in the later periods, is considered to be highly fictional (Birley, 1976, 7–22). Howartson (1997, 274) suggests, as a preferred and more reliable alternative, the works of Herodian of Syria, writing in Greek, *c*. AD 230, on the subject of Roman Emperors and military campaigns (in eight books), starting with Marcus Aurelius in AD 180 and finishing with Gordian III in AD 238.

Within this framework, therefore, we have many authors who provide a wide-ranging collection of information. Some describe the best materials to use for different processes, as with Pliny on fossil fuels and the best wood to use for charcoal or for use in shields (Pliny, *Hist. Nat.* 16.77), and similarly, Polybius on their construction (Polybius, VI.23.2–7). For descriptions of military actions and political events formative in organisational or equipment reforms, we have, for the earlier period, the writings of authors such as Pausanias (I.7.2), Polybius (VI.19.2), Plutarch, Sallust and Caesar himself (Caesar, *Bell. Gall.*), while for the Imperial period we have Cassius Dio, Tacitus, Josephus and Ammianus. For evidence on military life from the first-hand experiences of active serving members, we have Sallust, Caesar, Josephus and Ammianus, with advice on training and recruitment from Vegetius.

SCULPTURAL EVIDENCE

Sculpture and artistic representations in wall paintings and mosaics are in a sense the Roman equivalent of photography. They provide an image record over time, from the early Republic to the late Empire. Wall paintings and mosaics, however, are usually civilian in context and their contribution to our knowledge of military issues is limited. Sculpture falls into two main types, ceremonial and funerary, both having strengths and weaknesses in their usefulness as evidence. It is necessary, therefore, to consider the reasons as to why each was originally made, and who made it.

Ceremonial sculpture is generally high in artistic quality, made for public relations purposes, to promote the achievement of an individual, or his regime, not entirely unlike the propaganda artwork of the recent past. It uses conventions of dramatic poses to form images of power and success, and the convention of large triumphal figures, crushing smaller, weaker (barbaric?) opponents through the use of superior force. It is therefore not surprising that the majority of these monumental sculptures were erected during the Imperial period, the leadership depicted on each clearly feeling a need to promote its success to the people and its strength to any potential enemies.

As historians, we are always advised to have regard to potential bias within written histories, in that they are always written by the winning side, the vanquished, by necessity, being depicted with the extreme qualities of weakness, stupidity and malevolence in order to better promote the victor. Sculptural/artistic representations are to be viewed in the same light. As historical documents, their content may not accurately represent reality, but nevertheless they are still a valuable resource for historical sequencing, chronology and equipment, provided that their nature is understood.

There are a number of important ceremonial sculptures which are of boundless value to the study of Roman military actions and equipment. The most notable of these is Trajan's Column. Dedicated in AD 113, the Column was erected within Trajan's monumental Forum complex at Rome (built AD 106–113), inside a courtyard flanked by the Basilica Ulpia to the south side, the Greek and Latin libraries on the east and west (the Bibliotheca Ulpia) and the Temple of the Divine Trajan on the north (Davies, 1997, 43; Osborne, 1970, 1155). The whole complex of buildings, with the Column inside, was reputedly designed by the Syrian artist/architect Apollodorus of Damascus, who had accompanied Trajan on the Dacian campaigns (Davies, 1997, 43).

The Column consists of a pedestal base (with a small chamber housing the Emperor's ashes), a main column above, topped by a Tuscan capital with pedestal and statue at its apex (originally a gilded statue of the Emperor Trajan holding a spear and orb, but replaced by one of St Peter). There are a number of works written describing the Column, its purpose and methods of construction, and the artistic and historical merits of its decoration. In many of these works its height fluctuates between 150 Roman feet (44.07 metres) and 100 Roman feet (c. 125 feet, or 38.4 metres) to the base of the statue, and including the pedestal base (Osborne, 1970, 1155; Davies, 1997, 43; Lancaster, 1999, 419–39).

Lancaster (1999, 419–439) discussed in depth the methods of construction of the Column, from its foundations, its sequence of construction with other parts of the forum complex, and the sourcing of materials, and conjectured reconstructions of the lifting frame/tower used in its erection. Other authors, however, discuss the reasons for its existence – whether to mark the achievements of Trajan, or of the individual members of the army, in the campaign itself (Osborne, 1970, 1155); whether to celebrate Trajan's success (to justify the use of the Column base as a repository for his ashes; Davies, 1997, 63–5); or, as also suggested by Richmond (1982, 1), to mark the technological and constructional achievement of the architects (the height of the Column representing the height of the overburden of earth removed from the hill in order to build the forum).

The cylindrical pillar of Parian marble (formed from stone sourced from the Luna quarries, 300 km north of Rome) was provided with a central, helical stairwell. This is illuminated by small windows, barely visible within the exterior decorative spiral frieze of relief sculpture depicting Trajan's victory in the Dacian wars of AD 101–106. The relief winds around the shaft in twenty-three revolutions, 1 metre wide by 198 metres long (215 yards), which Davies (1997, 41) proposed may have been based either on the continuous illustrated scrolls (*rotulus*) or painted lengths of fabric wound around the columns of temples on feast days. It bears a pictorial documentation and commemoration of Trajan's victory in the two Dacian wars. It pictures symbolically the men who fought and died on both sides (Rossi, 1971, 14), and Richmond (1982, 1) believed that it depicted the 'best illustrations of the army' (undoubtably one of the most notable pictorial representation of the Roman army, used as a primary source by scholars for centuries, with many suggested reconstructions in academic and fine-art works based on its imagery). However, more recent opinions now agree that this image of the Roman army should be viewed with caution. While the artistic quality of the sculpture is superb, the representations of the figures depicted are highly stylised, and the equipment shown is of dubious accuracy.

Debate also surrounds the work of authors discussing the features and merits of the Column. Numerous works exist describing the Column, the methods of its construction, the reasons for its existence, and interpretations of featured events and equipment used, including Cichorius (1896), who produced a record of high-quality photographic images of the entire Column (from casts made in the 1860s by Napoleon III) still used by many modern authors (including Lepper and Frere, 1988). However, in more recent years, caveats have been voiced. For example, Bishop and Coulston, among others, refute the reliability of the depictions of equipment, which, although supposedly showing a 'snap-shot' of the military in the Trajanic period, do not reflect the hard evidence of actual equipment found in the archaeological record (Bishop and Coulston, 2006, 35, 254–9).

Similarly, interpretations of the stylistic conventions employed by authors such as Rossi (1971) have been seen by some authors as outdated. Rossi (1971, 14) suggested that the artist had utilised a convention separating visually the civilian legionary from the non-civilian auxiliary, by depicting all of the former in short tunic and bare legs, wearing *lorica segmentata* and carrying rectangular shield and *pilum*. However, other contemporary sculptural representations suggest mail was still being worn by some legionary troops at this time. For example, legionaries are depicted in *hamata* in the metopes of the Tropaeum Traiani at Adamklissi (Russell-Robinson, 1975, 170–1). Richmond suggested that these had been specifically provided with *hamata* to arm them against the Dacian *falx* (Richmond, 1967, 34–5; Russell-Robinson, 1975, 170).

The auxiliaries on the Column, in contrast, were depicted either in mail, short trousers (*bracchae*) and with oval shield, or in regional/ethnic costume, as with the Syrian archers (see plate section). Rossi also proposed the convention of using a single figure to represent a whole unit of men (not supported by Lepper and Frere, among others), the individual units being identified by their different shield designs. It is this information that Rossi (1971, 14) then used to produce his analysis of shield decoration in relation to specific units.

Many historians favour the proposed design conventions by Lepper and Frere (1988), who suggest a convention somewhat similar to the film maker's storyboard, with 'close-ups' to focus on incidents of important action. Richmond (1982, 2) viewed the Column as a 'picture book' of individual episodes showing the everyday activities of the army. These were then converted into a unified running sequence of interlocking scenes, produced by 'working up' the wartime sketchbooks of artists travelling with the army, whom he compared to the nineteenth-century journalist-artists (forerunners to modern TV and newspaper war correspondents). Each scene of the Column could then have been based on sketches made during the campaign, which would allow for more precise details of buildings, costume, accoutrements and physiognomy of participants (Romans, auxiliaries, Dacians and allies) to be shown. In his view, any mistakes would have been due to the stonecutter's interpretation of these drawings (Richmond, 1982, 5).

The work of Lepper and Frere, recognised as a major study of the Column, reproduces the Cichorius plates, although disappointingly reduced in scale, for reasons of economy, and so greatly diminishing the value of their efforts. Their work discusses the reasons behind the campaign but is, for the main part, a 'travelogue' attempting to relate the scenes depicted to the journey to Dacia undertaken by the army. They, however, give little attention to the actual equipment used, most of which refers to the mule train rather than the troops themselves (1988, 266–9), and which strongly references the work of Russell-Robinson (1975).

It has been suggested that the Column was initially only decorated on its pedestal base, with the main shaft left blank, the spiral frieze possibly having been a later addition by Hadrian when it became later used in its final phase as Trajan's tomb (Richmond (1982, 1). However, Davies (1997, 63–5) considered that if this had been the case, Hadrian would then have featured more prominently in the events depicted. She viewed the intended purpose of

Fig. 2 Scene from Trajan's Column showing legionaries in *lorica segmentata*, auxiliaries in mail (*hamata*) and archers in scale (*squamata*). (*Cichorius, 1896,* Die Reliefs der Traianssäule, 86)

the Column as primarily a funerary monument (the spiral motion of the frieze re-enacting ancient funerary rituals, processing around the shaft), despite its initial construction being four years before Trajan's death. In AD 117 Trajan suffered a stroke while on campaign in Syria. He then died on the journey home, in Cilicia (around 8 August), was cremated and his ashes returned to Rome sealed in a golden urn, which was deposited in the chamber in the base of the Column (Davies, 1997, 41).

Davies proposed that the Column was erected during Trajan's lifetime, designed as a tomb from its first concept, but with its purpose masked as a victory monument, to boost public support for the Emperor and his Dacian Wars (as the Emperor was not entitled to burial within the pomerium, but could only be honoured in that fashion by command of the Senate after his death). She considered that the chamber in its base had been deliberately designed to later accommodate Trajan's ashes and funerary altar, citing funerary sculptural motifs elsewhere within the complex while contrasting it with the lack of chamber in the Marcus Aurelius Column, which had never been intended to serve as a tomb. In her study of the commemorative imagery on the Column, Davies discussed the power of the dynamics of the architectural design in ensuring the perpetual memory of the Emperor in the minds of the ancient visitor, by exploiting the dramatic effect of emerging into the light at the top of the dark, helical staircase, and the subsequent vista from the summit across the Forum complex.

Ultimately, any discussion of the military equipment shown on the Column should consider that the accurate depiction of the Roman army was not its primary function. As discussed earlier, Richmond (1982, 1) believed that the Column served three purposes: its height was representative of the height of the cliff excavated to produce the Forum complex; a secondary purpose was as a war memorial to the two Dacian campaigns (the first consisting a series of expeditions leading up to the second campaign of organised conquest); and third, its intended function as a repository for the Emperor's ashes. Alternately, Davies (1997, 46–65) considered the Column to have been commissioned by Trajan as his future tomb from its conception, which he initially masked as a victory monument, to be adapted after his death as a permanent tribute to his memory. With this as its intended purpose, any accuracy of equipment, events or locations depicted would therefore have been secondary concerns.

The artistic conventions used on the Column, therefore, are arguably of greater significance than the study of the armour itself. At first glance, the representations of the equipment carried by the men appear to be of equally high quality, but closer examination of the specific armour types, such as helmets and *lorica segmentata*, suggests that these are not as realistic as they at first appear. They do not seem to resemble any real types which have ever been found. Helmets are unusually small and the buckle fastenings on the *segmentata* girdle plates would not be feasible. Representation of mail is often stylised as dots or wavy lines, some figures wearing plain tops (without the dots or wavy lines), which has led to suggestions of this being 'leather' armour. This theory was not supported by Russell-Robinson, however; he believed that the details may have been painted on instead, and this will be discussed in greater depth in Chapter IV.

Other similar stylised images exist on ceremonial monumental structures. These include the Great Trajanic Frieze (contemporary with Trajan's Column) incorporated into the later Arch of Constantine in the Forum Romanorum (Russell-Robinson, 1975, 182, plate 494), on the columns of Antoninus Pius (Russell-Robinson, 1975, 184, plate 497) and Marcus Aurelius (Russell-Robinson, 1975, 185, plates 498–9), and on the Arch of Severus (Russell-Robinson, 1975, 183, fig. 189). Although of undisputed artistic quality, it is a possibility that these monumental artists may not have had a significant personal experience of the military. They may have only ever seen the army in ceremonial uniforms, during triumphal marches, and possibly then only from a distance. They may not have had first-hand knowledge of specific equipment of units, which could then have been problematic for the depicted shield designs. That the shields have been found to have been decorated suggests that such decoration was commonplace, but the artist may not necessarily have assigned the correct design to the correct unit. If a modern artist were asked to draw a soldier, without benefit of a model, he may produce something soldier-ish, but not good enough to fool a fellow soldier. Similarly, these depictions of Roman soldiers may have looked convincing to the artist and the general public of Rome, but may not accurately reflect reality.

By contrast, the artistic quality of grave stelae is usually not as high, but this is compensated by the level of technical knowledge of the funerary mason. Because of their very nature, stelae will have been produced at relatively short notice, soon after the demise of the subject. They are not usually the highly decorated, well-planned, expensive works described above. They would probably have been produced by a stone mason attached to a unit, probably himself a soldier, whose main job would have been the production of numerous building blocks for construction projects – forts, gateways, aqueducts, and perhaps even Hadrian's Wall. While some were accomplished stonemasons, they were not necessarily artists in the sculptural sense. These 'stone cutters' are described by Tarruntenus Paternus as being among the list of men within the legion known as *immunes*, exempted from 'more onerous duties' (*Digesta: Corpus Iuris Civilis*, L.6.7; Campbell, 2000, 30).

They would have had first-hand, comprehensive knowledge of the equipment which they were trying to depict. Their accuracy, therefore, is on a level almost with a photograph. However, there are still some conventions at play which must be considered. Three main basic conventions can be seen in designs of funerary stelae. The deceased may be shown standing, facing forward; he may be seated, flanked by aspects depicting a banquet; or if he belonged to a cavalry unit, he may be depicted on horseback, possibly trampling an enemy under foot, perhaps followed by a smaller figure representing his groom. Again this latter convention is a symbolic image, as with the monumental sculptures, promoting the concept of Roman superiority. Noted cavalry stelae include those of Longinus, AD 43–61, from Colchester (Russell-Robinson, 1975, 106, plate 306); Flavinus of the Ala Petriana, from Corbridge (Russell-Robinson, 1975, 106, plate 307); and that of the recently discovered cavalryman from Lancaster.

In order to fit the image neatly into the given space, often large objects such as spear (*hasta*), javelin (*pilum*), shield or standard may be shrunken down considerably. Other features, like mail, as seen on monumental works, being difficult to reproduce in stone, may have been painted on, with the stone surface left smooth (leading many now to speculate on existence of leather armour). Objects, such as shields, would not be depicted fully in 3-D, as the sculpture would not require that level of depth, and so would be flattened, not possessing the true curvature of the original. Soldiers can be shown without helmets, so as not as to obscure the facial features, and to make the subject recognisable. In later periods, armour may not be worn at all, the subject depicted wearing his off-duty stand-down kit of tunic, belt and sword, which is of minimal use when studying the equipment.

EPIGRAPHIC EVIDENCE

Epigraphic evidence bridges the divide between literary and sculptural sources, although its value is limited. It can, however, provide clues as to identity, religious beliefs and the ethnic origin of the personnel at a fort, as well as which unit built a new fort, gateway or stretch of wall. There have been a number of items of Roman equipment found that are inscribed with their owner's name. In the Republican period, armour was bought by the individual soldier before the campaign. If not lost or damaged beyond repair, it would be brought home with him and, if not buried with him, may have been handed down to his successors. This is evidenced by the high incidence (around 49 per cent) of Iberian finds of Montefortino helmets dating from the Hannibalic or Punic Wars found in funerary contexts (Quesada Sanz, 1977, 153). It is also seen in the considerable age of the helmets in the Les Sorres shipwreck, which must have been heirlooms up to 400 years old by the time they were consigned for recycling (Izquierdo and Solias Aris, 2000, 1.11).

With the new 'professional' soldier of the Imperial period, equipment was issued on recruitment, leased for the duration of service and paid for by deductions from pay. Tacitus tells how soldiers had to 'pay for their clothing, weapons and tents' (*Annals*, 1.17). On retirement, or death, this equipment could be taken home by the individual, possibly accounting for occasional finds of military equipment in civilian contexts. More probably it would have been handed back, traded in to supplement the pension (to which he had been paying for many years). A soldier's equipment was valuable to him. Therefore, as a form of investment, many augmented their basic kit with the addition of decorative belt plates and more ornate swords, daggers and shield bosses, etc. Some items of equipment, being more expensive, or more relevant to personal safety, would rank higher in importance and are those items more likely to be marked with the owner's name for safekeeping. This could take the form of a simple engraving of the owner's name, and/or his centurion. Other items may be more elaborately decorated, as with the shield boss from a member of the Legio VIII found at Durham, England (Bidwell, 2001, 10, fig. 5A). These inscriptions can help to identify the original owner, his legion and perhaps his rank and ethnic origin, possibly providing dating evidence where loss can be identified with specific campaigns (as with the mail hook from Kalkriese). Some items have been found which bear more than one name inscribed on them, indicating that equipment was often handed on to other recruits, a process not dissimilar to that with modern armies (Bishop, 1985, 9). With the assistance of these multiple inscriptions, therefore, it is possible to build up an individual history for one specific item of equipment.

As armour is by design made to withstand substantial abuse, it can, and often does, remain in use for prolonged periods. With modern weapons, technology tends to cause premature obsolescence. However, in the case of traditional armour, as worn ceremonially by military units such as the Life Guards and Horse Guards, helmets and cuirasses may have been in use for centuries. I have purposefully made use of the living memories of J. R. Travis ('Bob'), a retired member of the British Life Guard cavalry, as they are one of the few remaining military units who still make use of traditional armour assemblages, as the closest comparative to the Roman cavalry still extant. His recollections included as a new recruit having to learn the history of each individual component part of his armour (his helmet, sword, cuirass and even boots), some pieces having seen action dating back to the Battle of Waterloo in 1815. The British army were not unique in their use of cuirass armour at that time, and much of the armour still used in the twentieth century was taken from Napoleon's cuirassiers and carabiniers after the battle for re-use by the British (including the cuirass used by Bob Travis), with some presented to the unit by Napoleon III, so use of the Life Guard's equipment for analogies would effectively be the same as use of their French or German equivalent (J. R. Travis Snr, pers. comm., December 1999).

ARCHAEOLOGICAL EVIDENCE

Caution should be exercised, however, in placing too much reliance on epigraphic sources for dating in the absence of other evidence of context. For example, epigraphy would not be an appropriate method to date artefacts which appear for sale on the international market without find location or dating context that can be corroborated in any other way. Many of these finds may originate from illicit excavations, perhaps aided by metal detectors, their new owners unable or unwilling to offer information on origin because of the risk of prosecution and financial loss. Their archaeological value, therefore, is almost nil. This, then, becomes all the more suspicious when inscriptions of previous Roman owners' names appear during 'cleaning' and 'conservation work', permitting retrospective epigraphic 'dating', as with the supposed Roman 'hybrid mail shoulder plates' which have been the focus for much recent debate. On closer inspection (which is not always possible where the objects are in private collections), some such inscriptions on artefacts have unsurprisingly been exposed as forgeries, which then devalues further what may have been an interesting and important find.

In reviewing the archaeological evidence for items of military equipment, we have to consider the nature of the finds, where they were found, what they were made of, and how they came to be 'lost'. Artefacts make their way into the archaeological record through a number of processes. They may be lost accidentally, through an act of random carelessness, or through some catastrophic event. They may have been deliberately discarded for some reason (perhaps because an item was of no value and had reached the end of its useful life, or perhaps the opposite case of a valuable item, discarded as part of a votive offering). This may then have relevance for dating of the artefact or implications for wear evidence. Some articles are therefore more likely to reach the archaeological record than others, and are more likely to appear through some methods than others.

High-value, high-status items are unlikely to be discarded deliberately at the end of their usefulness. If damaged in some way, it is likely that they would be repaired and when the original owner parted with them, it would be either through sale, theft or death of the owner. Small items, even of high value, may be lost accidentally (although the owner would normally take greater care not to do so) or through some catastrophic event. If this event were as a result of an attack on the owner, it is expected that such a valuable item would then become booty, hence the majority of finds from battle sites, such as Kalkriese, consist of low-value fragments dislodged from the main piece of armour (hinges, buckles, mail hooks, etc), with larger pieces only being found from locations from which looting was not possible (as for example at Kalkriese, where artefacts, including the cavalry face mask, were found under a collapsed earthwork; Bunz and Spickermann, 2006).

It is possible that high-status items may be stashed away at times of impending danger, with their owner unable to retrieve them later. This may even be a stolen item, stashed for later, thwarted retrieval, as was suggested for the 'Sword of Tiberius' (Bishop and Coulston, 1993, 73, fig. 38.2) and the Vindolanda 'standard' (Birley, 1977, plate 14). Some high-value items were never lost, but were deposited with no intention of future retrieval. This would be the case with items offered ceremonially or buried with a deceased owner. This is more likely to be so with items retrieved from 'native' contexts, perhaps graves of auxiliary troops or of enemy forces (plundered booty). Frequently, in the case of helmets and swords, these can exhibit signs of deliberate damage, to 'kill' the artefact, as seen with some of the Montefortino helmets from Iberian grave contexts (Quesada Sanz, 1977).

Occasionally, personal items that would have been considered relatively valuable to their owner (helmets, shields, swords, etc.) are found undamaged in water contexts (river or coastal). These may not have been deposited through any particularly ritualistic/religious action, but could have been accidental losses as a result of a catastrophic event. Particularly in this category would be the Durham shield boss of Legio VIII Augusta, found as a result of perceived coastal shipwreck, and several finds of helmets possibly lost during less than successful river crossings of the Rhine, and the River Po at Cremona. The latter have been associated with cautious confidence to the military action of AD 69 (Russell-Robinson, 1975), although ritualistic deposition can still not be ruled out.

By far the greatest number of items which find their way into the archaeological record are 'rubbish' – by that meaning low value, old, worn out, broken, often without any potential for repair or re-use (Bishop, 1985, 9). They are not always complete items, sometimes being just broken-off scraps, but although they would have been 'low value' to their owners, they can be invaluable as indications of wear damage. Caution has to be exercised here, however, not to lend too much weight to any apparent high-frequency occurrence of some items. Large numbers of an item may not necessarily imply its widespread use in preference to a known alternative, but may simply represent a less effective item which was more easily broken or more easily lost (as may be the case with the later *lorica segmentata* tie rings; Thomas, 2003, 109–13).

It follows that most items have had a history before their loss. They are unlikely to have been lost on the first day of manufacture and, in fact, the opposite is almost always the case, exhibiting signs of prolonged use, wear and possible combat damage. As with today, where modern Horse Guards wear cuirasses dating back several hundred years, Roman equipment passed through many hands during its useful life. Men would rarely take their kit with them on retirement. Having 'bought' it on lease through deductions from pay, they could then cash in their kit when they left, passing it on to new recruits. This can be seen evidenced in items bearing the names of more than one owner.

Some of the more personal items of kit could also have been taken home by veterans on retirement, as can be seen in occasional finds in non-military contexts, for example in graves and votive contexts. As grave goods are not often found in burials of ethnically Roman citizens, these are more usually indicative of auxiliary/provincial people, or may even represent equipment looted from their original owner (Quesada Sanz, 1977, 153).

Most finds of military equipment, however, do come from military sites. This is in part due to the nature of how the Roman army occupied a site, its use and re-use of materials, the logistics of manufacture and distribution of men and arms. Accepting that most armour would change hands throughout its period of use, and that troops moved around the Empire on campaigns and individuals possibly moved between units, the individual pieces of armour may be well-travelled from their place of origin/manufacture to their eventual loss/disposal/ deposition. Their loss may be accidental, although with the older, more worn items, it could be that the lack of effort to retrieve them was due to the object being close to the end of its useful life, its loss simply advancing slightly its inevitable demise.

Although the Romans were no paragons of virtue where it came to polluting their environment with industrial processes, they were quite efficient at recycling used materials (as evidenced on leather shield covers, from Vindonissa, Valkenburg and Roomburgh, some with re-used panels displaying stitching holes from earlier *tabulae ansatae*; van Driel-Murray,

1985, 43–54; 1989, 18–19; 1999, 45–54). Because of the effort expended in the production of even the smallest object, from raw material to end product, every effort would be made to prolong its useable life and to make use of residual parts at its termination, hence the caches of finds such as the Corbridge 'hoard' (where sections of multiple sets of pre-used *lorica* had been stored for repair and future re-use) and large pieces of tent panels, cut from the original object for re-working into patches or smaller items (as, for example, can be seen in the museum at Ribchester).

Despite this, however, some items were eventually discarded, finding their way into ditch in-fill with other non-recyclable waste. This process would be accelerated at times where the military were actively closing down a site and relocating. In these instances, even objects that were not necessarily irretrievably broken could be discarded. It is clear that when a military site was being decommissioned, everything was assessed for its future usefulness, value and portability. Bulky, lower-value items are particularly likely to be discarded at this time, whether broken or not. Anything which could be taken away for re-use would be packed up and taken with them, even to the extent of dismantling timber buildings. Whatever remained, whether unreusable, broken, old or worn out, would be burned and buried to prevent its use by an enemy. This is evidenced in the demolition fires at a number of sites, including Doncaster, Yorkshire (Buckland, 1978, 247), and in the quantity of finds from defensive ditches of forts, such as Newstead, Scotland (Curle, 1911, 56, 161).

Although it is inevitable that some rubbish would make its way into a fort's defensive ditches, if left, these ditches would quickly become blocked and cease to serve their primary function. It is logical to assume that these ditches would therefore have been rigorously maintained. This would then support the view that these items would have entered these ditches towards, or at, the end of the fort's period of military occupation.

Another feature of Roman military policy on decommissioning a site was to sabotage the water supply, also to render it useless to enemy forces. It appears to have therefore been a practice to deposit rubbish in the fort's wells, with the intention to both block and pollute them, and this may also include organic items, such as dead animals.

The practice of cleaning out a site when decommissioning it has therefore given us a large quantity of artefacts from a variety of contexts. These have the additional bonus of being in deposits which aid in dating fort wells and ditches – either dating the artefact where the decommission date is otherwise documented, or in dating the closure of the fort where found in context with other dating evidence (coins, pottery, etc). This then leads to the other issue relating to finds – differential survival. What we are able to find from excavation is influenced by a number of factors: the material from which the artefact is made; the likelihood of that material surviving in the conditions where it was deposited; the possibility of the site being damaged or redeveloped in later periods; and the probability of items being deposited in the first place (whether large/small, high/low status, easily broken, easily recyclable, worth stealing/looting). Objects retrieved from ditches may therefore possibly be either small, accidental losses (of high or low value and not necessarily broken) or deliberately disposed of. These would then be the sort of objects of no further use or value. They may be made of organic materials, such as wood, leather, textiles or bone (as seen in the many finds of leather scraps and worn-out leather objects from many fort sites, such as those at Ribchester and Vindolanda), or metals, such as iron or copper/brass.

The waterlogged, anaerobic conditions within a ditch would provide a high possibility of survival for organic material, although this could be further influenced by the acidic/alkaline properties of the surrounding fill matrix. Metallic objects, on the other hand, may fare less well, particularly the iron objects, although at some sites, where soil conditions are favourable, copper/brass objects can survive surprisingly well, as can be seen at Vindolanda, near Hadrian's Wall.

It is apparent, therefore, with the exception of a few objects deposited by genuine 'accidental loss' and subsequently rediscovered by equally random and accidental means (as with the river deposits), that the majority of artefacts are retrieved from predictable contexts, such as fort ditches. This then would suggest a further level of bias in the archaeological record – that influenced by choice of sites excavated. This factor must also be considered in civilian as well as military contexts. In the past there appears to have been a deliberate thought pattern at play in the choice of excavation locations. To some extent this would have been influenced by the visible nature of certain site types. High-status residences, with larger footprints and more substantial walls, are more easily pinpointed by aerial photography than are smaller, low-status buildings. In similar fashion, forts are often visible, not only in aerial photographs but also to the naked eye. Where these forts are situated within an urban context that developed later, the shape of the defences and, often, the internal road system can still be identified in the present-day town road plan. However, on a number of sites in rural contexts, the fort has been built in a hilltop, defensive position, and in these cases often has not seen any subsequent redevelopment with substantial walls, ditches and even internal roads and buildings visible. The visible nature of certain site types has therefore permitted more selective excavation.

Mindful of the increased probability of artefact survival in some parts of these sites, it would be tempting, if funding or time is not available, to cherry-pick these specific locations. It is possible, however, that these are precisely the areas that are necessary to define the boundaries of the site, with the added bonus of supplying dating evidence for period of occupation. However, in the case of high-status civilian sites, it does appear that preference is exercised in favour of the potentially 'richer' family rooms rather than the lower-status servant's quarters, workrooms and outbuildings, which is a shame as these are precisely the locations where most of the everyday activities took place.

Similarly, in forts where it has not been possible to excavate the full site, often only the defining ditches, bathhouses and officers' quarters have been investigated. It may be that the remainder of these sites have been left unexcavated as a deliberate measure for the highly commendable reason of protecting the underlying archaeology (as all excavation inevitably leads to destruction of the site itself), or may be left for a later date when improved excavation methods would render up greater information than currently possible. In these cases, we may in future be able to build a more accurate picture of the functions of these internal buildings where the majority of everyday activities took place.

In the case of sites investigated under time restraints as rescue excavations prior to subsequent redevelopment (as was the case with the Roman industrial site at Templeborough, near Sheffield, Yorkshire), these opportunities are now lost to us. In fairness, the excavations at Templeborough by Thomas May in 1916 and 1917 were actually re-excavations of a site previously stripped and damaged by nineteenth-century antiquarians, which is precisely the argument in favour of leaving a site unexcavated. However, as the entire site was then comprehensively bulldozed in preparation for the twentieth-century steel workings, to well below all archaeological levels, leaving the site until later was not an option available, and we can only be grateful for whatever information was retrieved from what was clearly a major industrial complex of considerable importance to the Roman iron/steel and weapon production and distribution infrastructure (May, 1922; Travis, 2005). Similarly, at Corbridge (Red House) a further 'rescue excavation', in preparation for a major road development, uncovered some lower-status, non-residential, internal buildings of the earlier fort, providing an insight into storage, cart garaging and possible *fabrica* workshops (Hanson et al., 1979, fig. 2). In order to gain a clearer image of the Roman military industrial and weapon production infrastructure, these are precisely the type of buildings that need to be examined.

It is to be hoped that more such sites could be excavated in the future, particularly in those areas with potential for redevelopment (that is, not in the relative 'safety' of the Hadrian's Wall tourist corridor, and not in the inaccessible hilltop locations, such as Hard Knott in Cumbria), and preferably without waiting until they should become threatened sites. It may be, however, that further development in the study of Roman armour lies in less densely populated parts of the world than in Britain, such as in the arid eastern regions, where preservation of material may be better and where remains may not be damaged or threatened by overlying later construction layers, or in re-evaluation of excavated material from these regions, as for example at sites such as Dura-Europos and Masada (the 1964–65 excavations of the latter being the subject of a recent final report; Stiebel and Magness, 2007, 1–94).

II

LORICA SEGMENTATA

The name *lorica segmentata* is a modern term (and although for reasons of consistency will appear italicised, should perhaps more correctly be used in non-italic format), used to refer to Roman segmented armour (unlike the terms *hamata* and *squamata*, for mail and scale armour respectively, which are terms also used in antiquity), the linguistics being discussed in greater depth by Simkins (1990, 11). The term *lorica* is known, in the context of 'body armour' or 'cuirass'. Although it is possible that the term *laminae* may have been used in antiquity to refer to iron plate armour, it is not clear whether these contexts may refer to the smaller plates of scale armour. In the absence of definite alternatives therefore, Bishop (2002, 1) chose to retain the term '*segmentata*' to describe an articulated, segmented cuirass, as shall the following discussion. Where articulated plate armour is used for limb protection, however, we have the terms *manicae* for arm protection and *ocreae*, for leg protection (greaves). The use of *segmentata* cannot be evidenced by the Romans before 9 BC at the earliest, and its use appears to cease by the third to fourth century AD. Its origins, however, may date back to much earlier periods, perhaps even to the Bronze Age, drawing on traditions from other cultures in the use of articulated plate armour for body and limb protection.

THE DEVELOPMENT OF ARTICULATED PLATE ARMOUR

The earliest known example of articulated plate armour, the 'Dendra cuirass', comes from the fifteenth century BC (Russell-Robinson, 1975, 147; Warry, 1980, 12; Bishop, 2002, 18). It is fashioned from wide, curved, copper-alloy plates, overlapping upwards, each plate tied to the one above by leather laces, the two halves, front and back, then separating for access. The width of the plate makes it less flexible than *segmentata*, as does the lack of vertical movement afforded by the front and back central fastenings of the latter, and arm movement must have been greatly restricted. Bishop (2002, 18) suggested a number of potential weaknesses, including the upward overlap rendering the armour more vulnerable to blows from above. This then could detach the internal leather ties, causing all lower plates to fall away, a problem that is not encountered in the more resilient Roman *segmentata*, where the plates are suspended from internal leather strapping. Its use for combat would have been somewhat limited. Its lack of flexibility, its weight and the length of the cuirass would have excluded its use on horseback. It would have also been an extremely expensive, high-status item, due to the cost of processing the amount of metal involved. It may, therefore, have only served a ceremonial purpose, or have been used for display/shock purposes by an otherwise non-combatant leader, although this interpretation is problematic, the crudeness of the workmanship tending to contradict the obvious expense of materials.

Articulated, laminated or segmental plate armour is also known from the fourth century BC onwards, particularly for cavalry limb protection, from other cultures in the steppe regions, such as the Parthians, and, perhaps through cultural exchange, from Hellensitic contexts. For example, a Hellenistic armguard, dating to *c.* 150 BC, was excavated from Ai-Khanum, constructed from around thirty-five overlapping curved plates and a larger upper plate at the shoulder. As this was a left arm assembly, it was interpreted as being for cavalry use, not being a right arm (sword arm) assembly (Bishop, 2002, 18). The continued use of segmented armour in other, non-Roman cultures, for arm and body protection, may also be seen in the depictions on the pedestal reliefs of Trajan's Column of captured enemy (Dacian/Sarmatian cavalry) equipment. However, as this is a sculptural depiction, its accuracy cannot be attested by archaeological evidence.

SCULPTURAL EVIDENCE

Until recently, our knowledge of Roman articulated body armour, the *lorica segmentata*, came almost exclusively from sculptural representations, the most famous of which being Trajan's Column. However, despite the artistic quality of the depiction of the figures, these are highly stylised representations, following contemporary monumental conventions, possibly executed by artists with little personal knowledge of military equipment. They also use the convention of showing all legionary troops in *segmentata*, with all auxiliaries wearing mail, which Rossi (1971, 100) proposed served for the purposes of separating visually the two. This has led to an assumption that *segmentata* was confined to legionaries alone – a view that has been challenged in recent years by increased archaeological finds of *segmentata* remains in non-legionary contexts. It is also possible that its use may have been influenced more by function within a unit/legion than by rank or citizen status. It must also be considered that by the Trajanic period *segmentata* had already been in use for a considerable period, with the images on the column representing later, developed forms, and also possibly therefore later period identity of usage. Other stylised, less detailed monumental sculptural representations of *lorica segmentata* can also be seen on the Great Trajanic Frieze incorporated into the later Arch of Constantine (Russell-Robinson, 1975, 182, plate 494), on the columns of Antoninus Pius (Russell-Robinson, 1975, 184, plate 497) and Marcus Aurelius (Russell-Robinson, 1975, 185, plates 498–9), and on the Arch of Severus (Russell-Robinson, 1975, 183, fig. 189).

Although by less accomplished artists, more accurate representations of military equipment often come from funerary stelae. However, the majority of these depict almost universally the use of mail rather than *segmentata*, which again calls into question its exclusive use by legionary troops. If *segmentata* had been in such widespread use, as is suggested by the images from Trajan's Column, one would have anticipated a far higher incidence of its appearance in these funerary stelae.

ARCHAEOLOGICAL EVIDENCE

The earliest actual finds of *segmentata* come from Austria, from forts on the *limes*, for example at Carnuntum (von Groller 1901a, 95). Here large quantities of military equipment, including several fragmentary pieces of *lorica segmentata*, were found in the Wafenmagazin deposits and reported by von Groller (although many of the finds are still not fully published). He interpreted the finds, based on Trajan's Column, as being a series of plates attached to a leather bodice. However, his interpretation was never reconstructed in metal and would not have functioned in practice (von Groller 1901a, 96, fig. 24). Subsequent contemporary artistic representations of Roman legionaries were then based on von Groller's interpretation (Coussin, 1926, 452–6).

At about the same time as the Carnuntum discoveries at the beginning of the twentieth century (von Groller, 1901b, plates 17, 18, 19), some *segmentata* remains were found in Britain, at Newstead, although these were in deposits of the later Antonine period and represented a more developed form, with fewer girdle plates and a different method of upper body closure. The plates found (one chest plate and a wide single back plate), were in fragmentary condition and were initially identified with the back plate to the front and incorrectly orientated by 90 degrees. The excavation of Newstead and Carnuntum being within a few years of each other, the initial reconstruction of this variant was again based on that of von Groller (Curle, 1911, 156). With the corrected alignment, and front to back positioning of the plates, it was later recognised that the girdle plates had been attached to the loops at the base of the chest, and wide, single, back plates by hooks on the top girdle plates. The brass-trimmed slots were then identified as being for horizontal fastening, either through pin and loop, turn key or, as more recently suggested, through leather strap and buckle (Poulter, 1988, 37).

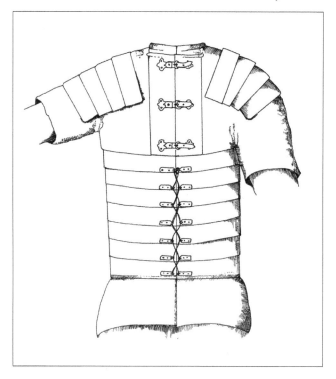

Fig. 3 Interpretation of *lorica segmentata* finds by von Groller, based on Trajan's Column depictions (von Groller, 1901b, fig. 23). (*Redrawn by J. R. Travis*)

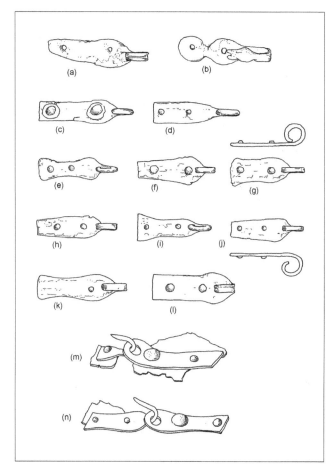

Fig. 4 A selection of *segmentata* tie loops: A & B from the Lunt; C to L from Carnuntum (from von Groller, 1901b, plate 17); M & N Corbridge type B/C suspension hook and loop, also from Carnuntum (from von Groller, 1901b, plate 18). (*Drawn by J. R. Travis*)

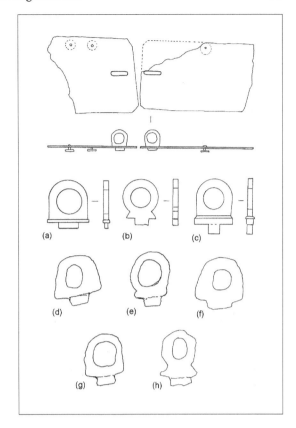

Fig. 5 A selection of *segmentata* tie rings:
A to C from Carnuntum (from von Groller,
1901b, plate 18); D to H from Caerleon.
(*Drawn by J. R. Travis*)

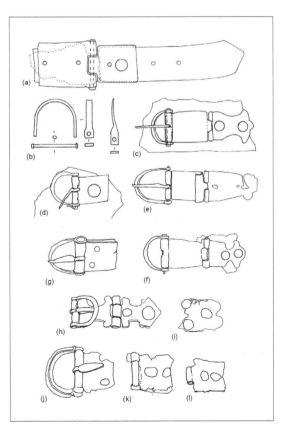

Fig. 6 A selection of *segmentata* buckles: A to
F from Carnuntum (from von Groller, 1901b,
plate 18); G from Caerleon; H to L from
Kalkriese (from Bunz & Spickermann, 2006).
(*Drawn by J. R. Travis*)

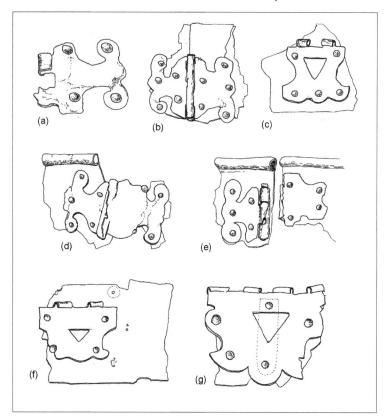

Fig. 7 A selection of *segmentata* hinges: A from Caerleon; B to G from Carnuntum (from von Groller, 1901b, plate XIX).
(*Drawn by J. R. Travis*)

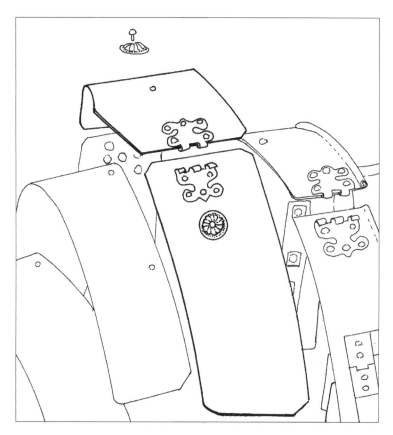

Fig. 8 Reconstruction of Corbridge Type A *lorica segmentata* with upper shoulder guards incorrectly aligned with 'points' outwards (after Connolly, in Russell-Robinson, 1975).
(*Redrawn by J. R. Travis*)

The next substantial discovery of *segmentata* plates came in 1964, at Corbridge, close to Hadrian's Wall, when a box was discovered containing parts of up to sixteen different but incomplete *lorica segmentatas* (Bishop and Allason-Jones 1988, 3). These appeared to fall into two basic typologies, A and B (with a possible subgroup C) – the Type As attaching upper bodies to girdle plates with buckles and leather straps, the Type Bs using hooks and loops (as on the Newstead). These finds were sufficiently complete to allow the now definitive reconstruction by Russell-Robinson (Russell-Robinson, 1975, 180, plate 491; Bishop 1998, 101, fig. 111). It also provided enough information to produce a more accurate representation of the Newstead variant.

Although there was some confusion over the dating of the finds, it appears likely that the Corbridge variants date from the late first to mid-second century AD, the Type A possibly being the earlier form, the more developed Newstead belonging to the later Antonine period (Bishop, 1998, 13; Curle, 1911, 56). However, more recent finds from an Augustan context, from Kalkriese, near Osnabruck in Germany, have now pushed back the first appearance of *segmentata* to the beginning of the first century AD (Franzius 1995, 69). This then provides a developmental sequence (and logical order for discussion) from this earliest known prototype at Kalkriese, to the Corbridge and later Newstead variants.

THE CORBRIDGE *LORICA*

The remains at Corbridge currently visible are those of a small garrison town, built on the Stanegate, of a mixed military/civilian nature, dating from the third to mid-fourth centuries AD. This overlies a series of at least four earlier military forts, dating from c. AD 86 to 163. The first excavations at the site, in 1906 by Leonard Woolley, outlined the defences, and those subsequently, from 1907 to 1914, extended this to include the central part of the fort. In 1930, HM Office of Works consolidated the remains and from 1934, although mostly between 1947 and 1973, Durham University ran a series of annual training excavations at Corbridge for its students (Bishop and Dore, 1988, 1).

The visible town is bisected (west to east) by the wide 'Stanegate' road. On the north side of this, towards the eastern end, is a large, forum-type complex. Richmond and Birley interpreted the town as a military depot (established at the time of Severus), and see this 'forum' as being a storehouse (Bishop and Dore, 1988, 2). This area (excavated as 'Site 11') overlies the *principia* (headquarters building) and *praetorium* (commanding officer's residence) of the earlier fort (Bishop and Dore, 1988, 3).

The *principia* is present throughout all four phases of the fort, initially built in timber and wattle/daub, with later stone cladding and eventual total stone rebuild (Bishop and Dore, 1988, 13). Around the *principia*, in the remainder of the Site 11 area, a number of different buildings have been identified during the different phases (granaries, barracks, hospital/ storehouse), the *praetorium* only appearing in Phase IV, initially in timber, later also rebuilt in stone (Bishop and Dore, 1988, 33).

In July 1964, when these training excavations were under the supervision of Professor Eric Birley and Charles Daniels, trenching was under way to investigate the earliest phase of this *principia*. The excavation clipped the corner of the ironbound wooden chest containing the hoard, which Daniels believed had been buried in the south-west corner of a room of the neighbouring Phase I building. This was a long corridor building, flanked on its eastern side by the ribbed, raised floor of a granary or storehouse. It was built close up to, and extending the full length of, the *principia*, with a series of small rooms on each side, interpreted by Daniels as a hospital or workshop (Bishop and Allason-Jones, 1988, 3). In his report on the 1974 excavations of the earliest fort (interpreted as an Agricolan supply base), close by at the Red House, Corbridge, Daniels interpreted similar 'hospital' buildings as workshops (*fabricae*), based on Schönberger's model from Künzing and Oberstimm (Hanson, Daniels, Dore and Gillam, 1979, 81). Daniels reported that wooden floorboards had been sawn through to dig a pit in order to bury the wooden chest, and that these had then been replaced. Later, the fire that destroyed the building had charred and shrunken the boards (Bishop and Allason-Jones, 1988, 4). If the hoard then belonged within this first phase, its dating would be within the range of *c*. AD 86 to 105 (Bishop and Dore, 1988, 3).

Bishop, however, disagreed with this interpretation by Daniels (Bishop and Allason-Jones, 1988, 4). He doubts that floorboards would have survived the destruction of the fire and believes that this burnt layer sealing the deposit is burnt wattle and daub from the later Phase II or III. During Phase II a building was erected close to, but not on top of, the burial site, which he believed to have been used as a store. The pit for the chest had then been dug through the burnt layer of wattle and daub from the demolition of this building, and the chest buried level with this layer. To strengthen this argument, he suggested that the technique exhibited in the manufacture of the enamel inlaid belt plate found within the hoard would have been 'rare in the first century but popular in the second century.' He therefore suggested a dating between AD 122 and 138 (Bishop and Allason-Jones, 1988, 5). This he assigns to Phase II, although the chronology described in his main work on the site (Bishop and Dore, 1988, 3) proposed that this would be the range for Phase III, Phase II being during the range of AD 105 to 122.

The illustration of this area in the publication of the hoard is somewhat confused (Bishop and Allason-Jones, 1988, fig. 1), showing both Phases II and III superimposed, as if in the same context. The area can be better understood in the reconstructed plans of Phase II and Phase III in the main report (Bishop and Dore, 1988, figs. 71 and 72). In both phases, the area where the chest was buried appears to be in an open, unused space. In both cases this is just north of a long, narrow building, built east–west, with a corridor on one side, a series of small rooms on the other side, interpreted in both phases as a storage building (Bishop and Dore, 1988, 135, fig. 28). If Bishop's argument that the pit being dug through the destruction layer of the earlier phase is followed, therefore, the deposit could date to any time between *c*. AD 105 and 138.

However, it is known that armour can, and still does (in the case of modern-day Life Guard ceremonial armour), remain in use for considerable periods of time, unless lost or damaged beyond repair by some catastrophic event. The armour from the Corbridge Hoard is in this respect no different, exhibiting signs of wear, damage and repair, appearing to be a collection of second-hand parts from a range of different cuirasses (none of which is complete), presumably waiting for possible future re-use (packed away for a rainy day). Its date of origin could therefore be considerably earlier than the range of AD 105 to 138 suggested.

The chest, once exposed, was not immediately excavated, recovery waiting until the end of the undergraduate excavation. The entire area around the box was then removed by undercutting and the whole assembly taken to the University of Newcastle Museum of Antiquities for controlled 'unpacking'. However, over twenty years elapsed between recovery and Bishop's subsequent publication, during which time he reports the laboratory notebooks, an inventory of the chest contents and at least one artefact went astray (Bishop and Allason-Jones, 1988, 1). With this in mind, it is hardly surprising that some inconsistencies exist within the published material. It is more surprising that more do not exist, and that almost forty years on, the majority of the finds can still be located and identified.

THE NEWSTEAD *LORICA*

Excavation of the Roman fort at Newstead between 1905 and 1909 by James Curle produced a wealth of artefacts, many attributable to deposition on the abandonment of the fort during the Antonine period. Some of these came from within the fort itself and some from the surrounding defensive ditches, consistent with the Roman practice of disposal of all un-reusable items on decommission of a site (Curle, 1911, 52–188). In a pit inside one of the side chambers of the headquarters building (*principia*) two pieces of segmented plate armour were discovered, later identified as a right-hand side breastplate and back plate of the variant of *lorica segmentata*, now named after this first find site. The plates were in poor, fragmentary condition and it is suggested by Bishop that the missing parts of this assembly (collar plate, upper shoulder guard and lesser shoulder plates), may have been present when originally deposited, but have not survived (Bishop, 2002, 46).

In 1906, further fragments of this Newstead-type *lorica* were found in the *praetorium* at Zugmantel, in deposits dated to *c.* AD259/60 (Thomas, 2003, 134–5). These provided an additional back plate (with remains of a copper-alloy closure fitting, along with a rolled edge at the neck) and fragments of a deep girdle plate with a rolled lower edge.

When discovered by Curle in 1905, the Newstead plates were initially interpreted the wrong way around, the back plate thought to be the front breastplate, and with the neck edge seen as the armhole. This was as a result of attempts to fit to von Groller's conception, using Trajan's Column, of plates riveted to a leather bodice, hinged at the back, lacing through holes at the front (Curle, 1911, 156). It was not until the von Groller interpretation was abandoned many years later that Russell-Robinson was able to attempt a credible interpretation of this variant (Russell-Robinson, 1975, 174). Drawing from contemporary finds from the Carnuntum 'Waffenmagazin' deposits from 1899 excavations (von Groller, 1901a, 95–113), Newstead and Zugmantel, he correctly aligned the breastplate and back plate (with the turned neck edge). He also estimated an assembly of six girdle plates (the lower one being extra deep, as at Zugmantel), suspended from the upper body assembly by suspension hooks and loops. In his interpretation, however, he connected the breastplates, collar plates and back plates by overlapping and riveting (rather than by use of hinges) to form a solid upper body assembly. For girdle plate fastenings, he proposed the use of tie rings, as had been found in numerous locations, suggesting a loop and pin system of lateral closure for breastplates and back plates.

Finds of Newstead-type plates and fittings from other sites have since added to this model, and also contributed to dating the span of its use. The Zugmantel deposits and those from Eining, Germany (back plate, collar plate, lesser shoulder guards and fragments of articulated arm guard), the latter dated to *c.* AD 299, push its use possibly to the fourth century AD (Thomas, 2003, 134–5). However, as these cuirasses may have been in use for considerable lengths of time before being discarded, this may be an overestimation.

Fig. 9 Chest and back plate of Newstead-type *lorica*, found at Newstead (from Curle, 1911, plate 22). (*Drawn by J. R. Travis*)

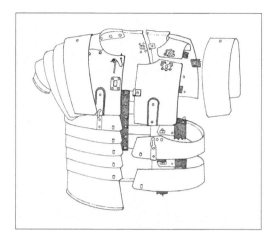

Fig. 10 Suggested reconstruction of Newstead-type *lorica segmentata*. (*Drawn by J. R. Travis*)

THE KALKRIESE *LORICA*

In AD 9, three Roman legions under the command of Quinctilius Varus were ambushed and defeated by Arminius (Cassius Dio, 56.18–22). One of the most interesting finds from the recent battlefield excavations was the breastplate from what is arguably the earliest example of Roman segmented armour. (Franzius, 1995, 71). There is a suggestion of possible *segmentata* parts from a yet earlier context from Dangstetten (Thomas, 2003, 127–9), although these are extremely fragmentary, making a definitive identification as *segmentata* problematic. It is highly unlikely that the one and only prototype was destroyed on its first incidence of use, and it is known that individual pieces of armour have always remained in use for long periods before decommission. Bishop, therefore, citing these Dangstetten artefacts, suggested that these early *lorica segmentata* may have been in use from 9 BC or earlier (Bishop, 2002, 23). However, although the material from Dangstetten, illustrated by Thomas (Thomas, 2003, 127–9, figs. 82.42–63), appears to be from *segmentata*, it consists of indeterminate bits of plate and buckles which may, or may not, be from *segmentata*. It has been known for scraps to turn out to be from something else on closer examination, perhaps arm protection (*manicae*), as at Newstead (Curle, 1911, plate 23), or as may be the case with some of the plates on display at Vindolanda. Therefore, although *segmentata* was probably in use pre-Kalkriese, the Kalkriese chest plate and collar plate are the only finds easily recognised as being *segmentata*, and it cannot be proven how widespread its use, even at the time of the Varus defeat.

Although Kalkriese initially only provided us with this breastplate and a few *lorica* fittings, and more recently with a mid-collar plate (Gryphius, 2003, 4), a reconstruction has been attempted using information from these and finds of early context non-Corbridge-style *segmentata* from other sites, including Britain.

SUMMARY

At the end of the Republican period, Roman legionaries and auxiliaries alike both traditionally wore mail (*hamata*), a style of *lorica* adopted from Gallic tribes of northern Italy, as seen on the Altar of Ahenobarbus, dating from the first century BC. Officers could wear mail, scale armour or muscle cuirass. Around the beginning of the Augustan period, it appears that experimental prototypes of a new form of *lorica* started to be introduced for some legionary troops – the *lorica segmentata*. The origins of *segmentata* are, however, enigmatic, the exact date and reasons for its development unknown. Certainly, segmented plate arm and leg protection is known from contexts of eastern peoples, as reflected in depictions of Sarmatian horsemen, although the trend in Roman armour assemblage towards the use of iron appears to derive from the influence of Gallic craftsmen.

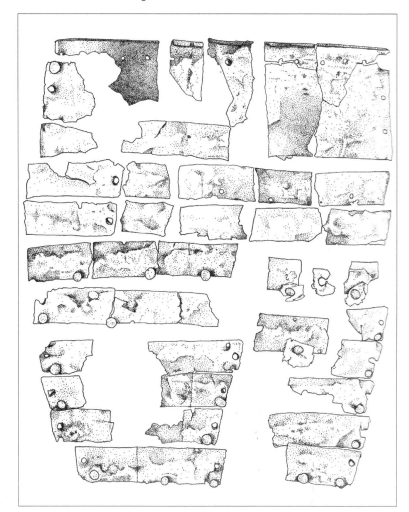

Fig. 11 Segmented plate armour from Newstead, probably from arm or leg protectors (from Curle, 1911, plate 23). (*Drawn by J. R. Travis*)

Fig. 12 Fragment of segmented plate armour from Vindolanda (inside view, rolled edge visible), interpreted as from *lorica segmentata* but more probably from arm protector, from position of rivet points. Also of note is the position of attachment loop at top left. (*Photo by J. R. Travis*)

The archaeological record is not entirely helpful. Pieces of plate armour are known from many locations, although many are small and fragmentary and could derive as easily from arm and leg protectors as from body armour. Although the finds of plate armour from the Kalkriese area, from combat contexts clearly dated to AD 9, are from recognisable *segmentata* components (breast and collar plates; Franzius, 1995, 71; Gryphius, 2003, 4), others, including those from Dangstetten, are less easily identified, the dating context of the latter to 9 BC being similarly of less solid determination (Thomas, 2003, 127–9).

In any event, it can be seen that *segmentata* probably did pre-date the Varian losses, at least in prototype form, and if the Dangstetten finds are correctly identified and dated, may date to the late first century BC. The possibility, therefore, is that this style of armour was developed in anticipation of the new weaponry and tactics of the opponents in the Germanic campaigns of the first century AD. However, it is known that Caesar was greatly concerned by the high losses suffered during his campaigns in Gaul and into Germania, initiating the large-scale re-kitting of his men using the skilled Gallic craftsmen (Caesar, *Bell. Gall.*). It is possible, therefore, that the first prototype forms of *segmentata* may have been initiated at that point, after witnessing the severe injuries caused by the Germanic-style tactics and slashing/hacking weapons, although there is of course no archaeological or literary evidence for this.

Alternately, although the ideology behind the development may stem from this point in time, practical development may have been delayed (by Caesar's death and the subsequent upheavals) and may not have once more been considered until Augustus similarly experienced severe losses in his civil war encounters and his campaigns in Pannonia and Spain (Cary and Scullard, 1979, 288–334).

In any event, this style of armour would offer greater defence against attack from overhead assault with hacking, slashing weapons, such as heavy swords and axes, or from downwardly directed heavy objects and projectiles. It is therefore not too surprising that most finds of *segmentata* come from hilly, frontier regions of the northern Empire, such as along the Germanic *limes* frontier (von Groller, 1901a; 1901b) and in Britain (Curle, 1911; Bishop and Allason-Jones, 1988). However, it is still not clear as to how comprehensively it was used, although probably not to the extent depicted on Trajan's Column (where it is used universally to depict all legionary troops), but possibly only being used for contingents of heavy infantry (these by consequence being most likely to be stationed in front-line positions). It is also possible that some of these heavy infantry contingents may also have been stationed at auxiliary forts (suggested by finds in non-legionary locations), their use being more determined by necessity of function rather than perhaps by citizen status. This existence of distinct 'heavy infantry' is evidenced from Josephus' descriptions of order of attack in his *Jewish Wars* (*Bell. Iud.*, III.123), although in these regions *segmentata* may have been more rarely used (due to confrontation by an entirely different opposing weaponry assemblage). It would, however, have offered ideal defence against the long, curved Dacian *falx* encountered in the campaigns depicted on Trajan's Column.

Segmentata remains have been found in Israel, at both Gamala and Masada, although not in large quantities (the finds from Masada consisting of just three tie loops, two hinged buckles and a lobate hinge), but nevertheless confirming Josephus' description of their use (Stiebel and Magness, 2007, 2–3, plate 3). In the context of the lengthy siege, in such difficult terrain, with the prospects of projectile assault from the defenders, its use is not contrary to that proposed in the more mountainous northern regions. The other forms of body armour, such as mail and scale, continued in use throughout this period, probably being still used by the majority of both legionary and auxiliary troops. However, both armour types also continued to adapt and develop, in answer probably again to changing opposition as the boundaries of the Empire expanded.

Again, *segmentata* fell out of use around the third to fourth century AD, returning once more to mail during the later Empire. The exact nature of this transition is unclear, although is more likely to be a gradual process rather than an abrupt cessation, but may have been in answer to changing enemy weaponry, or possibly as a result of economic factors, or a combination of both. The later forms of *segmentata*, as represented by the Newstead variants, do suggest a rationalisation of components, simplifying the number of girdle plates and upper body plates and reducing the use of leather strap fastenings (all potential weak points). It is possible also that in still later periods this process of adaptation extended to the formation of composite forms (in similar fashion to the composite mail and scale armour cavalry forms described in later chapters), with an example of one such composite appearing on the sculpture from Alba Iulia. Here *segmentata* girdle plates appear to be combined with small, rectangular chest plates (as seen with scale and mail shirts) and what seems to be a separate scale coif. Although it is not clear whether this particular sculpture represents military or gladitorial armour, in many cases the latter would have reflected the former, so the sculpture may in either event reflect military equivalents.

It is possible therefore that the move from *segmentata* was a gradual change, some of its more useful aspects being retained in other armour forms wherever these fitted to demands of the moment. However, as *segmentata* even at the height of its use may not have been as universally used as is currently believed to be the case, its gradual fall from use may be difficult to gauge archaeologically.

Furthermore, as most *segmentata* finds consist of small fragments, with only a handful of finds producing plates sufficiently large to be easily categorised, *segmentatas* across their geographical areas of use may have varied considerably, perhaps reflecting regional design features of numerous different craftsmen or workshops (our categorisations of Kalkriese, Corbridge and Newstead being artificial concepts). In reality there may have been dozens of variants in use at any time, the work of numerous different armourers and armoury workshops. Hopefully, as more military sites are investigated, more examples may come to light, expanding our knowledge of the level of uniformity and possible variants, along with time periods and purposes of use.

1BC/AD1	50	100	150	200	250
AUGUSTUS 27BC-AD14		VESPASIAN AD70-79	HADRIAN AD117-138	SEVERUS AD197-208	
	TIBERIUS AD14-37	TITUS AD79-81	ANTONINUS PIUS AD138-161	CARACALLA AD211-217	
	CALIGULA AD37-41	DOMITIAN AD81-96	MARCUS AURELIUS AD161-180	MACRINUS AD217-218	
	CLAUDIUS AD41-54	NERVA AD96-98	COMMODUS AD180-192	ELAGABALUS AD218-222	
	NERO AD54-68	TRAJAN AD98-117	CIVIL WAR AD192-197	SEVERUS ALEXANDER AD222-235	
KALKRIESE					
	CORBRIDGE				
		NEWSTEAD			
			ALBA IULIA		

Table 2.1 Timeline showing the approximate usage periods of *lorica segmentata*, in comparison to Imperial timeline.

III

LORICA SEGMENTATA
– Construction & Reconstruction

LORICA SEGMENTATA – COMPONENT PARTS

From the combination of evidence from sculptural and particularly archaeological sources, it has been possible to build an image of the common features and component parts of a basic *lorica segmentata*, although with some variation between typologies. Although the Romans were known to have widely used a form of copper-alloy known as *orichalcum*, in the absence of analysis, or where examination has been by visual means alone, the term 'copper-alloy' will be used in descriptions where appropriate.

Each *lorica segmentata* consists of two sets of horizontal 'girdle' plates (between six and eight plates depending on the variant), overlapping downwards, one set each side, riveted to internal leather strapping, joined at the centre back and centre front, using copper-alloy tie rings or loops. These are suspended from the upper body assembly, using either buckles and straps, or copper-alloy hooks and loops (again depending on variant) – each side consisting of breastplate at the front, between one and three back plates at the rear (depending on variant), linked by hinges to a collar plate. A shoulder assembly with five component parts then further protects the shoulder area on each side of the upper body assembly. The shoulder assembly on each side consists (working from the outside inwards) of two lesser shoulder plates, then two larger shoulder plates, overlapping downwards, linked to the upper body assembly by way of three internal leather straps, one at the front, one at the centre and one at the back. Any gap formed at the joining point between the shoulder and body assemblies is then covered by the upper shoulder guard, which overlaps both. This upper shoulder guard may be formed from a single piece (as in the Kalkriese and Newstead variants) or may be formed from three separate plates, front, middle and rear, joined by copper-alloy lobate hinges (as in the Corbridge variants).

As the hoard from Corbridge provided the remains of multiple sets of *segmentata*, it was possible using this material to theorise on the corresponding component parts of the more fragmentary variants from the later period Newstead and the presumed prototype Kalkriese, as discussed below.

NEWSTEAD

With all of the Newstead examples of *lorica segmentata*, the shoulder regions were damaged or missing, Russell-Robinson's reconstruction in this area being speculative. It was not until the discovery in 1989 of a Newstead-type right-hand-side back plate from Carlisle that this aspect of construction could be seen (Caruana, 1993, 15–17). This plate, although fragmentary and damaged, most of its lower half missing, retained its shoulder section, which displayed both evidence of an initial series of rivet holes, later replaced by repair or improvement with a large lobate hinge (64 mm by 48 mm), fixed by five copper-alloy rivets. Despite its fragmentary condition, the plate retained one of its fastening 'slots' (with copper-alloy rectangular cover plate, fixed by four rivets at the corners), and part of a lower suspension loop. This Caruana (1993, 17) used as evidence of the plate being of Newstead-type, from the assumption of only this variant using 'slot' closures.

The plate is considerably wider than any previous back plate, being at least 220 mm wide, which it is suggested could be either a chronological progression (this being a 'late' example of the variant), or from the cuirass being intended for a soldier with a wide back (Caruana, 1993, 17). The plate also appears to have two additional rivet holes close to the turned and flanged neck. This could then support the proposal by Poulter that the Newstead variant used an applied bronze strip to cover any sharp edges on the out-turned neck flange, these two rivet holes possibly serving to secure such a strip (Poulter, 1988, 31–49; Caruana, 1993, 17).

Poulter (1988, 37) also proposed an alternate method of lateral closure for the breastplate and back plates to that of loop and pin. He suggested a strap, looping through both slots, fastening with a buckle attached to one end of the strap. This system is similar to one initially proposed by Russell-Robinson in his early reconstruction made for Grosvenor Museum, Chester, in 1967, and bears similarities to that proposed for Corbridge Type B, based on my re-examination of the Corbridge material.

Bishop, however, suggested another alternate method for lateral closure, citing the plate from Zugmantel to support this view. He proposed a system of 'turning pins', secured by split pin, similar to that seen on some of the small, rectangular sports breastplates used with *hamata* and *squamata*. The plate from Zugmantel carries a rectangular/octagonal copper-alloy closure plate with just a small, round hole, which Bishop suggested could be used to accommodate a rotating 'turn-key' fitting (Bishop, 2002, 57). He also proposed a similar turn-key method of closure for the girdle plates, citing examples of girdle plates with slots, possibly to accommodate such turn keys, from Iza and Carnuntum (Bishop, 2002, 54, fig. 6.7).

However, this interpretation is still the object of much discussion among re-enactor groups, with experimentation on how these tie ring/turn-keys should be secured and fastened. Those tie rings found are not necessarily complete, their shafts being of varying lengths. One proposed reconstruction is that they should be perforated and secured on the inside with a split pin, although it is suggested that this would be a source of discomfort for the wearer. Another possibility is that the shaft would be peened/mushroomed to the inner plate, although this would of course prevent any rotation as a turn-key. It is also found through reconstruction that, left to their own devices, these turn-keys will rotate and work themselves back out, unless secured by either rods (individual or one long one), split pins or leather ties. If one long rod were used, presumably this would inhibit movement, although if smaller rods, or split pins, were used, they would indubitably have been lost with unfeasible regularity. If leather ties had been used, there could have been no perceived improvement over the previous tie loops system, apart perhaps from that of reduced manufacturing and replacement time (being cast fully-formed). This does still appear to be the more feasible method of use (the hole in the centre of these tie rings/turn keys being larger than those for existing sports-type turn keys, leather ties also being cheaper, easier and quicker to replace). However, no doubt the debate will still continue for many years to come.

Bishop also proposed in his reconstruction, based on the Carlisle example, that the upper body assembly (breastplate, collar plate and back plate) should be linked by large lobate hinges, rather than the solid rivets used by Russell-Robinson. This interpretation, linking large lobate hinges with Newstead-type *loricae*, allows individual finds of these large hinges to be categorised as Newstead finds, for example those from Great Chesters and Carnuntum. As new work on the Carnuntum 'Waffenmagazin' deposits has suggested an Antonine date, and finds of both Corbridge and Newstead types are now identified in the assemblage, Bishop suggested this may be representative of a changeover 'Antonine revolution' in military equipment (Bishop, 1998, 13). This then also provides a transitional overlap stage during the first half of the second century, where both Corbridge and Newstead variants may have been in use (Bishop, 2002, 49). However, this may just be indicative of regional differences, with individual workshops producing broadly similar but not identical products.

Similarly dating to within this timescale for Newstead-type armour, the sculpture from Alba Iulia, in Romania, appears to depict a military figure, wearing yet another variation of *segmentata*, along with segmented arm protection, or *manica* (Coulston, 1995, 13–17). Dated to a wide time band between Trajan's conquest and Aurelian's withdrawal from Dacia (from *c*. AD 106 to *c*. 270s), the figure carries a curved, rectangular shield with rectangular boss, similar to that found at Dura-Europos, and of the type usually associated with legionary troops. However, the use of the sword on the left argues for a later date (possibly second or third century), which is supported by Bishop, preferring a later date, after *c*. AD 200, based on the type of scale apparently used (Bishop, 2002, 92).

The *lorica* appears to have only four girth hoops, although this may just be a sculptural convention and not an accurate depiction. However, the difference to the conventional *segmentata* lies in the shoulder area. The *lorica* appears to combine articulated plates with scale, covering the neck and shoulder, fastened by two small rectangular plates in the centre of the chest, similar to the sports breastplates usually associated with mail and scale cuirasses. Coulston (1995, 17) views this as a 'hybrid' *segmentata*, but finds its use, combined with scale, as 'puzzling', considering that it would afford less protection than conventional shoulder plates.

However, the head of the figure is missing and the shoulder area damaged. The scale on the neck and shoulders and the rectangular closure plates appear to sit above, and separate to, conventional *segmentata* breastplates, which would have necessitated separate closure. It is possible, therefore, that this was not an integral part of the *segmentata* assembly below,

Fig. 13 Sculpture from Alba Iulia depicting soldier or gladiator wearing composite segmented armour. (*Drawn by J. R. Travis*)

but may have been an additional, separate coif-type protection for the head and neck area. The shoulder plates may have been omitted to prevent them tangling in the overlying scale, or it is also possible that the shoulder plates were present, but are now not evident due to subsequent damage to the shoulder areas of the sculpture.

What is clear, from the available finds of *segmentata* plates and fittings identified as being of Newstead type, is that there is still insufficient information for a definitive reconstruction, due to the poor, fragmentary state of the finds, and to the great variety evident within the assemblage. It may be that there is no Newstead type, but that numerous variants had by that time evolved. This may have been due to the length of time it had been in use, and also to the number of individual armourers who had each allowed his imagination to dream up countless improvements and adaptation to whatever current conditions dictated (enemies, weapons, climate, etc).

CORBRIDGE – INCONSISTENCIES IN THE PUBLISHED REPORT

In *Excavations at Corbridge – the Hoard*, Cuirass 5 is photographed (Bishop and Allason-Jones, 1988, 43, fig. 45) as a complete left-hand upper body assembly with its upper shoulder guard in its original position. In this assembly, the central plate has one straight side and one pointed side, similar to that from Cuirass 1. The crucial point of note here is that in this photograph the central plate of upper shoulder guard 5 is positioned with its pointed side inwards, towards the neck edge.

In Russell-Robinson's original reconstruction (Bishop and Allason-Jones, 1988, 101, fig. 111), he followed the format of this photograph of Cuirass 5 and also put the point of his central plate to the inside neck. However, in later constructions (Russell-Robinson, 1975, plates 491–3) working with P. Connolly (Russell-Robinson, 1975, figs. 178 and 180) he revised this opinion to put the point outwards, away from the neck. This was based on the published 'evidence' from the Cuirass 1 upper shoulder guard, which appeared from the illustrations to point outwards. The assembly from Cuirass 5 being the other way around (point inwards) was then assumed to have been due to its reuse from an earlier *lorica*, transposed onto the opposite side. Another argument towards this view was that, with the point towards the neck, the plate would dig into the neck on raising the arm. However, from my recent reassessment, it is clear that Russell-Robinson's original reconstruction with the point inwards was correct, the point sliding behind the neck when the arm was raised (the plate being shaped to the slope of the shoulder, making reversal impossible).

In the illustrations in the published report, the right-hand front, collar and back assembly of Cuirass 1 (Bishop and Allason-Jones, 1988, 26, fig. 26) is associated with right-hand upper shoulder assembly 1 (Bishop and Allason-Jones, 1988, 28, fig. 28). This is described as being assembled with the point of its central plate outwards, with its damaged outer plate (without decorated boss) being its front plate and its complete plate (with decorated boss) being to the back.

However, this opinion is based on the incorrectly drawn or printed patterns. The plates have been expanded outwards in the correct sequence, but have been flipped, so that the internal leather straps appear attached to the wrong side (Bishop and Allason-Jones, 1988, fig. 25). If expanded correctly, the assembly should open in the opposite direction. The upper shoulder from this cuirass may still, however, belong to the right-hand side, and correctly associated, depending on which of its end plates comes to the front.

On these end plates, one plate has a plain rivet; the other has a decorative boss. On Cuirass 2 upper shoulder guard, there is also one plain rivet and one decorative boss (Bishop and Allason-Jones, 1988, 32, fig. 32). This is shown, as with that from Cuirass 1, as having its plain rivet to the front. However, this plate could easily be turned around to bring the decorative boss to the front, as this is a plate with parallel sides (no pointed side), and there are no indications on the back of the direction of leather strapping. The upper left-hand assembly of Cuirass 3 (Bishop and Allason-Jones, 1988, 33, fig. 34) is also associated with an upper

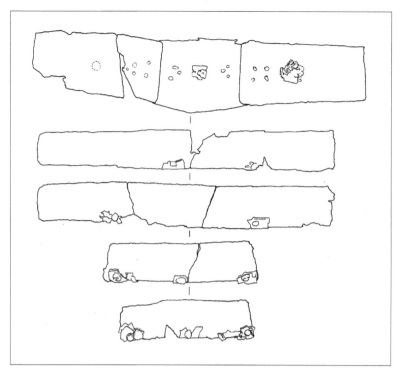

Fig. 14 Cuirass 5 upper shoulder assembly, with each plate 'flipped', which can be seen from the position of the traces of leather strapping, as shown in Bishop & Allason-Jones, 1988, fig. 25. (*Redrawn by J. R. Travis*)

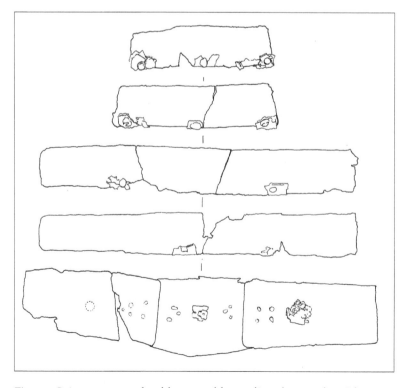

Fig. 15 Cuirass 5 upper shoulder assembly, re-aligned correctly, with centre point towards the neck. (*Drawn by J. R. Travis*)

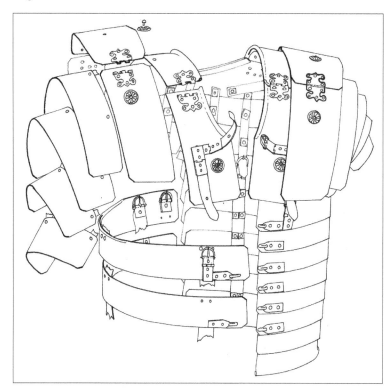

Fig. 16 Corbridge Type
A *lorica segmentata*,
amended to show
correctly aligned upper
shoulder guards.
(*Drawn by J. R. Travis*)

shoulder guard that has no definite point and has both one plain rivet and one decorative boss (Bishop and Allason-Jones, 1988, 35, fig. 36). However, from the slope on the end plates of this upper shoulder assembly, it is clear that, in this case at least, the plain rivet goes to the back. For purely decorative, aesthetic reasons, it makes more sense to have decorative bosses at the front, and plain rivets, if present, at the back. It seems plausible, therefore, that these other assemblies with plain rivets may also need to be flipped in the original illustrations to put their plain rivets to the back. These considerations of the illustrations were then borne out by observation of the original plates, which were found to be body-shaped (to indicate 'neck' side) and in profile, sloping with a gentler gradient to the rear.

WHERE FINDS ARE STORED

The finds of the Corbridge Hoard are currently stored in two separate locations: the Corbridge site museum and Newcastle University Museum of Antiquities (see Appendix). The plates are now in extremely fragile condition and very fragmentary, but it was still possible to identify each to the corresponding published illustration. Although it had been suggested that the plates had completely mineralised (L. Allason-Jones, pers. comm., February 2003), they were found still to be sensitive to magnetism.

On examination of the finds at Corbridge and Newcastle, most noticeable were the marked differences between them and *lorica* reconstructions currently in use by re-enactors. Not only were the bronze tie-loops, hinges and buckles so much more delicate, made from thinner metal, than their modern copies, but also all of the plates appeared to have been deliberately shaped and moulded to the body. This is in marked contrast to the flat plates of the reconstructions, which have been based on the published flat pattern/illustrations.

A full description of the individual plates can be found in the Appendix, 'Reassessment of the armour from the Corbridge Hoard', and in Table 3.2, 'Analysis of Corbridge Hoard armour stored at Corbridge and Newcastle'.

METALLURGICAL ANALYSIS

Due to time constraints, the reassessment of the Corbridge material was restricted to visual examination. Some metallurgical analysis work had been carried out, however, by A. R. Williams in 1977 and 1978, on two sections of *lorica segmentata* (pieces refs 5767 and 2199) from Vindolanda (Sim, 1998, 9). The description does not specify to what parts of the *lorica* these plates belonged, although their thicknesses were found to be consistent with those Corbridge upper body plates examined in this reassessment (ref. 5767 being between 1.8 and 2.9 mm and ref. 2199 being between 1.6 and 2.3 mm). Both plates were found to have oxidised sufaces with uncorroded centres, also appearing to be consistent with the condition of the Corbridge plates (which still reacted to simple testing with a magnet). Both plates were studied with a metallurgical microscope after first being polished and etched with natal (2 per cent).

In the first plate (5767), two bands were observed within the metallic structure, the lower band being mostly ferrite with rows of slag inclusions, the upper band containing both ferrite and pearlite (which is produced at higher temperatures), and having a carbon content of 0.3 per cent. The second plate (2199) also contained ferrite, with a band close to one surface where this was again mixed with a small amount of pearlite (less than 0.1 per cent carbon). Both plates were found to have further slag inclusions along the central section between the bands (Sim, 1998, 9).

Sim interpreted these findings to suggest that the plates had been formed by either folding and forging a bloom of metal, or by welding together two pieces of metal, chosen deliberately for their properties of soft ferrite on the inside and hard pearlite for the outer surface, where resistance to attack was required (Sim, 1998, 9). However, it is also possible that more pronounced pearlite formation on one surface may be due to that surface being heated to higher temperatures during the forging process, this side being inserted downwards, directly in contact with the heat source. This would also have been likely to be the case with the reproduction Kalkriese breastplate, which was heated with its convex, outer surface more directly into the heat source, to maximise the heating effect of the forge. In these circumstances any pearlite formation on the outer surface could have been more by way of a happy accident than by conscious mixing of metals with different properties, although the knowledge of this effect could prompt a deliberate process of choice.

In his presentation to the Carlisle Millennium Conference, October 2005, Sim also described further analysis of finds of *segmentata* and his attempts to reproduce similar plates working from bloom. He stated that he had been unable to reproduce the level of purity observed in the artefacts using charcoal as his fuel, as he had not been able to achieve sufficiently high temperatures (Sim, pers. comm., October 2005). He had, however, not been aware of the possible Roman use of coal as a fuel for forging, smithing and possibly also smelting (evidenced from sites such as Wilderspool, Manchester and Templeborough), which would have provided far higher temperatures than could be achieved by the use of charcoal alone (Travis, 2005), and would have produced results matching the level of purity sought by Sim.

CORBRIDGE – DISCUSSION

The current A and B typology of the Corbridge finds was based on the method of suspension of the girdle plates from the upper body, which on a Type A breastplate was by using horizontal and vertical leather straps and buckles (Bishop, 2002, 323). It can also be seen here just how delicate and fragmentary these plates now are, one Type A breastplate even showing signs of inexperienced museum repair, with the horizontal buckle now glued to the vertical strap. Despite the fragmentary condition, however, it is possible to see some evidence of repair to hinges prior to deposition, suggesting that these had been used and were either stored for future re-use or repair. Traces were also seen on one plate, close to the neck

Fig. 17 Corbridge Type A breastplate (cuirass 1)
– with incorrectly re-attached buckle.
(*Photo by J. R. Travis*)

Fig. 18 Corbridge Hoard remains – Cuirass 5
breastplate. (*Photo by J. R. Travis*)

turning, of a deposit, which could have been an applied solder of tin, pewter or some other material, to seal the crease from the elements. It may alternatively be evidence of surface tinning. However, it was not possible during this reassessment to analyse this deposit, which perhaps may be possible at some future date.

The assemblies all differed slightly, being probably the work of different armourers, made for individuals of different sizes, some of whom may have been left-handed, with buckles on the opposite sides. One notable feature, not apparent in the reconstructions, was the shape of the end of the girdle plates, being angled, not vertical, and also the size of the apparent overlap. This was much more substantial than in modern reconstructions and must have formed a more closely fitting and more solid cuirass. It was also found that double rivets were used to fix the internal leathers on each girdle plate. Many reconstructions skimp on this, using single rivets, which then cause too much horizontal sliding. As the internal leathering visible on the plates was mineralised, it was not possible to determine with absolute certainty what type of leather had been used, or what processing that leather had been subjected to. However, mindful of the stresses to which it would have been subjected, it would seem likely that cow hide would be preferable to thinner leathers such as goat, this being supported by the apparent thickness of the visible remains. Turned edges were found on the bottom plate of each set and at the underarms. On close examination, all appear to be folded, turned edges and not thickened by upsetting (hammering the plate on its edge) as suggested by Sim (2002, 62; Bishop, 2002, 102).

CORBRIDGE TYPE B – PROPOSED ALTERNATIVE METHOD OF CLOSURE

Breastplates of Type B were attached using loops on their lower edge to hooks on the girdle plates, as on the later Newstead variant (Bishop, 2002, 36). Again, in comparing the finds to the illustrations, it was noted that some details of the reverse sides of some plates had been omitted. In particular, the reverse of one Type B front plate, Cuirass 6, had the remains of a leather strap projecting beyond the centre edge, terminating in a torn end, suggesting that it had originally continued for some distance. This strap was attached to the plate directly behind the front fastening buckle. It had not been trimmed off and, in use, if it had served no purpose, would have been a great nuisance to the wearer. Its torn edge, however, suggested that its presence in the box was probably because it was awaiting repair.

In all of the finds of Corbridge B breastplates, only buckle sides are present. I would suggest that this rear strap is evidence of an alternative, different method of horizontal fastening on the Corbridge B variants. Instead of the leather strap which matches the front buckle being on the opposite plate, as on Type A, it may alternatively be this rear strap which then passes through a slot on the opposite plate, looping back to the buckle. If the non-buckle sides did not have a leather strap (susceptible to tearing), but a slot as proposed above, this may account for their absence in the Corbridge 'repair' box. This would then be a similar method of fastening to that more recently proposed by Poulter (1988, 37) for the later Newstead form, using strap and buckle instead of pins. The Corbridge B type then would appear even more closely to be a transitional stage to the Newstead. It may even have implications for the Newstead reconstructions, which are based on finds of sides with slots.

CORBRIDGE SHOULDER ASSEMBLY

The shoulder assembly is an area of inconsistency in most modern reconstructions, and again stems from printing anomalies in the original publication. In some places the wrong photographs have been printed, but one illustration has had a greater effect (Bishop and Allason-Jones, 1988, fig. 25). Here each individual plate of the shoulder assembly, listed as Cuirass 5, has been flipped vertically, giving the impression that it concertinas out in the opposite direction, with the point on the mid-plate of the upper shoulder guard pointing

Fig. 19 Corbridge Hoard remains – Cuirass 6 breastplate, rear view.
(*Photo by J. R. Travis*)

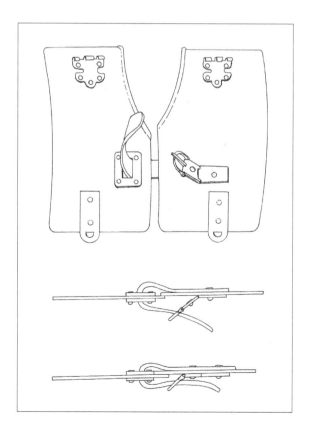

Fig. 20 Suggested alternate method of fastening – Corbridge Type B.
(*Drawn by J. R. Travis*)

Fig. 21 Cuirass 5 upper shoulder
guard (from above).
(*Photo by J. R. Travis*)

Fig. 22 Cuirass 5 upper shoulder
guard (from side).
(*Photo by J. R. Travis*)

away from the neck. This appears to have confused even Russell-Robinson. He altered his correct original interpretation for the incorrect later version, as can be seen on Connolly's line drawing (Russell-Robinson, 1975, 178, fig. 180), which was then widely used as a model by other reconstructors.

In comparison to the actual finds from Cuirass 5, however, it can be seen that the mid-plate points towards the neck. What is not apparent on the illustrations, because they are 2-D, is that the upper shoulder assembly is clearly body-shaped, sloping down to the contours of the shoulder. In profile, it is an inverted V-shape at the neck edge, and a more rounded U-shape towards the shoulder. The point of the mid plate, despite some suggestions that it would dig into the neck, sits slightly to the back of centre and would slide behind the neck when the arm was raised.

RIVETS, BOSSES, HINGES, ETC. – FUNCTIONALITY

In many current reconstructions worn by re-enactors or in museum displays, iron rivets are widespread. This choice of iron rivets appears to have been made, based on their obvious strength, in the absence of any information about the originals in the published reports. The weakest part of the *lorica* is the internal leather strapping, which through use eventually requires replacement, at which point the disadvantages of iron rivets become apparent. From the reassessment, it was found, however, that all rivets were of soft copper, which would have made them easier to extract when repairs became necessary.

For fixing brass fittings, such as tie loops and buckles, small dome-headed rivets had been inserted from the front and peened on the reverse. However, in contrast to the reconstructions, it was found on the originals that different rivets had been used to fix the internal leathering of the girdle plates and shoulder assemblies. Here rivets with flat heads of approximately 8 mm diameter can be seen on the inside, directly against the leathers, suggesting that they must have been inserted from the inside first then flattened on the outside. This also has implications for the assembly sequence, which must have been started from the bottom plate upwards – the opposite to current practice.

Roves were therefore not necessary and are rarely used, except in areas of later repair. This is in contrast to the Connolly reconstruction (Russell-Robinson, 1975, figs. 178 and 180), which uses roves on the inside behind every rivet. The only places where roves do appear to have been used were on the upper shoulder guards, where for constructional and aesthetic reasons, domed rivets have been inserted from the outside, through the metal, then leather, and require a solid surface to peen. The roves then prevent the rivet from pulling back through the leather, and because this is an area of extreme stress, decorative bosses serve a similar function on the outside.

KALKRIESE BREASTPLATE

Excavations carried out in 1994 at Kalkriese in Germany have uncovered a number of artefacts from an unrecorded context (Thomas, 2003, 130), possibly attributable to the Augustan period 'Varusschlacht' of AD 9, including a complete (left-hand side) breastplate of an early 'prototype' *lorica segmentata* (Franzius 1995, 71 and 76).

The plate shows signs of bronze edging. Thomas (2003, 130) reports a 'bronze U-shaped channel' covering the neck edge of the plate. There is also the possibility of brass edging on three of the other edges, with the exception perhaps of the top (hinged) shoulder edge, where it could have been an encumbrance. The plate is 188 mm in length and 135 mm in width, with a thickness between 1 mm and 3 mm. It is slightly convex, indicating body-shaping during the forging process. At the shoulder one side of a sub-lobate hinge remains, fixed by three dome-headed copper rivets, which would have attached the plate to a mid-collar plate (possibly similar to that described below).

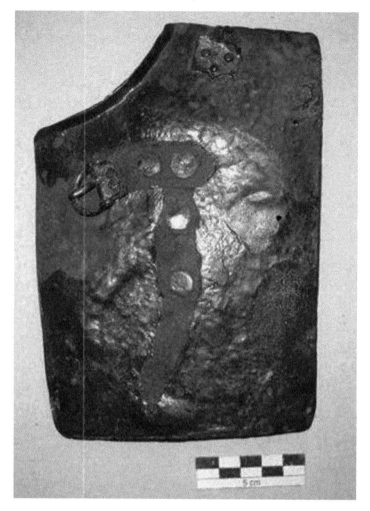

Fig. 23 Kalkriese breastplate. (*Photo by S. Wilbers-Rost*)

Fig. 24 Kalkriese breastplate – close up of sub-lobate hinge. (*Photo by S. Wilbers-Rost*)

The mineralised remnants of two leather straps can be seen, set at right angles, one vertical and one horizontal, fixed directly to the plate by large flat-headed copper rivets – the vertical strap presumably to serve for attachment to a corresponding buckle on suspended girdle plates (as with the later Corbridge A versions), and the horizontal strap for closing to the breastplate on the opposite (right-hand) side. This horizontal strap is terminated by a bronze buckle, the hinged buckle plate being attached to the leather by a small, copper, dome-headed rivet.

Two holes are visible on the outside (arm) edge of the plate, presumably used for the attachment of the plate to the shoulder assembly, by riveting to internal leather strapping. One hole is quite close to the edge, approximately 1.5 cm, and approximately 5 cm from the top edge. The second, lower rivet hole is approximately 10 cm from the top edge and set slightly further in, at approximately 2 cm from the side edge.

KALKRIESE MID-COLLAR AND BACK PLATES

Upper body plates have been found at Chichester, in Britain, dating from Claudian contexts shortly after the AD 43 invasion (Down 1978, 301, fig. 10.36 ii and iv: 1981, 164, fig. 8.28, 2). Although these are much later in date than those from Kalkriese, they do exhibit some similarities and differ sufficiently from the Corbridge finds to suggest that they belong to the earlier Kalkriese type, or at least a close variant.

The three plates found consist of a mid-collar plate, a back plate and a single-piece upper shoulder guard.

The mid-collar plate, despite using Corbridge-style lobate hinges, is much squatter and wider in shape, more closely resembling the recent find from Kalkriese, although, being made

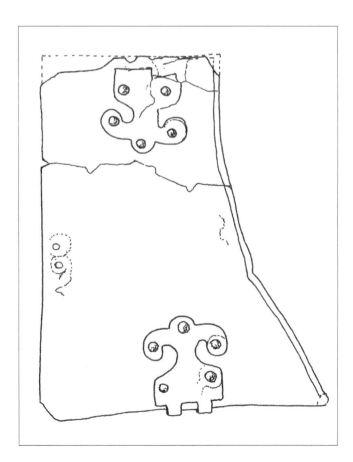

Fig. 25 Chichester collar plate, for comparison to Kalkriese plate (from Down, 1981). (*Redrawn by J. R. Travis*)

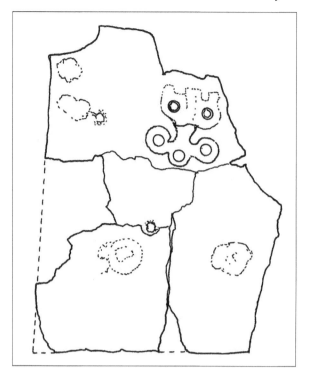

Fig. 26 Chichester back plate
(from Down, 1978, fig. 10.36).
(*Redrawn by J. R. Travis*)

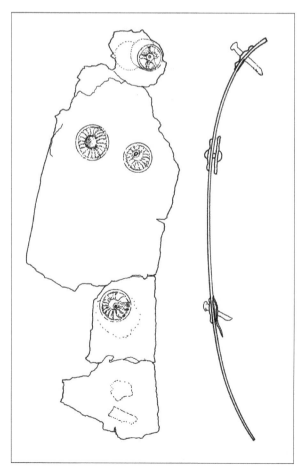

Fig. 27 Chichester single-piece upper
shoulder guard (from Down, 1978,
fig. 10.36). (*Redrawn by J. R. Travis*)

of double-thickness plate, it does not need the brass protective neck edging (Down 1981, 164, fig. 8.28, 2).

The second plate (Down 1978, 301, fig. 10.36 ii), although described in the published report as a shoulder plate, can only be interpreted as a back plate, which can be seen by rotating the illustration and aligning the position of the hinge. In this way the other rivet holes on the plate can be interpreted as being for closure fittings and internal leathers, although the resulting back plate is significantly deeper than the narrow Corbridge-style back plates. However, whereas on the Corbridge type three narrow plates of similar depth are used, to give a similar balanced appearance with this wider plate only two such plates would be necessary each side.

One possible Kalkriese upper shoulder guard from Vindonissa has been identified by Bishop as being a front or back lower plate from a three-part assembly, the identification being based on the Kalkriese-style hinge (Bishop 2002, 27, fig. 4.5). However, it appears to be extremely wide for an upper shoulder guard, which may have made mobility very difficult. An alternative interpretation of this plate may be as a fragment of back plate, which then makes more sense of the remaining rivet holes.

The Chichester upper shoulder guard consists of a single plate, unlike the Corbridge three-piece hinged units, with paired sets of decorated bosses (Down, 1978, 301, fig. 10.36 iv). One reconstruction using this plate has suggested its use combined with mail, part of the argument for which being the long, bent shank remaining on the central rivet (Bishop, 2002, 74, fig. 8.8). However, it is unlikely that it was used with mail, as it would be very difficult to put on and would probably not remain attached for long before tearing. When used with Kalkriese plates, however, with slightly different internal strapping arrangement to the Corbridge version, it allows full use of both side rivet holes on the Kalkriese breastplate. Furthermore, when attaching to internal leathers, top central rivets do tend to leave a long shank as on the Chichester original. I have therefore assigned this single-piece plate to the Kalkriese form as it differs significantly from the Corbridge three-part, and comes from an early Claudian context. However, it is possible that this is a later transitional variant, or may just be representative of the work of a different armourer.

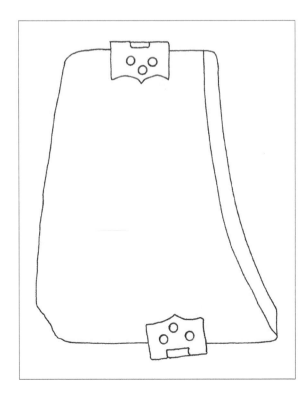

Fig. 28 Kalkriese collar plate (from photograph by Gryphius, *Varus Kurier*, 2003). (*Drawn by J. R. Travis*)

At the time that the reconstruction was commenced, the breastplate was the only known *segmentata* plate found at Kalkriese. The remaining parts of the reconstruction, therefore, were purely conjectural, based on presumed similarities to finds of early Claudian contexts elsewhere, specifically those from Chichester. However, since completion of the project, further excavation at Kalkriese located a mid-collar plate which bears strong resemblance in shape to that from Chichester. This has only been briefly published in the excavation's magazine, *Varus Kurier*, and it is not clear how closely the finds are associated (so in probability not from the same *lorica*), although being from the same battle context, must be contemporary in date (Gryphius, 2003, 4).

KALKRIESE GIRDLE PLATES

There is no evidence from Britain, and very little elsewhere, of girdle plates positively identified as Kalkriese-type. A few fragments of plates have been found in Europe, at Vindonissa and Dangstetten (Bishop 2002, 25), which may be girdle plates. However, it is not possible to say with any certainty how many were used each side, whether they were brass-trimmed, or how they were fastened. The Corbridge remains appear to show eight plates per side with Type A, and seven with Type B. One set from Stillfried has been found which appears to have been asymmetrical – seven plates one side, eight on the other (Bishop 2002, 47). However, it was observed from use of reconstructed armour that eight girdle plates will cause bruising to the left leg on the average man during normal use – picking up shield, forming shield wall, etc. Therefore, the number of plates may be a typological progression, possibly the work of different armourers, or perhaps just due to the sets being made for tall or short men. As with modern armies, soldiers traditionally throw away any kit that causes problems. This could explain the asymmetric set from Stillfried, possibly where sets have been 'mix-and-matched' for comfort. With this in mind, the reconstructed Kalkriese has been made with only seven plates each side, being best suited to the individual intending to wear it.

KALKRIESE – METHOD OF CLOSURE

There has been some discussion on the method of closure of the girth hoops. In Bishop's *Lorica Segmentata Volume 1*, he suggested that as no Corbridge-style tie loops have been found associated with Kalkriese armour, something cruder must have been used, such as simple holes with thong threaded through. Alternately, he suggested the use of front and back buckles and straps, as seen on Trajan's Column (Bishop 2002, 27). In considering these possibilities, the following drawbacks come to mind:

- With simple hole and thong, the thong would abrade on the edge of the hole and the thong would probably soon tear.
- When the *lorica* is not being worn, the girdle plates of the *segmentata* usually concertina into themselves. If buckles were to have been used, they would probably damage or jam when the *lorica* is in its collapsed form.
- Furthermore, not only does Trajan's Column date to a much later time, when it is presumed design improvements would have been made, it is widely accepted, even by Bishop, that it is a much-stylised representation which cannot be taken as an authentic view of actual equipment.

However, although Corbridge-style tie loops have not yet been found in Augustan contexts, they have been found in Claudian contexts, in Europe and in Britain, dating close to the invasion, such as at Hod Hill and Chichester (Down 1978, 292, fig. 20). For this reason, and in the absence of any evidence to the contrary, tie loops have been used on the reconstruction.

RECONSTRUCTION OF THE KALKRIESE

To test the potential compatability of the Kalkriese plates to those from early Claudian contexts in Britain, such as those from Chichester, it was decided to construct a hybrid *lorica* using both sets of plates, following as closely as possible the materials and methodologies of construction from the later Corbridge finds. The first stage in the reconstruction process was to make a cardboard mock-up using the finds from Kalkriese and Chichester as a basic template, but with minor adjustments in order to fit the intended individual.

The pattern pieces were then translated into sheet steel blanks before forge-shaping breast, collar and back plates, alternating between heating and hammering into sandbags. The neck edges of all plates were then out-turned before reheating and the brass/copper-alloy edging attached. This was applied only to the neck edge itself on the back and collar plates, but also around all of the outer edges of the front plate, as this has been suggested on the original find. There is the possibility that this may have been omitted on the edge where it would have been joined to the collar plate, as at this point any edging may have prevented the hinge from lying flush to the plates (however, on testing on the reconstruction, this was found not to be the case, so neither proving nor disproving the possibility).

Once the forge-blackened plates had been cleaned up by lightly polishing, the two halves of the upper body were ready to be assembled, using two small sub-lobate brass hinges on each side. The three plates of each half were offered up and the positions of the hinges marked. The hinges were then attached first to the mid-collar plate, so that the angles of the front and back plates could be adjusted to fit the body. Rivet holes were punched, first through the hinge plates, then through the body plates to match, flattening from the reverse to counter the dishing caused by the punch. The hinges were also laid on a flat anvil and struck close to the hinge pin to produce a flat back surface which would sit flush with the body plates. The hinges were then attached using small dome-headed copper rivets,

Fig. 29 Kalkriese reconstruction: collar plate completed – forged, fitted with copper-alloy trim, but still forge-blackened, in unpolished state. (*Photo by J. R. Travis*)

Fig. 30 Kalkriese reconstruction: back plate completed – still in forge-blackened state. (*Photo by J. R. Travis*)

inserted from the outside, then mushroomed and peened flat on the inside. Rivet holes were also punched for the attachment of the vertical and horizontal fastenings and the internal strapping of the shoulders.

The horizontal and vertical straps and buckles were then attached using larger flat-headed copper rivets, inserted from the outer surface. These were again peened on the inside, only using strengthening roves in positions where the same rivet was also being used to secure leather strapping on the inside. The internal vertical fastening straps were also then used to suspend the lower back plates from the upper plates.

Girdle plates were bent to the shape of the body, starting with the upper hoop. This plate was also reduced in height on the under arm top surface by turning over the edge. With the top plates shaped to the body, the lower plates were then bent so that each fitted inside the one above. The front and back end edges were then cut at a sloping angle, after allowing for an area of overlap. The positions of the internal straps were then marked on the inside, along with the positions of pairs of rivet points close to the top edge of each plate. Tie loops and buckles were attached to the plates prior to assembly, in the same way that the hinges were attached to the upper body, apart from the lower two hoops which were not intended to be fastened.

Finally, the girdle plates were assembled from the bottom plate first, working upwards, the rivets passing from the inside and being peened on the outside. The rivets were flat-headed, around 8 mm in diameter, and made from soft copper, so that they could later be removed more easily when re-strapping is necessary. The lesser shoulder plates were assembled in similar way to the girdle plates, working from the outer plate inwards, overlapping subsequent plates to conceal and protect the rivets on the plate below. When the assembly was complete and attached to the upper body plates, it formed an unprotected gap. Covering with the single-piece upper shoulder guard (the final piece to add) then protected this gap.

Unlike the previous plates, it was not possible to attach the upper shoulder guard using rivets inserted from the inside. For this reason, the small, domed copper rivets passed through strengthening bosses on the outside, the metal of the plate, the leather strap, and finally through a fixing rove. This allowed a solid surface for the rivet to be peened against, and prevented the rivet pulling back through in use. Furthermore, because it was a particularly awkward place to get a rivet into, the top centre rivet inevitably ended up with a considerably long shank, bent over inside, in exactly the same way as the Chichester plate.

KALKRIESE – POSSIBLE VARIANTS

As with the Corbridge *lorica*, Bishop has suggested two variants for the Kalkriese: Type A, closed by straps riveted directly to plates (as on the Kalkriese breastplate) and Type B, using fixed buckles, as have been found as separate small finds at Kalkriese and other contemporary sites (Bishop, 2002, 27). However, from experiments during reconstruction, it was apparent that this distinction between hinged and unhinged buckles is more likely to be determined by the position and function of use. For example, any buckle used for the front vertical fastening of the top girdle plate to the upper body has to be hinged. When the vertical strap is fastened, the breastplate has to pass down behind the hinge to be able to get the pin into the strap. If the plate cannot pull down behind the buckle, it will not fasten close enough and will form a gap, defeating the purpose of having the armour.

For the inside back buckles this does not apply, and simple fixed buckles are adequate, as are initially the simple strap and buckles used for the horizontal closures. It is only with prolonged use that these would experience tearing, which must have eventually led to the hinged buckles and straps on the later Corbridge varieties. I would rather suggest that any possible A and B typology would be more likely to centre around the transition from sub-lobate to stronger lobate hinges, probably by the time of the invasion of Britain, and as are exhibited in the finds of Kalkriese-style plates from Chichester.

FINISHING/POLISHING

There has been much discussion over the finishing and subsequent treatment of the *lorica segmentata* in use. Within the re-enactment contingent, a variety of treatments are employed, some being less authentic than others, which then leads on to the general divide between reconstructions made by academics for museum display and those made by enthusiasts for living history display. One aspect which all of these reconstructions have in common, that of Russell-Robinson and the above described Kalkriese reconstruction included, is the use of modern materials. As none of us have access to a genuine Roman foundry or leather processing *fabrica*, some compromises have had to be made, with choice wherever possible to the nearest equivalent, for example the use of vegetable-tanned leather rather than chemically processed. The metal used, however, has in all cases been modern sheet steel, the facilities for producing an authentic Roman billet of iron from authentic raw materials not being available. Even if a Roman-style furnace were to be used, the resulting billet would never be exactly comparable to that produced in antiquity for numerous reasons. The same sources of raw materials and fuels could never be duplicated due to their seams of origin being worked out/extracted centuries ago. In addition, the metal produced would be affected by modern background atmospheric pollution during the smelting process, along with water-based pollution during any quenching process, making chemical differences to the metal at microscopic level.

This does not mean that any reconstruction using modern materials is entirely without merit, as these can be a valuable aid in testing construction techniques, general wear damage, and indicating areas liable to frequent repair. The work of Williams, on metallurgical examination of existing plates, and that of Sim, on reproduction of Roman billet, negate the necessity for a complete reconstruction of *lorica segmentata* (or any other specific items of military equipment), using fully authentic materials.

The range of general wear on modern reconstructions would also never exactly replicate that experienced by the 'real thing', again in part due to use of approximate equivalent materials not exactly responding as would the original, but also due to it never being

LORICA SEGMENTATA COMPONENT PARTS	Kalkriese	Corbridge A	Corbridge B/C	Newstead (Connolly)	Newstead (Bishop)
Ferrous Plates					
Breastplate	2	2	2	2	2
Collar plate	2	2	2	2	2
Back plate(s)	4	6	6	2	2
Lesser shoulder plates	4	4	4	4	4
Larger shoulder plates	4	4	4	4	4
Upper shoulder guard plates	2	6	6	2	6
Girdle plates	16	16	16	12	12
Fittings					
tie loops	24	24	24		
tie rings				20	20
Pin & loop/strap & buckle				3	3
suspension hooks			6	6	6
suspension loops			6	6	6
buckles (hinged)	2	4	2		
buckles (unhinged)	6	4			
straps (hinged)		4			
straps (unhinged)	8	4	2		
hinges (lobate)		8	8		8
hinges (sub-lobate)	4				
Rivets					
small dome headed	86	135	118	33	113
Dome headed	18	10	10	30	6
Flat headed	146	122	144	102	102

Above: Table 3.1 List of component parts of *lorica segmentata.*

Opposite: Table 3.2 Analysis of Corbridge Hoard armour stored at Corbridge and Newcastle.

LOCATION	CUIRASS (M Bishop)	FIG (M Bishop)	BOX	CORBRIDGE A/B	RHS	LHS	USG	LGE SH'DR	SMALL SH'DR	CHEST	BUCKLE SIDE Y/N	BACK	COLLAR	G'DLE	FRONT OR BACK	Tie loops	Buckle	Hinge	Average thickness	Rivet material	Rivet size (mm)	Boss diam (mm)	NOTES
Corbridge	1	29	CO23085	A			f												3.4	cu	9.7	28.5	
Corbridge	1	29	CO23085	A			m												3.4	cu	9.7	24.6	
Corbridge	1	29	CO23085	A			b												2.9				Back piece part missing from diags (part w/o boss)
Corbridge	1	29	1215	A			b																part lower back USG
Corbridge	1	29	1215	A	1			2															
Corbridge	1	29	1215	A	1				2														
Corbridge	1	29	1215	A	1							1											rv deep backplate?
Corbridge	5	42	CO23082	A		1													2.4	cu	8.0		plates extend lower at back
Corbridge	5	42	CO23084	A		1		2											2.1	cu	8.0		plates extend lower at back
Corbridge	iv	63	CO23079	A		1								2					1.8				ends of bottom 2 girdle plates
Corbridge	iv	63	CO23080	A		1								1	Bk	o	fe		1.7	cu	8.0		fragment top girdle plate with inside buckle
Corbridge	iv	63	CO23081	A		1								7	Bk	5	fe		1.7	cu	8.5		5 with tie loops - part missing from diag
Corbridge	iv	63	CO23083	A		1								7	Fr	6	cu		1.6	cu	8.0		6 with tie loops - part missing from diag
Corbridge	iv	63	n/k	A		1								8	n/k	o			1.7	cu	9.0		fragments of 8
Newcastle	6	49	1218	BC	1					1	Y					3	cu	cu	3.7	cu	9.0		breastplate, iron loop, signs of alternate fastening
Newcastle	6	49	1218	BC									1				cu	cu	2.7	cu	12.0		collar plate
Newcastle	6	49	1218	BC	1							2					cu	cu	2.6	cu	9.0	2.6	top 2 backplates
Newcastle	2	31	2	A	1					1								cu	2.6	cu	8.0	3.4	part breastplate
Newcastle	2	31	2	A	1							1						cu	3.4	cu	7.0		part pl1 back
Newcastle	2	31	2	A	1								1					cu	2.2	cu			collar plate
Newcastle	3	34	2			1				1							cu	cu	2.7	cu	4.5		hinge twisted & damaged, torn on third loop
Newcastle	3	34	2			1						1					cu	cu	2.0	cu	4.0		pl 1 back with buckle
Newcastle	3	34	2			1							1					cu	2.5	cu	10.0		hinge on front part repaired with large rivets
Newcastle	i	54	3	A			1							8	Fr			cu		cu			fragments of 8
Newcastle	5	45&44	3			1	1																USG - back part missing
Newcastle	4	40	4		1		1													cu			decorative boss to front
Newcastle	3	33	1217		1																		
Newcastle	3	33	1217						2				1										
Newcastle	3	33	1217			1		2				3											
Newcastle	4	26	1187		1												Y		2.9	cu			horizontal buckle now glued to vertical strap
Newcastle	1	26	1187		1					1							Y	cu	2.7	cu			
Newcastle	1	26	1187		1					1							Y	cu	2.0	cu			
Newcastle	v?	66	1210	B	1									7		9			2.0	cu			
Newcastle	iii?	60	1210	A?		1								5		3				cu			

subjected to the same use and abuse. Although a re-enactor may use his *segmentata* for many years (some groups, such as the Ermine Street Guard, having now been in operation for over thirty years), it will have only been subjected to occasional wear, with an unrepresentatively high degree of cleaning and maintenance in between. It would, quite rightly, never have been tested to catastrophic levels by full combat with the intended/potential demise of the occupant. Within these constraints, however, it is possible to see the operational limits of the armour, its flexibility and those areas most likely to fail through repetitive movement (hinges, fastenings, internal strapping, etc.). This may then suggest possible reasons for chronological developments apparent in the typological sequence, from Kalkriese, through Corbridge, to Newstead.

The examination of the Corbridge material, however, indicated that the plates were not just produced from flat sheet metal, unlike modern reconstructions, including that of Russell-Robinson, but had been forge-shaped to follow body contours, breastplates and back plates being slightly convex, and the collar and shoulder plates sloping to the shape of the wearer. It was a deliberate intention with the Kalkriese reconstruction, therefore, to combine a mixture of flat sheet metal on the girdle plates (as used in the modern reconstructions) with forge-shaped plates for the upper body, in order to in some way test the differential wear damage.

Initially, the first apparent difference to current reconstructions was with the tendency for the breastplates to separate, leaving a triangular gap in the lower, central position. It was suggested by Bishop that this could be minimised by use of a padded undergarment to raise the shoulder area (Bishop, 2002, 80). From use of the Kalkriese reconstruction, a padded undergarment was found, in practice, to be beneficial (the wearer experiencing significant discomfort, along with multiple cuts and abrasions, with no such undergarment). However, it was also found that such a high level of padding was not necessary if the plates were correctly shaped, as this 'gaping' phenomenon did not occur and light reinforcement of the shoulder area was sufficient. As the Corbridge examples appear to be close-fitting, it seems probable that overly substantial padding worn underneath (or too much bulk from an over-wide tunic) could cause undue pressure on the underarm nerves, leading to a 'dead' arm. In consequence, although some form of undergarment was probable, indeed would have been necessary, it was unlikely to be as substantial as that worn under mail (*hamata*).

With further exposure to the elements through continued use, however, an additional advantage was noted between the flat sheet and those plates that had been forge-shaped, the former being more adversely affected by corrosion. Although when forging was complete, before the *lorica* was assembled, the plates had been cleaned and 'polished', they had retained a darker patina (possibly due to an increased content of carbon inclusions) in comparison to the untreated sheet, which appeared to then impede corrosion. It is possible that the hardened outer layers (with higher levels of pearlite) of the plates examined microscopically by Williams may have exhibited similar resistance to corrosion (Sim, 1998, 9).

This does not, however, mean that the original *segmentatas* would necessarily have been left forge-blackened, as suggested by some re-enactors. It is known from literary sources (Josephus, *Bell. Iud.*) that Roman soldiers did polish their armour, and it would be reasonable to believe this to be the case. Polishing the armour would inhibit unnecessary corrosion from surface soiling and regular cleaning would allow the owner to recognise early signs of impending wear damage and so effect timely repairs, avoiding any unpredicted and catastrophic combat failure.

It has been suggested that the armour may have been in some way provided with a protective coating, although this was unlikely to have been the high-gloss chrome finish exhibited among some of the re-enactment contingents, nor, due to the high costs involved, would it be likely that the armour would be silvered. It is possible that tinning may have been used, although there is no evidence for this, apart from the possible 'gunky' deposit on one of the Corbridge breastplates (which only chemical analysis could identify or disprove). It is more likely that, in common with most medieval plate armour, the surface was just cleaned and polished, perhaps retaining the slightly darker forge patina.

IV

MAIL (*LORICA HAMATA*)

The most widely used form of Roman body armour was mail, or *hamata*. It was versatile and virtually classless, used by both legionary and auxiliary troops, by officer classes and lower ranks alike, serving both infantry and cavalry purposes, with just minor functional variations between. Its continuous use can be seen spanning almost the entire history of the Roman army, although exhibiting a developmental sequence in its design which echoes both the similar developmental changes within the organisational structure of the army itself, and the changing nature of enemy weaponry and tactics with expansion into new and alien territories.

Its structure is formed from a lattice of interlocking metal rings, either formed of iron or copper-alloy (although iron was the most commonly used medium), each passing through four neighbours, two above and two below, producing a fabric resembling loosely (from a distance at least) that of knitted wool. The mail may be formed from either closable rings of wound wire (their ends either butted together, welded or riveted), or from solid rings, punched from flat sheet metal. These may then be combined in the same garment, with alternate rows of solid and closable rings.

The armour produced is both light and flexible, allowing the wearer full freedom of unimpeded movement. The thickness of the basic materials used, whether the sheet metal used for solid rings, or the wound wire, would not appear to offer substantial protection, particularly in combination with all of the corresponding 'holes'. However, in practice the fabric produced will absorb and dissipate the force of a blow (perhaps from a sword strike) over a larger area, with minimal damage to the integrity of the structure, other than the loss of a few links, which are easily and cheaply replaced. This makes it ideal for use in close combat situations against most forms of weaponry, with the exception of direct projectile strikes (missile or arrow).

ORIGINS

The origins of mail are unclear, lying probably with nomadic peoples of non-literary or sculptural traditions, although with a general consensus of the Celts being the probable originators, and with the Romans 'borrowing' the technology from observation of Gaulish examples (Russell-Robinson, 1975, 164; Feugère, 2002, 74). The date of the earliest example is similarly vague, with Russell-Robinson citing a reference to finds from fifth-century BC Scythian tombs (Piggott, 1965, 240; Russell-Robinson, 1975, 164). Feugère, however, cites Ciumesti in Romania as the earliest example, dating to the third century BC (Feugère, 2002, 74). What is apparent is that its use was known to Celtic people by the fourth and third centuries, its earliest pictorial representation being that of a Galatian mercenary at Sidon (Russell-Robinson, 1975, 17, fig. 17), at least pre-dating its earliest appearance among the Italic peoples. However, its use at that time was probably restricted to higher-status, aristocratic members, due to the labour-intensive, high cost of manufacture, with lower-status warriors fighting unarmoured.

The fourth century BC saw many changes in the arms and associations of the Italic peoples. At the commencement of the period, the peninsula was rife with frequent wars between the many individual states, the Roman and Samnite peoples being major players in these conflicts, other regions forming alliances with either side. This led to a widespread interchanging of ideas, technologies, weapons assemblages and fighting techniques, culminating by the end of the century in a homogenous set of equipment, with an adoption of the longer oval shield (*scutum*) and missile weapons (javelin and *pila*) from the Samnites and southern allies, and a change in fighting techniques from the hoplite phalanx to the manipular formation, Some regional differences perpetuated (which Burns sees as forms of 'us *v.* them' expressions of group identity and affiliation) and other differences were positively encouraged. For example, Diodorus related how Dionysius of Syracuse engaged craftsmen to equip his mercenaries, as he believed they would fight better with familiar equipment (Burns, 2003, 66). Other equipment was abandoned in favour of better models, where seen in use by 'foreign' allies or opponents, evidenced by trends towards helmet types better suited to cavalry use (as with the Athenian Boeotian helmet), or with better visibility, hearing and ease of manufacture (for example the Apulo-Corinthian, Samno-Attic, Greek Pylos, or the Celtic Montefortino; Burns, 2003, 70).

At the same time as adopting the Montefortino helmet from the Celts/Gauls, the other part of the Gallic basic assemblage, mail, was also assimilated, offering by far superior protection to the 'Italic' contemporary alternatives of simple pectoral plates (*cardiophylax*), or the Samnite triple-disc cuirasses. Burns, however, also proposed that the adoption of the Montefortino helmet and mail cuirass was not entirely due to the improved features and ease and economy of manufacture, but to its 'neutral' (non-Italic) origin, which would not have caused offence by echoing any one regional identity following all of the fourth-century BC 'conquests' (Burns, 2003, 73).

As mail was a valuable commodity, each shirt representing many man-hours of painstaking work, and once made, being easy to maintain, it could remain in use for considerable lengths of time, possibly handed down to multiple owners. Archaeological examples are therefore rare, and where found, frequently consist of amorphous, highly corroded lumps from which it is impossible to determine garment design.

SCULPTURAL REPRESENTATIONS

The best evidence for the designs of mail shirts comes, therefore, from sculptural representations, and as many of these are datable (either from identification of individuals on grave stelae, or from propaganda monuments of known events), a developmental progression of styles can be constructed. However, mail is a difficult concept for any sculptor to represent, and which was attempted using a variety of methods (possibly in part reflecting regional artistic styles), some of which in this early period particularly could be open to misinterpretation (as in von Groller's interpretation of mail finds from Carnuntum).

For example, in some representations such as the second-century BC victory frieze from the Temple of Athena at Pergamum (Russell-Robinson, 1975 164, plate 459), and the early first-century BC column at Mavilly (Russell-Robinson, 1975, 169, fig. 176), the sculptor appears to enlarge the rings by four to five times, to make them easier to distinguish, although evidence from actual finds (albeit much later in date) suggest this large size to be unlikely (Feugère, 2002, 75; Russell-Robinson, 1975, 169). Other representations, however, attempt to portray mail in more abstract forms, for example depicting only the lower parts of the rings, using rows of semi-circles, like shallow u-shapes, as on both the Altar of Ahenobarbus, dating to around 100 BC, and the similarly dated Vachères warrior, from the end of the first century BC (Feugère, 2002, 75; Russell-Robinson, 1975, 169).

Slightly less detailed and cruder, but similarly abstract methods can also be seen on other later dated representations of mail, for example using rows of rectangular holes (as on the Osuna reliefs; Russell-Robinson, 1975, 164, fig. 175), a scatter of triangular shapes (as on the late Augustan period trophy relief at the Musée Borély), or using wavy/zigzag lines (set vertically, as on the Palazzo Ducale relief, Mantua, or horizontally, as on Trajan's Column; Feugère, 2005, 75; Russell-Robinson, 1975, 169).

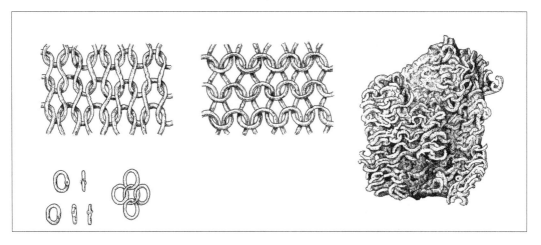

Fig. 31 Mail finds from Carnuntum, with interpretation by von Groller (from von Groller, 1901b, plate 20). (*Redrawn by J. R. Travis*)

Fig. 32 Gallic warrior from Vacheres, late first century BC, wearing *lorica hamata* with shoulder doubling (a) front view and (b) side view. (*Artwork by J. R. Travis*)

Fig. 33 Altar of Ahenobarbus, featuring soldiers in *lorica hamata* with Celtic-style 'cape' shoulder protection, carrying oval shields with long vertical *spina*.
(*Photo by Marie-Lan Nguyen/Wikimedia Commons*)

In many other representations, however, all attempts at simulation of the individual rings appears to be abandoned, with the cuirass outlined but left otherwise blank. This has been identified by some as depicting 'leather armour'. However, both Feugère (2002, 75) and Russell-Robinson (1975, 164) considered leather to be impractical as armour, suggesting that the cuirasses would have been painted with the missing detail later. It is quite possible that many Roman sculptures would have been intended to have been viewed painted, rather than in the bare state we see them today, a suggestion borne out by reports of traces of paint found on Trajan's Column in 1833 (Wheeler, 1971, 178).

Sculptural representations may also not necessarily offer totally reliable impressions of reality, with many of the examples cited being stylised and idealised depictions of real events portrayed for propaganda purposes, the combatants equipped with the best armour and weaponry. This is particularly evident in those monumental sculptures of the second and first centuries BC, where mail appears to be worn almost universally. However, in contrast, Polybius (VI.23) reports that at that time only those able to meet the property requirement were permitted mail, with poorer men, or those from more remote communities with less advanced equipment, still using simple square brass breastplates, which could only offer minimal protection (Burns, 2003, 78).

Similarly, sculptural representations in later periods, such as those on Trajan's Column, where all legionary personnel are depicted universally in segmented plate armour (*lorica segmentata*) and auxiliary troops in mail, may not entirely reflect reality. There are many aspects of the Column which suggest that many artistic conventions are at play, for both political propaganda and cultural purposes, as discussed in greater detail elsewhere. However, what can be noted, particularly in mail representations, is the way that the armour moulds itself to the body of the wearer, as a means to suggest the prime physical prowess of the Roman military rather than in any attempt to imitate the true appearance of how a real mailshirt would hang. This is in contrast to the more realistic depictions on earlier sculptures, these particular examples perhaps representing the pinnacle of a period of strong propagandist artistic imagery. Alternately, it may perhaps reflect a return to the Hellenistic ideal of the perfection of the human body, with men as the central figures, rather than those of the gods.

DESIGNS

The use of mail by the Roman military can therefore be visualised using sculptural representations to produce a sequence of stylistic development in design, from the second century BC, spanning the Republican period, into the Imperial and down to the sixth century AD, showing at least five distinctly different designs.

During the last century of the Republican period, two different designs can be seen: the continuance of the older 'Gaulish' or 'Celtic' style, and its replacement by the newer 'Greek' design, the latter being the more commonly seen, both styles being sleeveless, reaching to mid-thigh length, their differences lying in the method of additional shoulder reinforcement.

In the Gaulish-style cuirass, additional protection is provided to the upper arms and shoulders by a 'cape' of mail, as seen clearly depicted on not only the early first-century BC statue of Mars from Mavilly, Côte d'Or, but also still in use at the end of the first century AD by soldiers of Gaulish background (Feugère, 2002, 101; Russell-Robinson, 1975, 169). In the second, 'Greek' style, two large, wide shoulder protectors (formed as an extension of the back) pass over the shoulders, partly covering and protecting the upper arm on some examples, fastening on the front. In some cases these are simply tied down to the main cuirass body, whereas in other examples lateral movement is prevented by use of horizontal fasteners.

Again variations can be seen here over time, with examples from the earlier Republican period using rectangular bars (as on the second-century BC victory frieze of Aemilius Paulus at Delphi, the Altar of Domitius Ahenobarbus and also on the Pergamum frieze), whereas the later examples, from the late Republican and Augustan periods, use a system of double hooks, with snake-headed terminals, fixed to a central rivet (Russell-Robinson, 1975, 164, Feugère, 2002, 101). Examples of these serpentine hooks are also known archaeologically from many sites, including Chassenard (Feugère, 2002, 100, fig. 122), where the owner, A. Blucius Muci(anus), had also engraved his name (Feugère, 2002, 75; Russell-Robinson, 1975, 164, 169).

The shoulder protectors on a number of sculptures (both early and later examples) appear to have been bound at the edges, probably using leather, as seen on that of the first-century BC Celtic Vachères warrior (who features early use of the serpentine closure hooks), and later on the Arch of Orange, dating to the early first century AD (Feugère, 2002, 75; Russell-Robinson, 1975, 169). It is possible that the full reverse area may have been leather covered, which would not only strengthen the protector, but would minimise any possibility of snagging on the main cuirass body beneath. In contrast, the protecting 'cape' on the earlier Mavilly Column is interpreted by Russell-Robinson not to have been bound or backed, noting the way in which the mail appears to 'fall' in a more natural way, folded backwards and tied by laces (Russell-Robinson, 1975, 169; Feugère, 2002, 75). A similar design of cuirass appears to have been in use by both cavalry and infantry troops, although those of the former would have been provided with short side slits, for ease of use on horseback, with both examples teamed with a belt to transfer the weight of the armour from the shoulders to the waist and hips (Russell-Robinson, 1975, 164).

By the end of the first century AD, the basic body shape changed again, with the bodice shortening to hip length. However, this trend towards shorter cuirasses can be seen in a few (perhaps prototype) examples, one on the Arch of Orange (dating to AD 26/27) and another on the stela of Caius Castricus, from Budapest (both with waist-length, short-sleeved bodices,

Fig. 34 Caerleon Museum mail and snake hook. (*Photo by J. R. Travis*)

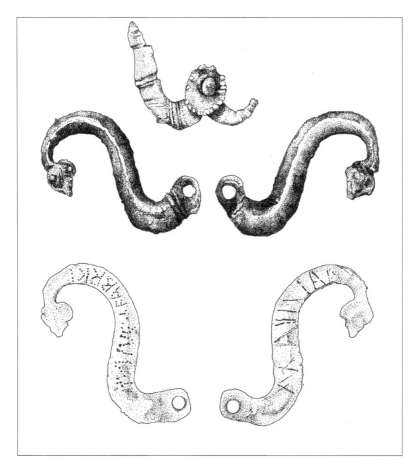

Fig. 35 Kalkriese snake hook (after Bunz and Spickermann, 2006).
(*Drawn by J. R. Travis*)

without shoulder protectors, but with the addition of pteruged skirt and arms), although at that time the earlier forms appear to be still the norm.

By the second century AD, both infantry and cavalry can be seen in these simple, short-sleeved cuirasses, reaching to hip level or occasionally to upper thigh, although those used by cavalry were still being provided with the short side slits, as seen on the stelae of both Flavius Bassus, from Cologne, and of Flavinus of the ala Petriana, from Hexham Abbey (Russell-Robinson, 1975, 169; Webster, 1998, plate 14b). This shorter length by consequence reduces the weight of the garment, negating the need for a belt to transfer the weight to the hips from the shoulders, swords now being seen suspended by a *balteus* over one shoulder, slung diagonally across the chest. This shorter-style cuirass would have offered greater freedom of movement – reducing the weight of armour to be carried by the wearer, without reducing too greatly the level of protection offered – and can be seen in use in two slight design variations on the Tropaeum Trajani at Adamklissi (where the shirts are plain and straightedged) and on both Trajan's and Marcus Aurelius' Columns (where both terminate in pointed edges, or 'dags'; Russell-Robinson, 1975, 169).

As none of these examples are provided with shoulder protectors, and several reliefs show individuals from different angles (showing the front, side and back of the garment), it should presumably be possible to see any evidence for openings/closure around the neck, shoulder or back, the absence of which suggested a simple 'pullover' style, which would have required a sufficiently large opening for the head to pass through. This would also suggest that the cuirass may not have been as tightly fitted as the imagery on the Trajan's Column examples suggest, the reality being perhaps a little more loosely fitting (although the fabric of mail does allow for a level of elasticity).

From the third century AD (Antonine period), a fourth style of cuirass can be seen, with a looser shape, short sleeves and a lengthening hemline. Although shoulder doubling had now gone (which used to permit additional protection to the neck area, by drawing the extra layer in to cover any wideness of the neck aperture on the main garment), a new method of closure can be seen on the body of the cuirass. This comprised the addition of small, copper-alloy closure plates on the chest, shaped at the neck edge to allow for a close-fitting neck. These decoratively embossed plates are known from a number of sources, following two slightly different designs, the most common being using two equally sized rectangular plates, closed by square-headed, perforated pins and slots, or less frequently by two assymetrical plates, forming a trapezoid shape, closed by an integral hook and slot system, as seen on the example from Bertoldsheim. This method of closure is seen used on both mail and scale cuirasses (and will be discussed therefore in greater detail in the subsequent chapter on scale armour), and on the composite forms (consisting of a combination of scale, mail and also possibly a quantity of larger plates).

Sculptural representations of this style of cuirass are rare, with few monumental sculptures known between the death of Severus in AD 211 and the rule of Diocletian in AD 284. Russell-Robinson suggested that during this period the infantry was more lightly armed, perhaps with just the protection of leather, although mail and scale continued to be used by the cavalry, their use increasing while that of infantry was reducing, citing views of infantry in possible leather armour on the Arch of Severus (from AD 203; Russell-Robinson, 1975, 171). Some images do exist of armour of the period, however, on frescoes from the synagogue at Dura-Europos depicting the Battle of Ebenezer, and on a grave stela of an unidentified legionary of possibly similar date from Brigetio, Hungary, with soldiers seen in knee-length and elbow-length, loose-fitting, unbelted mail and scale, some also wearing hooded coifs, presumably fashioned of the same fabric as the cuirass (Stephenson and Dixon, 2003, 44; James, 2004, 110).

Similar designs appear to apply to both infantry and cavalry alike, with cavalry now abandoning side slits in favour of long front and back central slits, which are more practical on horseback, allowing the bulk of the garment to separate centrally and fall down on each side of the horse, with the added bonus of offering both protection to the rider's legs and the sides of the horse.

Several examples of mail coats of this period were found at Dura-Europos in the Tower 19 countermine, one fully and one almost complete (along with the remains of their original owners) and several others in fragmentary condition (over thirty fragments are listed, but many possibly from the same garment). All examples found are thought to have been of this simple, loose-fitting, 'pullover' style, although the presence of a mail hook of the earlier Imperial style suggested some residual use of shoulder reinforcements (James, 2004, 111).

James (ibid.) reports that all examples are of iron, with some decorative use of copper-alloy, using the standard construction of each ring being connected to four others, but reports that corrosion of the iron prevented any determination of whether butted, overlapped, riveted or stamped rings had been used (ring sizes of 8 to 9 mm diameter by 1 mm thickness being identified where possible). He does, however, report the use of stamped and butted copper-alloy rings for decoration, but as these mostly occur as edge trimmings, in areas where strength is not a priority, this does not preclude the use of riveted iron mail in the main body of the garments.

One of the Dura examples (the almost complete example, catalogued at number 379), provided evidence of its simple 'pullover' design, with a slit for the neck (trimmed by three rows of copper-alloy rings), and sleeves reaching to just below the elbow (or possibly wrist length, as they had perhaps ridden up on the owner at death, as had also the body of the cuirass, preventing any accurate estimate of length). The cuirass was also found to have a trident-shaped ('heraldic') design fashioned on the chest by use of copper-alloy rings to contrast with the iron rings of the main fabric. This has been interpreted as possibly being a Sasanian heraldic device, which may indicate that the deceased was one of the opposing Persian forces. Nevertheless, the shirt's construction was much the same as that of the other examples found, indicating a standard armour type of universally widespread use (ibid.).

This cuirass was also found to have been worn over an undergarment of a light-brown fibrous material, which appeared not to have been of a woven construction, and which James interprets as possibly being the remains of a padded felt 'arming doublet', possibly the *thoracomachus* (or *subarmalis*) as described in the *De Rebus Bellicis*, and the use of which will be discussed in greater detail in the next chapter (James, 2004, 116).

This style of looser, knee-length, sleeved cuirass then continued throughout the fourth and fifth centuries, down to the sixth century, but without the embossed closure plates, this now replaced by a wider neck aperture. During this period of use, length fluctuated once more, from the knee-length cuirasses, as seen on the Arch of Diocletian, where infantrymen can be seen in belted, loose-fitting, knee-length cuirasses, one man in mail and the other in scale (Stephenson, 2001, 35, fig. 9), and as described for cavalry use by Procopius in his *History of the Wars* (I.1 9–15), to the later Byzantine period 'hooded coats of mail reaching to their ankles' as described by Maurice in his *Strategikon* (I. 2).

However, it is not clear as to how universal the use of the rectangular closing plates had been with cuirasses of the earlier third century AD, and as to how much the cuirasses of the fourth to sixth centuries should be seen as a separate type. Certainly, closure plates and turning key fasteners of Type 1 plates were found at Dura-Europos from this period, but none were found attached to any of the examples seen on the victims of the Tower 19 countermine collapse, these being of the simple, slit-necked type, the closure plates possibly belonging to scale cuirasses.

Similarly, an iron mail shirt found at South Shields, England, in the burnt remains of a barrack building from the late third to early fourth century AD fort, may have been of similar construction to those at Dura-Europos (Croom, 2001). The mail was found in a corroded heap which, when cleaned, revealed a construction of alternating rows of 7 mm diameter solid (probably welded) rings and 8 mm diameter, slightly oval-shaped, riveted rings (formed of wire 1 mm thick), closed by rivets with domed heads (around 1 mm diameter) through flattened terminals (1.75 mm across; Croom, 2001, 55). The mail had fallen to the floor after the commencement of the fire (suggesting possible methods of storage by hanging on a peg, heaping on a shelf, or in a bag), with products of burning above and below the remains, the shape of the remains suggesting the lower opening to be below the heap, the neck hole on the top, to the right of one out-flung sleeve of indeterminate length (Croom, 2001, 55).

Although in her interpretation Croom describes the third-century use of closure plates, none was subsequently found on x-ray examination of the remains (Croom, 2001, 55). This would suggest either that the mail shirt was not complete (either unfinished or awaiting repair/reuse), or had not made use of such plates (as on the Dura examples). This, then, would further strengthen an argument against widespread use of closure plates, which being in all known examples to have been intricately (and presumably expensively) decorated, may have been reserved to officer or cavalry use, with plainer, slit-necked versions used by the greater numbers of infantry lower ranks.

CONSTRUCTION AND RECONSTRUCTION

In order to test materials, methodologies and time factors involved in the manufacture of a mail cuirass, it was decided to reconstruct a reproduction garment, following the process through from the winding of the wire to the finished product. The finished article then offered opportunity to field-test this against various weaponry, with and without any associated padded undergarment.

Any reconstruction of a mail shirt would have to take into consideration a number of factors: the materials used (iron or copper-alloy); the size of rings to be used (external diameter and gauge of wire); method of closure (butted, overlapped, riveted, welded or solid); direction of assembly (horizontal or vertical); and overall design (from the long Republican Gaulish or Greek styles, to the shorter Imperial, or the longer, sleeved pullover styles of the later Empire), some styles clearly requiring a far greater quantity of rings than others, representing a greater cost in man-hours.

It is possible to make simple mail by butting or overlapping the joints in the rings. This is quicker to braid and therefore less labour intensive than any other methods. However, it is not as strong a construction. Most archaeological finds do appear to have at least some of the rings riveted. A riveted joint is stronger than a butted joint but it also requires much more concentration of effort, and is harder on the eyes, etc., being more of the work of a jeweller than of an armourer. It is possible that all rings may be riveted but this would be much more labour intensive. Another alternative is to use a mixture of riveted rings and solid rings. These solid rings could be formed in either two ways. They could be punched out of a flat sheet as solid washers, or they could be butted rings, threaded back onto a metal rod, reheated and hammered to weld the joint, the latter being the method suggested to produce the solid rings used in the mail shirt from South Shields (Croom, 2001, 55).

As size of rings varies greatly, it is possible that not all were made in the same way. Some rings, for example, are very small and would have been extremely difficult to rivet, although the example at Caerleon Roman Legionary Museum of very small gauge copper-alloy rings show signs of at least some of the rings being riveted, as were similar finds of very small mail from both Mainz and 'The Lunt', Coventry (3 mm diameter). Depending on the status of the wearer, higher-status mail may have been more substantially constructed, particularly in the case of these finer gauges of mail which Russell-Robinson believed to have belonged to wealthy owners (Russell-Robinson, 1975, 173).

By examining remaining medieval mail on display at the Royal Armouries, Leeds, most examples are found to have been riveted, either on every ring or on rings alternating with solid ones. There are examples of even minute rings being riveted so it is not impossible that all sizes could be joined this way. Examples of horse armour, however, were frequently found to be simply butt-jointed. Although these examples were intended for an animal, not a human, it is possible that if mass-producing for low-status legionary or auxiliary use, butt joints may have been used in order to kit out a large group of men quickly. It is possible in these cases that the individual soldier would gradually replace sections of his armour with patches of the more robust riveted mail later, eventually replacing the entire mail suit.

This practice has been witnessed among re-enactors who have kitted out in a hurry. These modern suits are never intended to be tested in combat conditions, and lives will never depend

Fig. 36
Caerleon
Museum mail
– close up
showing-rivets.
(*Photo by
J. R. Travis*)

upon them. Modern butchers are known to still use mail, in the form of hand protectors, these also being of the more easily and quickly produced 'butt' construction, so clearly this slightly inferior form is not without merit, offering better protection than no mail at all. However, as a suit of mail may remain in use for many years, even generations, and many men may inherit mail fully formed, it would only be instances where entire legions were kitted out from scratch where there would be a need to produce armour quickly. Therefore, it is more probable that the majority of mail would have been more robustly constructed, using some combination of riveted or half-riveted rings.

DIRECTION OF 'KNITTING' – HORIZONTAL OR VERTICAL?

The majority of archaeological finds of mail are fragmentary and often highly corroded. Full garments are infrequent finds and where found may be rolled, folded or heaped, so displaced fragments could have come from almost any part of the garment and any orientation; thus as a consequence, it is not always possible to tell in what direction the rows were laid down. However, direction of construction will have consequence to the properties of the finished garment, in elasticity and level of protection. If the fabric is produced using horizontal rows, the weight will stretch out the pattern downwards with gravity, forming a more open pattern. The stretching quality will still be produced with either direction of construction, shortening the piece if stretched widthways.

Vertical rows in contrast will give a closer, denser pattern, with the weight of the garment pulling downwards, closing up the knit and narrowing the piece, although again it will stretch widthways, shortening the piece. Vertical construction, however, will produce more stretch widthways, and horizontal construction will give more stretch vertically, so in consequence: vertical construction will give a closer weave but horizontal will use less rings.

In the absence of a great deal of archaeological evidence, some suggestions could be made based on sculptural evidence. As discussed previously, mail is a difficult concept to portray sculpturally, with many depictions being greatly stylised and simplified, some depicting chain by circles, dots or holes, or just left plain for features to be painted on later, so here the direction of construction would not be apparent. However, some depictions use a convention of vertical wavy lines (as on the cavalryman on the relief in the Palazzo Ducale, Mantua) or

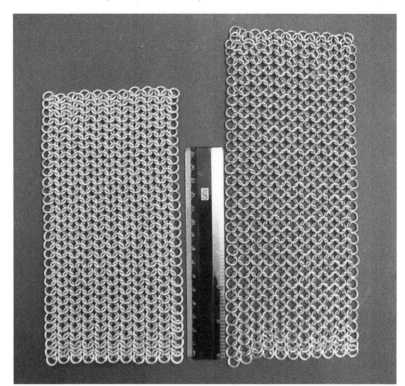

Fig. 37 Close-up view of reproduction mail showing degree of 'stretch' (reconstruction by H. Travis). (*Photo by J. R. Travis*).

vertical zigzags (as seen on some examples on Trajan's Column, which would be suggestive of vertical construction), whereas other examples use shallow semi-circles to suggest horizontal rows (such as on the Altar of Ahenobarbus and on the Vachères warrior; Russell-Robinson, 1975, 164; Feugère, 2002, 74). Further, some *hamata* is shown to terminate in triangular shapes (or 'dags') at the hem (as seen, for example, on the columns of both Trajan and Marcus Aurelius, as used by a variety of troops: auxiliary, hamian archer, officers, etc; Russell-Robinson, 1975, 169). This triangular shape is found to form more easily if rows are constructed horizontally. Therefore, in these cases the fabric may be a horizontal structure. Some sculptures depict mail coats with small sleeves, and some later examples are seen to have full sleeves. Vertical rows would make this structure easier to build, especially as sleeves would then need to be inserted into the fabric of the main garment. This then would allow the mail to fall over the shoulders, leading straight into the sleeve.

From a study of existing suits of mail, little remains dating to the Roman period which would prove conclusively direction of construction, other than the examples from the single location and dated context of the Tower 19 countermine at Dura-Europos, which appear from the photographic evidence to have been formed using vertical construction, and which then transposes into the horizontal when carried over on to the sleeves, as proposed above (James, 2004, 118, figs. 52–61). However, as mail has been used over many centuries (even being used today for protective gloves for butchers) this continuity of tradition suggested that analogies could be drawn from other time periods where available, many such examples existing from medieval and Viking contexts. Some of these examples can be seen on display at the Royal Armouries, Leeds – some of European and some of oriental origin. It was found that all of the mail suits seen at Leeds Armouries, including coifs and shoulder capes, use vertical rows, although these are obviously much later in date than Roman, and all include sleeves. Vertical construction may therefore lend itself more to sleeved garments where 'dagged' hems are not required.

Mail was developed by the Celts, before the Roman period, continuing to be used throughout the Empire and into the later Viking and medieval periods without any apparent break. Therefore, the skills required to produce it would have been handed down through the generations, and methods of construction presumably would also have been continuous. There is no evidence against horizontal rows, and it could have been easier to build the simpler bodice forms with this method. However, if there had been any requirement for sleeves, it would more probably have been the vertical method employed. Therefore, following the medieval examples seen, and using the rationale of continuity of tradition, the decision was made to use the vertical method of assembly in the following reconstruction.

PATTERN

There are several possible patterns of linking the rings, depending on how many rings join into each other. The standard pattern where each ring connects with four neighbouring rings is the most usual form. Similar to this, but more rarely found, are forms with six or eight connections, which would give a denser weave. Another form, sometimes described as 'Italian', is a more open pattern, lower in density, with no particular direction. In this form, there is one row of rings with four connections, linking to each other and the rows above and below, using two of each vertical and horizontal rings. An example of this form used in the Roman period can be seen from a second-century AD Thracian burial from Catalka, in Bulgaria (Stephenson, 2001, 48, fig. 16), although this was not found in a Roman context.

MAKING THE RINGS

Before the mail shirt can be constructed, a sufficient quantity of rings must first be prepared. For solid rings this would involve punching out the shape from a flat sheet, which for uniform thickness may have been produced using mechanical presses (or possibly even hot rolling or large-area trip hammers, as suggested by Fulford for the production of scales; Fulford et al., 2004, 201). The individual rings could then have been punched from this sheet using a punch and die, first punching the inner diameter by perforating the sheet using a small die, then completing the ring by punching over each hole using a larger die, producing rings of flat, square cross-section (Sim and Ridge, 2002, 100–1, figs. 44 and 45).

Fig. 38 'Italian'-pattern mail. (*Drawn by H. Travis*)

The remaining 50 per cent of the rings used will need to have the capacity to open and close, in order to link to neighbouring solid rings. This would then be formed from wire, making rings of the characteristic round cross-section. However, if solid rings are not to be used (as described above), it is also possible to produce 'solid' rings by forming 'open' rings, closing 50 per cent before construction commences (using either the butted, riveted or welded methods of closure). This process may therefore be broken down into a sequence of stages, not all of which would necessarily need to be performed by the same person, with varying levels of skill required.

These were:

i)   Making the wire.
ii) Winding the worm.
iii) Cutting the rings.
iv) Reforming the rings.
v)   Preparing riveted rings.
vi) Producing any 'solid' or 'closed' rings in advance of construction.

MAKING THE WIRE

The first stage in the production of the 'open' rings (before any winding and cutting of the bare wire) would have to have been the production of the wire itself, although it may have arrived at the workshop already in wire format, being perhaps pre-processed elsewhere. Nevertheless, the wire would still have had to be produced, even if not at the same location as the construction into mail. For the purposes of the reconstruction, pre-formed wire was sourced from a modern iron foundry, built above the location of the former Roman fort and industrial *fabrica* at Templeborough, South Yorkshire.

The process would have commenced initially with an ingot/billet of metal, hammered into a rod of as narrow a gauge as possible at the smith's hearth. This would then have been reduced in diameter by passing through successively narrower holes in a 'drawplate' until the required gauge of wire was produced. A number of these drawplates have been found, some from Roman contexts (for example from Vindolanda, and Altena, Germany) and others from later periods (for example plates from Staraja Ladoga, Russia; Hedeby, Germany; By and Bygland, Norway; and Mastermyr, Sweden, all from Viking contexts; Sim and Ridge, 2002, 102; Armbruster and Eilbracht, 2006, 32).

An illustration depicting the medieval production of wire using a drawplate is also known from the Mendelsche Zwölfbrüder-Stiftung, Nürnberg (Armbruster and Eilbracht, 2006, 32, fig. 9). In this a worker can be seen seated on what appears to be a swing, suspended from the workshop ceiling, producing wire, held in tongs, by pulling it through a drawplate (a series of holes being visible) which is set vertically in a heavy block (possibly a tree stump or butt). Armbruster and Eilbracht, in their discussion of the production of Viking gold wire, cite similar drawplates still in use in modern-day workshops, but in their example with the worker holding the plate between the feet (Armbruster and Eilbracht, 2006, 32, fig. 10).

The plates in use in the modern-day workshop, as with the Viking period plates, are almost identical to those from the Roman contexts, indicating a continuous tradition. The plates in most cases are of iron, although that from Staraja Ladoga was of high-zinc brass (also a notably hard material). They each have a series of differently sized, conically-shaped tapering holes, through which the wire is pulled (Armbruster and Eilbracht, 2006, 32, fig. 10). Sim proposed that these tapering holes could be produced using either a round punch (for round-sectioned wire), or a square-sectioned punch (for flat-sided wire), the differing sized apertures produced by varying the depth of the punch. The angle of the taper would also determine the 'reduction ratio', with a lower angle reducing the wire by less for each pass than a steeper angle, requiring more passes through smaller apertures, but requiring less force to do so (Sim and Ridge, 2002, 102). There is no evidence, archaeological or literary, from the Roman period to suggest any use of mechanical processing to provide the required

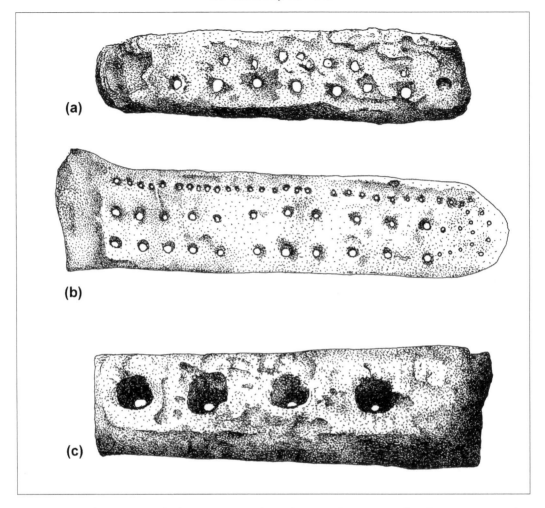

Fig. 39 Drawplates – (a) & (b) from Staraja Ladoga (from Armbruster & Eilbracht, 2006, 32) and (c) from Vindolanda (from Sim & Ridge, 2002, 102 fig. 46). (*Redrawn by J. R. Travis*)

force to draw the wire, but both the medieval illustration and the modern-day example cited indicate that this was a process which could be accomplished by a single worker (Armbruster and Eilbracht, 2006, 32, figs. 9 and 10).

TOOLS REQUIRED

Mail construction is a highly specialised craft, and as a consequence requires a specialist toolset, each part of which has been developed to meet a particular purpose:

- To form the 'worm' – a set of pliers with which to hold the wire, and a rod of the same size as the internal diameter of the rings to be made, around which the wire will be wound. This rod can be metal or wood (the origin of the term 'wormwood'), as long as it is sufficiently strong, with a handle at one end and a small hole at the other large enough to take the first end of the wire.
- To cut the 'worm' to form the rings, strong, long-nosed metal cutters are required, which will work more efficiently if the lower jaw is supported in a vice. Cutters are also required to cut the tiny rivets from strips of sheet metal.

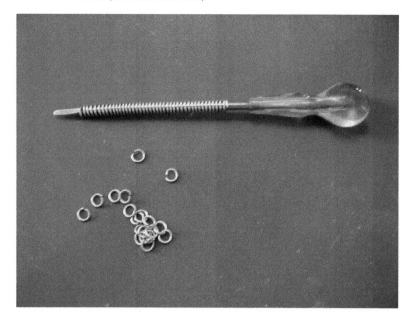

Fig. 40 Winding
the 'worm' to form
rings from wire
(reconstruction by
H. Travis). (*Photo
by J. R. Travis*)

- To flatten the riveting area at the opening of the ring, a pair of heavy, wide-nosed pliers is used to hold the ring, and a hammer to strike the top of the pliers.
- To form the rivet holes in the flattened rings, a small metal punch and an anvil with a small semi-circular groove on one edge, shaped to fit the ring, holding it in place while the tiny rivet holes are punched.
- To braid the shirt, two pairs of small, strong pliers will be needed; one pair with a flat, wide nose for the left hand, and a pointed pair for the right hand. Traditionally, these tools are given bird names, the wire-cutters being named 'condor', the wide braiding pliers the 'duck', and the narrow, pointed braiding pliers the 'woodpecker' (Klostermann, 1997).

CONSTRUCTION

The mail shirt has to be made to fit the man, and therefore each will be an individual garment, with different measurements. A basic tabard form can, however, be made with average proportions, possibly slightly smaller than average, which can then be expanded to fit the larger man before joining the side seams. Once the neck and shoulder assembly is completed, it is possible to fit the piece to the individual, expanding the shoulder width and neck hole if necessary, and ensuring the correct depth of arm holes from the shoulder. This is the most complicated part of what is a fairly simple form, the hardest part being the shaping of the neck. The remainder of the body is formed by just two rectangles, attached horizontally to the chest and back to give the required length, and joined up the side seams.

However, a complete mail shirt is a heavy and unwieldy object with which to work. When work commences, it will fit easily on the lap, and can be carried out almost anywhere. As a piece of mail grows, it becomes more difficult to manipulate, sliding off the lap, and a larger work area, or flat table, is required. It is easier, therefore, to work with smaller pieces, only joining them together into the main form later. Furthermore, as building mail is a mind-numbingly boring activity, as a motivational factor alone, it is preferable to work on smaller, narrower pieces which grow in length quicker than to build up rows which are the full width of the finished suit. Obviously, at some time it will be necessary to work with the full suit when assembling the smaller pieces, and at this stage a large, flat work area will be useful.

Although it is possible, if using open rings, to braid every individual ring in turn, it is more practicable to work two rows at one time. If using half open rings and half closed rings, as would be the case with punched solid rings or welded rings, this method of two rows at one time would be necessary. Before commencing any braiding, two quantities of open and closed rings should be prepared. This may not necessarily be all of the rings, but sufficient to allow an uninterrupted period of work. If all of the rings in the piece are to be riveted, half of these should be completed now before assembly. The open rings, whether to be riveted or butted, should be prepared so that the joining area overlaps slightly. This is because, when the ring is gripped on each side by the 'duck' and 'woodpecker' pliers and twisted to open, the gap will open out slightly. When the ring is twisted back to close, this gap will open out a little bit more. It is imperative that there should be no gap at all in the finished closed ring once assembled. Any such gap, when combined with any gap in the neighbouring attached ring, could allow the two rings to separate later, particularly with butted rings. This problem is more acute with narrower-gauge wire rings, and with riveted rings any such gap would make the alignment of the tiny rivet holes difficult. The prepared rings can then be grouped on wire loops and heated in a hearth, covered by carbon-based fuel, to anneal and carburise the metal. Any rings that are intended to form welded rings will now fuse, forming 'solid' rings.

As previously mentioned, it is preferable to make the mail in smaller pieces. The first stage in making one of these pieces is to start with a simple chain of the required length, and then to extend this chain by adding further rows. This first part is traditionally known as a 'septett' (Klostermann, 1997), formed by a simple chain, five rings in length, with every alternate link being double rings, so that there are seven rings in all.

Either a simple chain can be built first, with the alternating additional rings added later or, more logically, these double rings may be inserted straightaway at the outset, using the solid or pre-closed rings. Although it will be more practicable to form a much longer chain, the smaller constituent part of the septett will be used for ease of describing the method used. As the 'knitted' pattern produced will form offset alternating rows, the following convention will be used for the purposes of counting the numbers of rings in a chain and rows completed. The length of the chain will be counted using only the open alternate rings, the septett below being then three links in length. This will then form a single row, with numbers 2, 4, 6 and 7 being discounted, and the row forming the extension to the septett then being the second row.

As it is suggested that the body of the mail be worked in smaller pieces, to be 'stitched' together at a later stage, an initial chain of twenty-five rings would be a manageable size to start with. Therefore, by producing pieces of work of twenty rows in length, each will contain approximately 1,000 rings. In reality, these pieces will consist of twenty rows of twenty-five open rings and twenty-one rows of twenty-four closed rings. Therefore, the piece will contain 1,004 rings, 500 open and 504 closed.

Each septett in this first row is then extended by opening it out flat and working into the upper ring in each of these double pairs (numbers 6 and 7). Care has to be taken in this first extending row to ensure that the pattern of the septett is lying flat, without any twists. Although it is possible to commence working at either end of the chain, the convention will be followed of working from right to left. In this way, as in the diagram below, the first open ring, number 8, will be looped under ring number 7 below. Two closed rings, 9 and 10, are then slipped on before it is closed.

This second row is then formed by similarly working into the remaining upper ring of the septett. The next open ring, number 11, is passed through rings 10 and 7 from above, re-emerging through ring 6. An additional closed ring, number 12, is then slipped on and the ring closed. In the same way, the next open ring, number 13, will be linked through its neighbouring rings with another closed ring added. It can be seen then that, by building a row of open rings, the second offset row of closed rings is also added. Even if building a mail of simple butted rings, the same technique can be used and will give a more efficient method of construction.

Once several of these pieces have been completed they can be 'stitched' together, horizontally and vertically, to form larger pieces, avoiding the need to work with large heavy pieces of mail until most of the rings have been linked. The area of the neck will, however, require working with a fairly large piece as it will need equal shaping up both sides. This is quite simple shaping however, and can be achieved by working a couple of rows straight

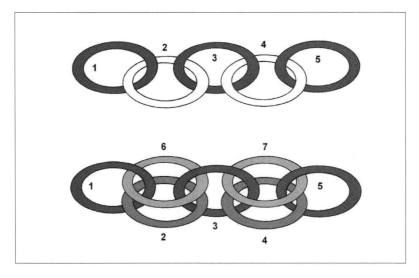

Fig. 41 Forming the 'septett'. (*Drawn by H. Travis*)

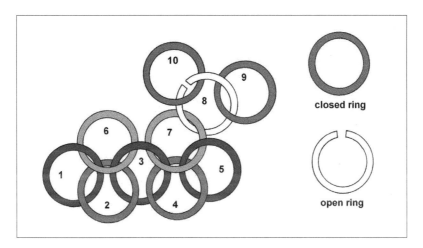

Fig. 42 Extending the 'septett'. (*Drawn by H. Travis*)

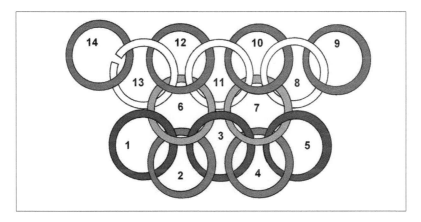

Fig. 43 The completed second row of the extended 'septett'.
(*Drawn by H. Travis*)

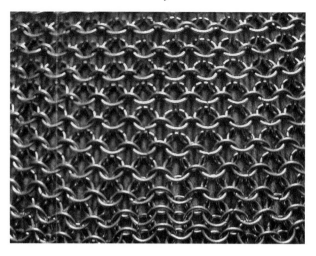

Fig. 44 Close-up view of reproduction mail (reconstruction by H. Travis). (*Photo by J. R. Travis*)

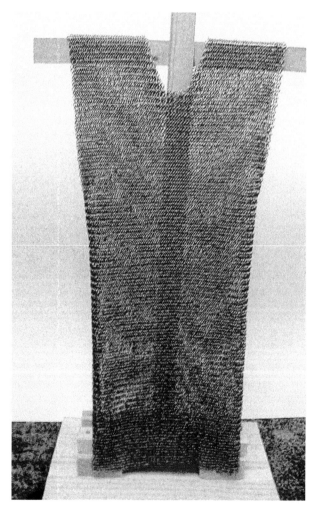

Fig. 45 Completed reproduction mail (reconstruction by H. Travis). (*Photo by J. R. Travis*)

at the front, then leaving several rings in the centre of the row, and reducing on each side by omitting the inside end ring of each row until the required width is reached, in a similar manner to knitting a neck hole for a woollen garment. Then, after a few rows of working straight without reduction, a couple of rows can be worked, increasing by one ring each row. The back panel can then be 'stitched' on to one shoulder, crossing the gap of the neck, and 'stitching' to the opposite shoulder. As the resulting neck hole will probably then be too narrow for a close fit around the neck, it may be necessary to remove a vertical row down for a few centimetres from the centre of the back neck to form an opening.

SHAPING

Additional shaping may be required if constructing coifs, shoulder capes, or for the triangular end decorations sometimes seen on sculptures of officers, auxiliaries, Hamian archers, etc. These peaked triangles, sometimes called 'Gizehcorners' or 'dags', are simple shapes formed by reducing equally on both sides for several rows. Some modern makers of mail (Klostermann, 1997) suggest building parts of the body with these triangular Gizehcorners to obtain a quicker effect and to reduce frustration during the long process of mail building, filling in the triangular gaps later. However, this would hamper slightly the flow of building horizontal rows, requiring more thought when filling in these gaps, and may have the opposite effect, creating greater frustration later.

Another form of shaping, used for widening the diameter of a tube, perhaps for an upper sleeve, or for shaping a cape, is the 'trumpet' seam. This is achieved by inserting periodically an additional open ring, with its corresponding closed ring. Further additional open rings are then inserted immediately above the first on subsequent rows. By building six equally spaced trumpet seams on a closed circular chain, a flat circular shape with six segments will form, as found in some Celtic shoulder cape-type constructions. A similar reduction shaping can also be achieved by reversing this process, linking one ring into three instead of the two in the standard pattern, which will reduce the number of rings in the next row.

KNITTING THE MAIL

The process above then describes the basic structure to be formed, but does not yet describe how this is to be achieved by 'knitting' or 'braiding'. In order to actually braid the rings, the two pliers, the 'duck' and 'woodpecker' are used. With the 'duck' in the left hand and the 'woodpecker' in the inside of the right hand, pick up an open ring with the thumb and index finger. With the opening pointed upwards, thread this ring through the first two neighbouring closed rings to be linked from above, re-emerging through the third ring from below. Holding the right hand side of the open ring in the 'woodpecker', slip on the next closed ring.

Then grip the left-hand side of this ring with the right-hand side of the 'duck', enclosing almost half of the ring. Then, holding the 'woodpecker' still, twist the ring towards you with the 'duck' until the open ends of the ring meet. If making a butted joint, twist the ring slightly more than is needed so that it will spring back to the correct position when released. It is imperative that as close a fit as possible is achieved to minimise the remaining gap in a butted joint, or otherwise to correctly align the rivet holes in a riveted joint. Next, for a riveted joint, release the 'woodpecker' and, still holding the ring in the 'duck', place it in the groove on the edge of the anvil. Fit the tiny rivet through the small holes in the end of the ring with the right hand and compress to close.

DISCUSSION

This procedure for picking up, linking and closing the rings, with practice, takes approximately 5 to 6 seconds for butted joints, and for riveted joints approximately 10 seconds for each ring. This, though, is in reality adding two rings each time because of the pre-closed rings. This means that it is possible to braid in one minute, twenty butted or twelve riveted rings, or in one hour 1,200 butted or 720 riveted. Theoretically, this would mean that a 25,000 ring mail shirt would take approximately 35 man-hours to make, excluding processing time to make and prepare the rings.

However, this is not a realistic calculation and would never in practice be achievable, as with the other stages of the process. Humans are not machines, and being a natural resource they need the essential breaks for toilet breaks, eating a meal, having a drink, stretching, itching their noses, etc. Some parts of the process will also take longer than straightforward braiding, for example when shaping the neck, trying on and fitting to the body. In addition, prolonged use of the pliers to braid, and of compressing the rivets, would place unnatural strains on the arms, hands and fingers. Although after a few thousand rings the hands do accustom themselves to the strain, initial blisters leading to areas of protective hardened skin, this rate of assembly would be unsustainable. This rate of assembly is possible for only short bursts of activity, after which the arms tire and the concentration lapses. The true rate of assembly, therefore, would be much lower. In one sustained, timed experiment a block of 1,000 rings was actually produced in 2 hours 30 minutes, without comfort breaks.

This then gives a rate of assembly of one open and one closed ring every 18 seconds, an overall rate of 9 seconds per ring. This, then, is three times longer than the ideal calculation. Based on these new values, then, it would be possible to braid 400 rings in one hour, and a 25,000 ring mail shirt would take approximately 62.5 hours. Therefore, for the purposes of calculation of assembly time, this value will be used as the most realistic.

This, however, does not agree with the suggested timings proposed by Croom (2001, 55) in her discussion of the mailshirt from South Shields. She reports that a replica shirt constructed by the Arbeia Society had used 54,000 rings. As this reconstruction was of the later loose-fitting, knee length design, with elbow-length sleeves, and as the rings used were reportedly of 7 mm external diameter, as opposed to the 8 mm rings used in the reconstruction above (6 mm internal diameter using 1 mm gauge wire), producing a slightly denser fabric, it is not entirely implausible that it would contain this many rings. However, she then estimates timings for production based on Sim proposing 215 man-days for production, considerably more than the above reconstruction suggested. It was unclear, however, whether this estimation was for the construction of the shirt alone, or whether it included the additional processes of winding and cutting the rings, preparation of rivets and production of the 'solid' welded rings, so this further comparative data must be factored into the discussion (see Table 4.2). It was also unclear as to how many man-hours were included in the estimated man-days, so calculations have been based on both a 7-hour and a 12-hour day.

Even by factoring in the additional processes of winding, cutting and preparing the rings prior to braiding, however, a timing of only 22 seconds per ring can be seen. Multiplying this by the 25,000 rings needed, this would mean a total of approximately 153 man-hours, which would then suggest a total of 21.8 or 12.7 man-days for 7-hour and 12-hour working days respectively. Even doubling these timings to estimate the time required to produce a garment of comparable ring quantities to the Arbeia example would only indicate a 25–26 man-day maximum, far less than the 215 days suggested by Sim. It can only be assumed that this calculation must also have factored in the production of the drawn wire, perhaps from bloom stage, but even so, this would still seem to be a somewhat excessive estimate.

A further cautionary note must be drawn on the acceptance of these values. It was reported by a family of Iron Age re-enactors from Archeon, Netherlands, who were also professional jewellers (pers. comm., 2002), that they had completed a suit of medieval-style mail, in a hurry, in 10 days (although this being just the time for basic assembly, not including all of the additional preparatory stages). This apparently was only made possible by working from dawn to dusk daily, with all meal preparation and babysitting performed by their mother-in-law, which may mirror the possible role of the extended family in antiquity. If it is assumed here working for 10 days at 12 hours per day for two people, this would suggest a total time of 240 hours (still significantly less than the Arbeia example, which would have been comparable in size and ring quantity).

However, a medieval shirt, being longer and including sleeves, would probably contain 50 per cent more rings. This, then, would give a comparable time of 120 hours, which would double the experimental sample figures. This example therefore highlights the problems associated with applying time and motion principles to mail production, the unsustainable rate of assembly, and the effects on this of even the most basic human comfort breaks and motivation. It is therefore not likely that mail production would have been carried out as a single activity for any sustained period, but would more probably have been fitted into a more varied routine of other tasks.

CONCLUSION

The early Roman army of the sixth century, and until the start of the fourth century BC, used the basic hoplite equipment and phalanx formation derived from a Hellenic model, as depicted on the Certosa situla (Zotti, 2006), with shield, helmet, greaves and body armour, in order of importance and value depending on personal status (Livy, *Hist. of Rome*, I.43). By the end of the fourth century BC, after frequent 'war' actions (over land and resources) between the Romans and the Samnite peoples with neighbouring regions allying on either side, a homogenisation of armour can be seen, regional variations merging, assimilating the best features of each (Burns, 2003, 62–3, 72). Following defeats by Gallic Celts at Allia in 386 BC (Livy, *Hist. of Rome*, IV.59), the Romans witnessed their superior mail body armour, and also assimilated this into their own assemblage, at least for the more wealthy members, along with the Gallic Montefortino helmet (Burns, 2003, 70). However, even by the First Punic War of the third century BC, Polybius (VI.23) reported that only the wealthy few were using this 'improved' mail, the majority still using the very basic simple chest plates.

By the Second Punic War, however, the Roman army had once more reorganised, increasing the number of legions, admitting poorer classes of men and introducing an annual selection of temporary conscripts, with volunteers encouraged by a small allowance, to bolster manpower for the new legions (Quesada Sanz, 1997, 155). The second century BC saw further revisions to the organisation and identity of the Roman army, initiated firstly under Gracchus and later under Marius, with greater relaxation of recruitment restrictions (boundary and financial), an overall increase in manpower, restructuring of the manipular legions into cohorts and some redesign of equipment (Campbell, 2000, 6). Many of those newly eligible were unable to afford their own equipment, which was instead provided by the use of mass production in state-owned 'factories' (Paddock, 1985, 146).

With further relaxation of citizenship following the Social and Civil wars of the early to mid-first century BC, the increase in the number of legions to twelve, and the increase in the level of 'payment' to volunteers, more new equipment was required to equip the newly formed additional legions, and to re-equip existing legions before and after conflicts, for example with Caesar in his Gallic wars using Gallic craftsmen, known for their skills in metalworking and armour production. Although the exact locations of these Gallic 'state-owned' factories are unknown, it is suggested, in the case of helmet supply, that these would be in regions known to be friendly to Caesar, in particular the Coolus district of Marne, close to the Rhine. It is therefore possible that mail, being originally a Gallic/Celtic armour type, may have been similarly sourced.

After a short period of relative peace around the end of the first century BC and the start of the first century AD, production then recommenced to re-equip the legions in advance of the Germanic campaigns. Around this time, new features appear to have been introduced to the military assemblage, possibly in preparation for the weaponry and tactics of the new opponents. However, despite the development of new, segmented armour for 'heavy infantry' specialist troops, the other forms of body armour, such as mail and scale, continued in use throughout this period, probably being still used by the majority of both legionary and auxiliary troops. However, both armour types also continued to adapt and develop, in answer probably again to changing opposition as the boundaries of the Empire expanded.

Initially, in the first century AD, cuirasses greatly reduced in length to hip length, also losing the additional shoulder doubling, making the armour much lighter and more flexible to use,

Piece	Dimensions	Estimated no. of rings		
A	22 rings x 87 rows	(22 x 87 x 2)	=	3,828
B1	3 rings x 33 rows (bottom) x 35 rows (top)	(3 x 33 x 2)+(3 x 2)	=	204
B2	as B1	(3 x 33 x 2)+(3 x 2)	=	204
C1	2 rings x 33 rows	(2x 33 x 2)	=	132
C2	as C2	(2 x 33 x 2)	=	132
D1	8 rings x 40 rows (bottom) x 33 rows (top)	(8 x 33 x 2)+(8 x 7)	=	584
D2	as D1	(8 x 33 x 2)+(8 x 7)	=	584
E	17 rings x 87 rows	(17 x 87 x 2)	=	2,958
F1	44 rings x 72 rows	(44 x 72 x 2)	=	6,336
F2	as F1	(44 x 72 x 2)	=	6,336
		Total rings		21,298
Additional Shoulder piece				
Piece	Dimensions	Estimated no. of rings		
Back panel	22 rings x 50 rows	(22 x 50 x 2)	=	2,200
Side piece x 2	22 rings x 15 rows each	(22 x 15 x 2)x2	=	1,320
		Total		3,520
Estimated total rings = 24,818 (21,298 main body + 3,520 shoulder piece)				

Table 4.1 Basic mail shirt dimensions (based on rings of 6 mm inner diameter).

Time taken to:	Seconds per ring
Wind 'worm' and cut rings	5
Prepare closed rings and open rings prior to assembly	8
Link and rivet rings	9
Total time per ring	22

Table 4.2 Time and motion summary.

while also being quicker and cheaper to produce (an important factor when large bodies of men were required to be mobilised at short notice (Russell-Robinson, 1975, 164–9; Feugère, 2002, 75). Later, from the third century, perhaps in answer to changing tactics and weaponry, the shape of both infantry and cavalry body armour changed once more. Mail and scale cuirasses are both seen to lengthen, becoming looser-fitting and developing sleeves of varying lengths (those for cavalry use developing a central front and rear slit for ease of riding and for added protection to the legs of the rider and flanks of his horse; Stephenson and Dixon, 2003, 44). It is also around this time that the segmented armour appears to fall from use, its function perhaps being no longer necessary against this different type of enemy weaponry, or perhaps due to its higher cost of production (mail and scale being cheaper and easier to make and repair).

It would appear, therefore, that at different times in the history of the Roman military, production may have alternated between small-scale private industry and large-scale, 'factory' mass production. Although the production of mail is not a complicated process, some stages do require varying levels of skill, dexterity and strength. It is clear that the production of the wire does not require the use of large factories and can be performed in small-scale workshops (as is still done today in some less technologically advanced societies), although the process does require some physical strength.

There is an alternate possibility that the process of manufacture may not necessarily have been carried out by military personnel in the *fabricae* inside a fort or specialist 'factory'. It could have formed part of a local village-based economy, with the whole family, possibly even the whole village, being involved in the process, with similar arrangements known from the medieval period. This may have been a similar arrangement to that of medieval weavers, where different parts of the process were completed by husband, wife, children, extended family, etc. In the case of mail production, however, there are some parts of the process which would not be possible for all members of a family.

The winding and cutting of the 'worms', for example, would have also required a level of physical strength probably only possible for the adult males of a society (military or civilian) for any sustained length of time. The braiding and riveting of the links do not require such a high level of physical strength and would have been possible for any adult family member. However, as it would have required accurate closure of the links and working with the very small rivets, it may not have been possible for the elderly members of an extended family with lower levels of manual dexterity and poorer eyesight. Here, older children may have had the strength to use the pliers, although not for any sustained periods, but may not have had the manual dexterity required for accurate closure of the rings. For similar reasons, they would be unlikely to have played a major part in the preparation of the pre-closed rings or in the punching of the rivet holes.

Less skilled or less physically strong workers could have assisted with one of the most irritating parts of the process, however. Once prepared, the open rings tend to tangle up with one another, and the assembly time is often lengthened greatly by separating individual rings before they can be threaded in. In a military *fabrica*, less skilled workers (or in a village community, perhaps children) could assist with this process by separating these tangled individual open rings prior to assembly. In addition, the elderly and younger family members, by completing the normal household duties, could have released the adult members for more prolonged work periods.

V

MUSCLE CUIRASS
(*LORICA MUSCULATA*)

SCULPTURAL REPRESENTATIONS

The muscle cuirass is usually depicted in sculptural representations associated with officers, generals and Emperors, with continual use through the Republican period down to the fifth century AD. Although no Roman examples of this type of armour have been found, it is considered most probable that, as with earlier Greek and Etruscan models, they would have been fashioned in bronze (Russell-Robinson, 1975, 147). It is possible that leather could have been used, as it is light to wear and easily moulded to shape if boiled (which would also harden the leather), but even very thick and hardened leather (*cuir bouillée*) would offer little protection in combat (and it is known that even the most decorative 'ceremonial' armour may be expected to serve in combat conditions), compared to bronze. As a medium, *musculata* can be highly polished, moulded to give the impression of an athletic physique, and decorated with embossed or appliqué symbolic and mythological ornaments, lending itself readily to the role of ceremonial armour. It is seen, therefore, in sculptural representations not only of high-ranking officers, but also of troops serving in high-visibility ceremonial positions, such as the Praetorian Guards. Their armour (as indeed is the case with modern-day troops serving ceremonial functions, such as the Life Guards) intentionally reflects the nostalgic glory of more archaic periods, for example the second-century AD Praetorian relief at the Musée du Louvre (Goldsworthy, 2000, 2), and that of a Praetorian centurion on the Column of Antoninus Pius (in the Vatican Museum; Russell-Robinson, 1975, 147).

However, despite this high-status use in later periods, the muscle cuirass had previously served less prestigious purposes. In addition to the highly decorative, high-waisted version, as depicted being worn by all officer ranks on Trajan's Column, paired with a double skirt of *pteruges*, a second style is seen with more defensive qualities, reaching down over the hips and curving down over the abdomen (Russell-Robinson, 1975, 149). This style, in its less decorative forms, appears to have been used more universally for lower ranks in earlier periods. For example, on a Republican-period relief of a bireme in the Temple of Fortuna Primigenia at Palestrina (also in the Vatican Museum), two of the marines depicted are shown wearing simple versions of these hip-length muscle cuirasses (Russell-Robinson, 1975, 147). Similarly, a late fourth to early third-century BC terracotta statue from a vase from Canosa depicts a helmeted and seated warrior wearing a high-necked, sleeveless cuirass which reaches over the hips, curving down at the front, demonstrating not only this lower ranking use, but also emphasising the longevity of service of this style of armour (Feugère, 2002, 71).

ORIGINS

Russell-Robinson saw the origin of this cuirass in the early armours of Bronze-Age Greece, citing as an example the fifteenth-century Dendra armour (Russell-Robinson, 1975, 147), although this being a heavy, inflexible arrangement of overlapping tubes, it perhaps shows more affinity with the *lorica segmentata* designs. This style, however, then developed into a more practical form covering only the ribcage area, which, through the Classical and

Hellenistic periods, came more to follow the musculature of the body, and by the fifth century BC, the use of hinges improved movement and flexibility further. It is probably, then, this shorter-bodied Greek ancestor which is reflected in the later Imperial Roman officer cuirass (Feugère, 2002, 73).

While Greek body armour to the fifth century took the form of full-bodied muscle cuirasses as described above, the Italic armours from the seventh to the fourth centuries were much simpler, offering less protection, consisting of just a pair of discs 20 to 50 cm in diameter, held in a harness front and back known as the *cardiophylax* (as it only protects the heart area; Feugère, 2002, 73). Examples of this armour type can be seen on a seventh-century BC statue from Capestrano and also on a sixth-century BC painting from Ceri, and was known to have been in use in Anacona, Campania, Corsica and southern France, forming the rudimentary basis for the superior Samnite 'triple-disc' armour developing from the fourth century BC (Feugère, 2002, 73).

The 'triple-disc' cuirass consisted of three large disc shapes on the chest and back, two above and one below, forming a triangular pectoral. It is suggested that it developed originally in the central Apennine region, with its earliest examples being found from the later half of the fifth century BC (from the necropolis at Alfedena, in the Abruzzo), becoming more widespread in areas of Samnite influence during the pan-Italic warfare of the fourth century BC (Feugère, 2002, 73; Burns, 2003, 70).

The fourth century BC appears to mark the pivotal point in the nature of both Roman military equipment and the organisation of the army (with the development of the manipular legion), the two being inextricably linked. At the start of the century, Italy was made up of a number of separate city states, each with their own armies, equipped according to their own individual traditions and forming alliances and fighting among themselves on an annual basis, mostly driven by a need for land and resources. The Roman people and the

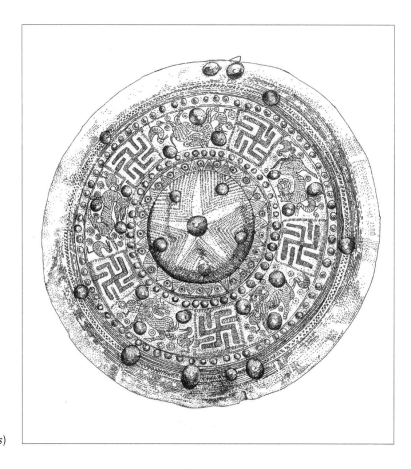

Fig. 46 Simple circular heart guards – *cardiophylax* (or *kardiophylax*): (a) Bronze disc with repoussée bosses and punched and incised animals, birds and geometric designs. Etruscan, 675–625 BC. The armour type is found inland in Etruria and in east, central Italy, worn backed with leather, as armour to protect the heart (*kardiophylax*), held in place by straps passing over one shoulder and under both arms. British Museum (GR1867.5-8.374). (*Artwork by J. R. Travis*)

Samnites were the two major players in these conflicts, the other Italic peoples casting their allegiances for either one side or the other. For example, at the start of the fourth century BC, Rome entered into a conflict with the neighbouring Etruscan state of Veii, the latter being supported by people of Aequi and Volsci (Livy, V.38–44, VII.19, VII.29, IX.20). As the century progressed this conflict escalated, drawing in more, and eventually all, of the neighbouring Italic peoples, expanding the boundaries of the areas involved and the size of the armies on each side (Burns, 2003, 62–3).

This interaction of peoples with different traditions, fighting techniques and armour assemblages brought about a sharing of the best ideas and styles. This modification of the armour assemblage was also part of a wider modification of fighting techniques and tactics. For example, according to Livy, at the beginning of the fourth-century period, the Roman army fought in hoplite-style phalanx formation 'like Macedonians', using round shields (Livy, VIII.8). Their opponents, the Samnites, however, had traditionally fought in more flexible open formation, using javelin and early forms of *pila*, and carrying longer oblong shields (*scuta*) from the fifth century BC. During the fifty years of Samnite wars from 343 to 293 BC, the Romans had time to evaluate the potential of this different assemblage and fighting technique, and particularly following their defeat by the Gauls at Allia in 386 BC, they introduced a series of reforms: the payment of soldiers, the use of Samnite-style oblong shields (better suited to defence against missile weapons such as javelin and *pila* in open formation fighting), and the use of manipular battle formation rather than the hoplite-style phalanx (Livy, IV.59; Plutarch, *Camillus*, 40.4)

As their fighting tactics were adapted for manipular formation and the weaponry assemblage modified to suit, this more open formation fighting then required a more efficient method of body protection than had been afforded by the simple *cardiophylax*. To some extent the Celtic mail cuirass and Montefortino helmets had been adopted from the Gauls in the early fourth century BC (the Montefortino being a simple, efficient helmet type, lending itself readily to methods of mass production), but the mail, although offering a far superior body protection, was very expensive to make and outside the resources of the majority (Burns, 2003, 70).

The Samnite triple-disc, however, offered a substantial improvement over the simple *cardiophylax* without maximum outlay. Under Samnite influence, in coastal regions with historic Greek and Etruscan cultural links and Greek-style armour and weaponry traditions (such as Campania, Lucania and Apulia), rectangular anatomical breastplates with stylised musculature began to appear from the mid-fourth century as a hybrid between the old Greek-style muscle cuirass and the Samnite triple-disc, with many common features between the two (Burns, 2003, 72; Feugère, 2002, 73). Both styles consisted of front and back pectoral plates with shoulder and side linking plates, although on some examples hinges are substituted for the triple-disc style ring attachments, the rectangular plates often featuring also an applied wave-pattern decoration along the borders, similar to motifs seen on red-figure vases from the same regions (Burns, 2003, 72).

This style of cuirass appears to have been used throughout the third and second centuries BC by pre-Marian reform Republican legionaries, with the probability of manufacture in central and southern Italy (areas where the style appears to have originated; Feugère, 2002, 73). One contemporary view of the use of this style of cuirass can also be seen on the third-century BC ivory relief from Palestrina on two heavily armed warriors (possibly Roman, although not proven), who are also seen to be equipped with greaves, lance, crested helmets and an oval shield (Feugère, 2002, 63, fig. 65). Feugère considers that the use of this armour type must have been limited, despite its regular occurrence on coinage (which may have served propaganda purposes only), as no examples have yet been found.

However, lack of finds does not necessarily prove rarity. Certainly a sizeable number of Montefortino helmets have been found, but many of these have been in funerary contexts. Helmets and swords do appear to hold a particular importance to the individual, and this could explain the preponderance of helmets found in funerary contexts rather than other body armour. The cuirass, however, is an efficient, valuable, high-status piece of equipment

Fig. 47 Emperor Augustus depicted wearing muscle cuirass as may have been worn by senior officers of the Imperial period. (*Artwork by J. R. Travis*)

which would have remained in use for considerable lengths of time, potentially handed down to later generations for reuse (as evidenced in more modern-day Life Guard cuirasses, many of which have seen centuries of use; JR Travis Snr, pers. comm.), and at the end of their usefulness, representing a large volume of bronze plate, would have no doubt have been recycled as a valuable resource, and unlikely to have been discarded.

Its use, however, may indeed have been limited (as Feugère suggested) for the additional reason of its cost; in a similar way, the use of mail may have been restricted to the wealthier (Feugère, 2002, 73). The Roman legionary of the second and first-century BC Republic is typically portrayed on sculptural representations, such as the relief of Aemilius Paulus and the Altar of Domitius Ahenobarbus, as wearing the best available equipment of Montefortino helmets, mail cuirass and carrying the oval *scutum* (Burns, 2003, 71). However, this view may be idealised propagandist art, with the reality being more basic, as described by Polybius. He states that mail would have only been available to those meeting the property requirement of 10,000 drachmae, with the majority from poorer and more remote communities still using a square (24 cm) brass plate (*cardiophylax*) protection, with the plain muscle cuirass, undecorated apart from its stylised simulated musculature, fitting in between these two extremes (Polybius, VI.23).

MUSCLE CUIRASSES OF THE IMPERIAL PERIOD

The muscle cuirasses of the first to fifth centuries AD however, in contrast to those of earlier periods, are often highly ornate, with applied or embossed decoration, with potentially two differing body styles depicted: either the Hellenistic, high-waisted style, best suited to cavalry, or the more common hip-length, curving down at the front abdomen, Republican style (Russell-Robinson, 1975, 149). The most decorative design used is a central Medusa head motif, with paired griffins on the ribs and scrolled tendrils on the abdomen. A common alternative design substitutes winged victories for the griffins, and either Minerva, weapons or trophies in the central position, for example the motifs of victory and divine supporting figures seen on the Prima Porta Augustus at the Vatican Museum. Russell-Robinson proposed that these decorative motifs may have been embossed on the cuirass, in similar fashion to decoration seen on cavalry helmets (as for example on the Ribchester helmet), or may have been made separately and applied with rivets and/or solder (as some of the applied brass designs on Imperial iron helmets; Russell-Robinson, 1975, 152).

Variation is also seen on the sculptural representations in the way that the pectoral plates are joined and the style of shoulder straps used, some being archaic, Greek-style, the others the newer Roman-style, the former having right-angle cutaway shapes on lower extreme corners. Shoulder straps appear to have been hinged to the back plate, with the ends tied down to rings on the breastplate. Other examples have matching straps to the rear, but Russell-Robinson in his discussion suggested that these may have been fixed and unmoveable (Russell-Robinson, 1975, 149). He also suggested that many of these sculptural representations may not be founded in reality at all, some examples exhibiting impractical features, such as unfeasibly narrow, short, tight sleeves. He proposed that many of the sculptural representations may be intended for propaganda purposes, the subject having been given a choice, perhaps from a catalogue of drawings, for an idealised image of himself to be disseminated across the Empire, and may not be representative of any 'real' armour worn by the subject (Russell-Robinson, 1975, 149). Until examples are found, it is impossible to prove or challenge the existence of this armour type during this later phase of the first to fifth century AD as being either real armour or images of fantasy, drawing on nostalgic memories of an archaic age. However, its existence on lower-ranking officers, albeit symbolically, on monumental sculptures such as Trajan's Column would tend to favour its existence, at least in a limited capacity.

VI

SCALE ARMOUR (*LORICA SQUAMATA*)

Scale armour, as with the muscle cuirass previously discussed, was used by the Roman army for a considerable length of time, from the earliest days of the Republic through to the later stages of Empire, spanning over 800 years, although its origin reaches back to over a millennium earlier. This longevity of use has been attributed by many, including Russell-Robinson and Feugère, to the ease of its manufacture and repair (Feugère, 2002, 74; Russell-Robinson, 1975, 153). It consists of rigid plates of copper-alloy or iron (although in earlier periods any other resilient material may have been used, such as wood, thick, hardened leather, ivory, etc), sewn or wired to each other and a flexible backing garment (of fabric or leather), allowing free and flexible movement for the wearer, and providing an impressive and pleasing aesthetic effect when polished, giving an appearance like snakeskin, fish scales, or bird plumage (Feugère, 2002, 74).

The individual scales are simple to cut to shape, the attachment perforations being easily made with even such simple implements as a hammer and anvil, and at a modest cost that compares favourably against mail or plate armour, which Russell-Robinson thought made it ideal for equipping large bodies of auxiliary troops economically at short notice, and led Feugère to suggest it as ideal for use by second-rank troops and cavalrymen (Feugère, 2002, 74; Russell-Robinson, 1975, 153). It is closely related to the armour type known as 'lamellar', which is similarly made of rigid plates laced together, but in view of a few fundamental differences (in that the lamellar plates are laced to each other, but not to the backing garment, the lacing being visible on the exterior surface, and the overlap direction being reversed to upwards) this will be discussed separately.

ORIGINS

The origins of scale are not clear, but it would appear to have been in use back into the early Bronze Age, if not earlier, probably originating in the east. Russell-Robinson suggested a date at least into the seventeenth century BC for origin, with archaeological evidence from both Egyptian and Hittite contexts dating to the fourteenth and thirteenth centuries BC where it already appears in a fully developed form (Russell-Robinson, 1975, 153). For example, an impression of a fourteenth-century warrior can be seen depicted in an incised image on a fragment of a clay vessel from the Hittite site of Boğaskoy, in Turkey (although MacQueen suggested that the figure depicted may not represent a Hittite warrior, but an Aegean or West Anatolian opponent; 1986, 63, fig. 34). His body armour has been interpreted by MacQueen as a sleeveless jacket, possibly of leather, decorated with a series of concentric circles, worn over a scale shirt with elbow-length sleeves with fringed ends (although alternately this 'jacket' could represent some form of solid cuirass). The elements of this armour which appear to have been of scale (either separate sleeves, or parts of an underlying scale shirt) can be seen as a series of horizontal lines with lateral zigzag pattern, which may represent the method of attachment of the scales.

A number of scales were found at the same site, presumably from a near-contemporary context, which could offer some clues as to how such scales could have attached (MacQueen, 1986, 63). The scales are flat at one end, rounded at the other, with a central lengthwise

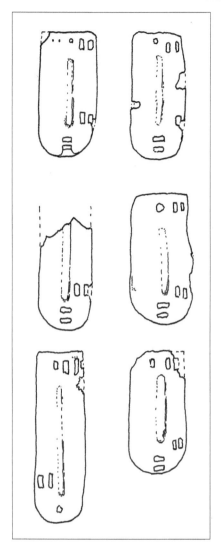

Fig. 48 Hittite scales – bronze, from Bogazkoy (after Neve, from MacQueen, 1986, 63, fig. 33). Average height *c*. 6 cm. (*Drawn by J. R. Travis*)

reinforcing rib, which does not quite reach entirely to each end, allowing for closer overlap with the rows above and below. The scales are each pierced with a series of holes, some round and others rectangular in shape. Paired holes can be seen down one side (top and bottom), which suggested that the scales may not have overlapped laterally, but would have been attached side by side to the backing. However, other holes (some single, some paired) at the top and bottom centre could have allowed overlap vertically, producing a semi-rigid effect more like lamellar-type scales.

Evidence of early use of scale can also be seen from Egyptian contexts, from both artistic representations and archaeological remains. A series of bronze scales have been found in the palace of Amenhotep III in Thebes, one of which retains traces of a textile backing, suggesting a method of construction to hold the assemblage of scales together. The scales are long and leaf-shaped, flat at the top with rounded corners (the top end narrower than the lower end), the lower end curving to a rounded point. Again a lengthwise central spine reinforces the scales, and a series of holes served to join them to each other and to the backing. Holes again can be seen top and bottom centre, with paired holes set diagonally at top right and bottom left, suggesting construction being laid side by side in horizontal rows (without overlap), then each row overlapping the row below by about one third in an offset, staggered alignment which would have produced a semi-rigid structure (Wise, 1987, 20).

1 Kalkriese reconstruction: completed *lorica* modelled by J. R. Travis. (*Photo by H. Travis*)

Left: 2 Re-enactors of Deva V. Victrix (Chester's Roman Guard) portraying legionaries wearing lorica segmentata (on the left, Corbridge type A; on the right, Newstead type).
(*Photo by H. Travis*)

Below: 3 Kalkriese reconstruction: cardboard mock-up.
(*Photo by J. R. Travis*)

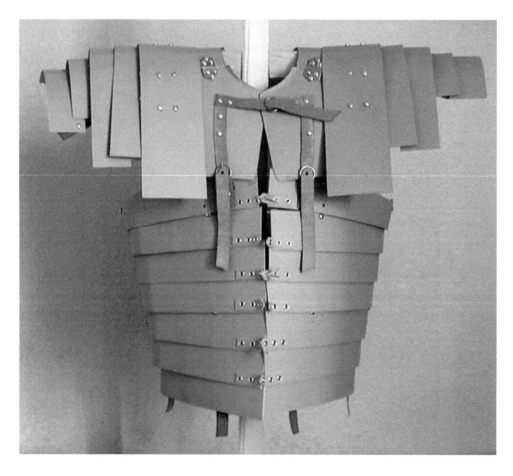

4 Kalkriese reconstruction workshop: attaching copper-alloy neck trim to plates. (*Photo by H. and J. R. Travis*)

5 Kalkriese reconstruction workshop: back plates with neck trim attached, for body shaping. (*Photo by H. and J. R. Travis*)

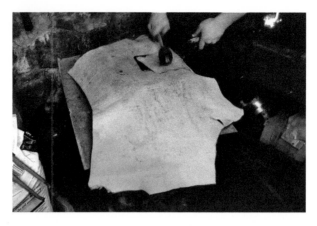

6 Kalkriese reconstruction workshop: plates heated in forge and hammered to shape on soft bed of sand and leather for support. (*Photo by H. and J. R. Travis*)

7 Kalkriese reconstruction workshop: breastplate completed (body-shaped, neck trim attached) but still forge-blackened. (*Photo by H. and J. R. Travis*)

8 Kalkriese reconstruction workshop: lesser shoulder guards bent to shape. (*Photo by H. and J. R. Travis*)

9 Kalkriese reconstruction workshop: rolled edge applied to lower girdle plates, and underarm areas of top girdle plates reduced in height at mid-section, to prevent 'dead arm' to wearer. (*Photo by H. and J. R. Travis*)

10 Kalkriese reconstruction workshop: girdle plates bent to body shape of intended wearer.
(*Photo by H. and J. R. Travis*)

11 Kalkriese reconstruction workshop: girdle plates fitted inside each other, marked to length to allow for overlap.
(*Photo by H. and J. R. Travis*)

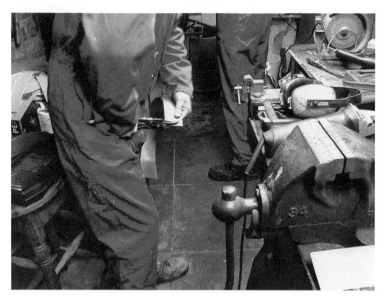

12 Kalkriese reconstruction workshop: girdle plate overlaps trimmed to match. (*Photo by H. and J. R. Travis*)

13 Kalkriese reconstruction: breastplate – forged, fitted with copper-alloy trim and polished ready for application of hinges, buckles, etc. (*Photo by J. R. Travis*)

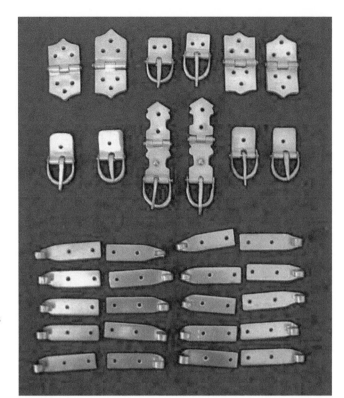

14 Complete set of fittings for Kalkriese reconstruction: four sub-lobate hinges; two front vertical buckles; two horizontal strap buckles (front and back); four vertical internal back buckles; and twenty tie loops (for five fastening girdle hoops and two hoops remaining 'open'). (*Photo by J. R. Travis*)

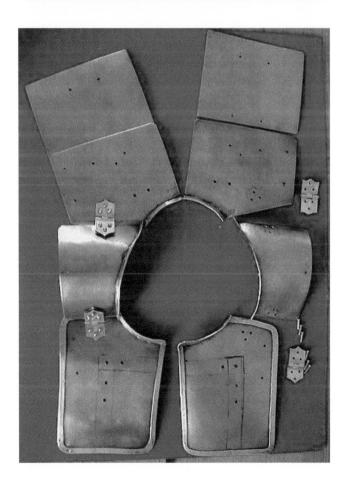

15 Kalkriese reconstruction: upper-body plates arranged and marked up for assembly with copper-alloy fittings (hinges, buckles, etc.). (*Photo by J. R. Travis*)

16 Kalkriese reconstruction: internal leather strapping of the upper body and shoulder assembly. (*Photo by J. R. Travis*)

17 Kalkriese reconstruction: girdle plates shaped, fitted together and marked ready for riveting to internal leathers. (*Photo by J. R. Travis*)

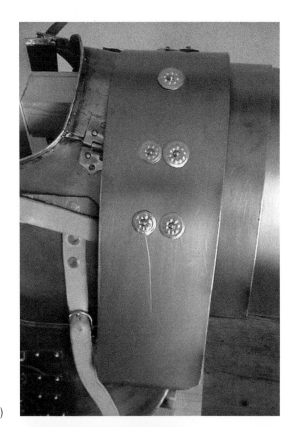

18 Kalkriese reconstruction: exterior view of upper shoulder assembly. (*Photo by J. R. Travis*)

19 Re-enactor and author Will Llawerch portraying Iron Age/Celtic warrior, wearing Montefortino helmet with Celtic-style cheek pieces and mail cuirass with Celtic/Gallic-style 'cape' shoulder doubling, as seen on early first-century BC statue of Mars from Mavilly, Côte d'Or. (*Photo by H. Travis*)

20 Re-enactors of Deva V. Victrix (Chester's Roman Guard) portraying Emperor Domitian (left) and legionary standard-bearer, *signifier* (right), wearing mail cuirass (*lorica hamata*), with shoulder doubling closed by serpentine-style closure hooks. (*Photo by H. Travis*)

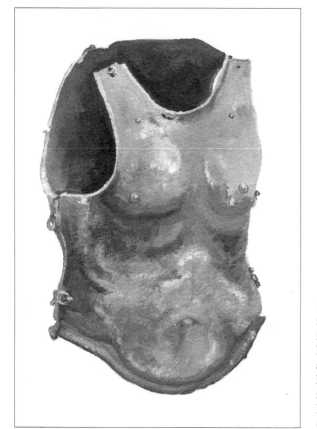

21 Muscle cuirass with anatomical musculature. South Italian from Greek influence, 350–300 BC, from tomb near Naples, probably made for a cavalryman as it splays at the hips. Cuirass is full-length, unlike shorter ones (which were made to be worn with bronze belts). British Museum (GR1842.7-28.712). (*Artwork by J. R. Travis*)

22 Bronze muscle cuirass (rectangular), south Italian, 375–325 BC, originally attached by rings to hinged shoulder pieces and side guards. British Museum (GR1902.4-28.2). (*Artwork by J. R. Travis*)

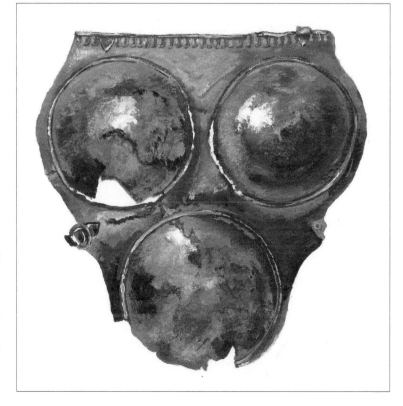

23 Bronze triple-disc breastplate. South Italian, 400–300 BC, from Ruvo. This would have had matching back plate, side plates and hinged shoulder plates. The type evolved after 400 BC, not from single-disc version (Bronze 373), but from the rectangular muscled one. Small discs represent pectoral muscles and the larger one the abdominal. British Museum (GR1856.12-26.665). (*Artwork by J. R. Travis*)

Above left: 24 Roman 'hoplite' soldier of early fourth century BC, wearing a simple pair of small discs (*cardiophylax*) linked by a series of rings, helmet, leg protectors (greaves), and carrying a small, round *hoplon* shield. (*Artwork by J. R. Travis*)

Above right: 25 Samnite warrior of early fourth century BC, wearing triple-disc cuirass, carrying long rectangular shield (*scutum*) and projectile weapons (javelin and prototype *pila*). (*Artwork by J. R. Travis*)

Above left: 26 Roman legionary of the later Republican period (following the 'reforms' of Marius), wearing mail cuirass, bronze helmet of Coolus ('Mannheim') type (simply shaped, without crest knobs), and carrying oval shields ('Fayum'-style) and the new improved *pilum*. (*Artwork by J. R. Travis*)

Above right: 27 Auxiliary cavalryman of the Imperial period, wearing mail cuirass and 'sports' masked face helmet. (*Artwork by J. R. Travis*)

Above left: 28 Imperial-period officer in scale cuirass. The transverse helmet crest indicates the rank of Centurian. (*Artwork by J. R. Travis*)

Above right: 29 Late Empire legionary wearing loose-fitting, long-sleeved scale cuirass (as depicted in the 'Battle of Ebenezer' fresco from the Synagogue, Dura-Europos, and on the Arch of Diocletian, late third to early fourth century AD). (*Artwork by J. R. Travis*)

30 Scythian/Sarmatian archer, his costume based on Bosphoran funerary stela of Rhodon. He is depicted wearing a quilted/padded over-tunic or *subarmalis*, carrying Scythian-style recurved bow and *gorytus* (side quiver for both bow and arrows) decorated with Scythian-style animal motifs. (*Artwork by J. R. Travis*)

31 Syrian archer, as depicted on Trajan's Column, wearing ankle-length flowing tunic, short mail cuirass and eastern-style conical helmet. Tunic colour unknown, but depicted in green, based on conjectural interpretation of Hamian archer stela from Housesteads fort, Hadrian's Wall. (*Artwork by J. R. Travis*)

32 Scythian armoured horsemen, wearing combination mail and scale body armour. Based on Scythian cataphract-style armour of sixth to fifth century BC and Scythian armour with iron scales, fifth century BC from Lingul. (*Artwork by J. R. Travis, after Negin, 1998, 72, plate 5, and Feugère, 2002*)

33 *Clibinarius,* with armoured horse wearing 'trapper' of copper alloy scales on textile backing with leather edging, as found at Dura Europos. Based on Dura-Europos graffito and finds photographed in James, 2004. (*Artwork by J. R. Travis*)

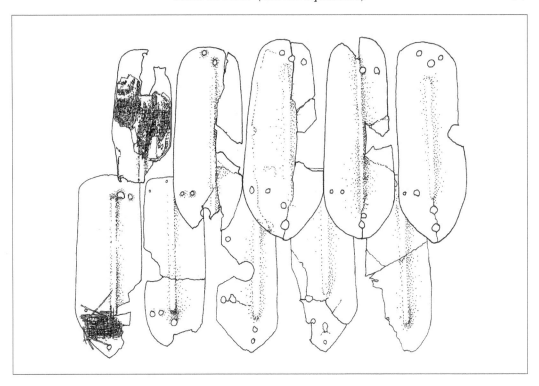

Fig. 49 Bronze scales from fourteenth-century BC armour, found in the palace of Amenhotep III in Thebes. Parts of backing garment (fabric or leather) still visible at top-left (from Wise, 1987, 20). (*Drawn by J. R. Travis*)

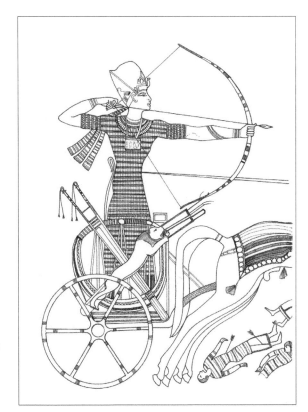

Fig. 50 Detail from a relief at Ramesseum, Thebes, depicting Rameses II at Qadesh, wearing a full-length scale coat (from MacQueen, 1986, 49, fig. 25). (*Redrawn by J. R. Travis*)

A further impression of Egyptian scale construction can be seen in an illustration of armour from the tomb of Rameses III (Wise, 1987, 21), which shows a long coat of scale with a high neck and short sleeves (a similar coat of ankle-length scale with short sleeves can be seen in an image of Rameses II at Qadesh, trampling a series of enemies under his chariot; MacQueen, 1986, 49, fig. 25). The former shows a construction of round-ended scales, set side by side, aligned vertically. A 'hole' visible at the lower end of each scale would have fixed each scale to the one below, with a short 'line' on the top right-hand side of each scale possibly representing vertical cording (Wise, 1987, 21). Again, this structure would have been semi-rigid in the vertical plane, but more flexible than the previous example in the horizontal direction.

Slightly later in date, a corselet of rawhide scales was found, attached to a linen backing, in the tomb of Tutenkhamun, dating to around 1322 BC, which suggests that other materials than bronze would have been used. Although inferior to bronze, rawhide can provide a strong and resilient surface, a material of sufficiently adequate impact resistance to be still used for construction of shields at Dura-Europos in the third century AD. Again, further examples of Egyptian scale come from the tenth-century BC tomb of the Pharoah Sheshong. These, however, show the improved method of construction found in later cuirasses, whereby the scales overlap their neighbours horizontally (albeit only by one fifth of their width), producing a double thickness over much of its surface (Russell-Robinson, 1975, 154).

Although these fourteenth-century BC finds may indeed be the earliest evidence for scale, this does not prove conclusively any point of origin. Its use does increase in the east and north, with fourth-century finds of bronze scales in tumuli in southern Russia, and a set of composite mail and scale Scythian armour with iron scales from Lingul, dating to the fifth century, but its use remained rare in Greece, and it does not appear at all in Celtic regions. As the uptake of new ideas and technologies has been shown to be driven by appearance of a new, better suggestion, and considering that the Greeks and Celts were already using a superior product (the muscle cuirass and mail shirts respectively), it would seen reasonable to expect that they would not have taken up the use of scale. This therefore suggested to Russell-Robinson and Feugère, on the balance of probabilities, an overall origin in the east with a movement through Cyprus and Greece into Italy, its uptake boosted by recruitment of eastern auxiliaries (Russell-Robinson, 1975, 154; Feugère, 2002, 74). Indeed, most of the Roman sculptural representations and archaeological evidence (scale being a frequent find on most sites, although complete cuirasses are not known) does come from the later Imperial periods of the first to sixth centuries AD, and within this time span alone, a developmental progression of design, and a variety of functions, identity and status are known.

CONSTRUCTION

Although more examples of scale are found than of mail, this is hardly surprising due to the small size of the component parts of the latter, and does not imply any greater level of use. In fact, quite the opposite is probably the case. Bearing this in mind, many sites produce a small quantity of scale (notable finds being from Dura-Europos, Syria; Straubing, Germany; and Carpow, Scotland), with other sites such as Carnuntum and Newstead producing hundreds, but from a mixture of differently sized plates from multiple shirts. No site, however, has yet produced an entire, complete cuirass, the closest example being the bronze shirt from Lake Trasimene (now in the Royal Ontario Museum; Russell-Robinson, 1975, 154), although that reconstruction is entirely conjectural, consisting by the time of its discovery of just a quantity of separated scales.

Among the examples of scale found, a variety of sizes, quantity and arrangement of perforations can be seen. Where scales have been found in association with others and traces of backing material, a variety of constructional techniques are seen (for example, sometimes rows of scale may have been aligned above each other, or alternatively offset like roofing tiles). This has been demonstrated by Clemetson, who catalogued finds of known scale in

Britain (along with some suggested constructional methods), using variation in shape, size and perforation pattern (finding forty-six different types across twenty-five sites), as von Groller had previously done at Carnuntum (where he identified thirty-six types at the one single site; Clemetson, 1993, 8–10; von Groller, 1901a, 85).

At Newstead (excavated between 1905 and 1909), a deposit of 346 copper-alloy (brass) scales was found in a pit in the *principia*, many of which were still fastened together, providing an insight into methods of construction. The scales were of a uniform size (2.9 cm by 1.2 cm by 1 mm), shape (square-topped with a rounded bottom), and thickness, showing a uniform pattern of perforations (five holes, set in a vertical pair on each side and one larger hole at top centre). They had been fastened together horizontally, using ties of square sectioned brass wire or strips, threaded through the smaller side holes, overlapping the right side of each scale over the left side of its neighbour. Each horizontal strip had then been laced to a backing fabric (possibly of leather) using leather thongs, passed through the large holes at top centre (Curle, 1911, 158; Feugère, 2002, 98).

At Carpow in Scotland (excavated in 1979), a piece of folded scale armour was found in a shallow pit in the *praetentura* (Coulston, 1992, 21). The size of the site (11 hectares), coupled with the presence of substantial stone internal buildings, suggested a probable legionary *vexillationes*, Severan in date. On conservation, the top layer of the folded deposit was removed, exposing the remains of the textile backing and also the method of construction. The copper-alloy scales (15 to 16 mm by 13 mm) were again of uniform shape (rectangular

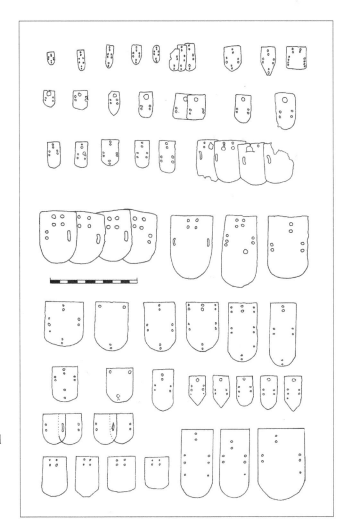

Fig. 51 Variety of scale types found at Carnuntum, from von Groller, 1901b, plate 15 (below scale), and at Dura-Europos, from James, 2004, 136, fig. 82 (above scale). (*Redrawn by J. R. Travis*)

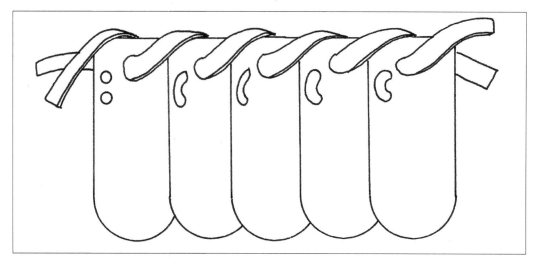

Fig. 52 Method of lacing Newstead scales (from Curle, 1911, fig. 12). (*Redrawn by J. R. Travis*)

with rounded lower corners), size, thickness and perforation pattern (although a different pattern of holes than those at Newstead). Each scale was perforated by six holes, set in three vertical pairs, one pair at top centre and one pair a short distance lower down on each side. The scales were then laid in rows overlapping their neighbour, wired together with bronze wire strips 1 mm wide, threaded through the side holes and bent over at the back. Linen S-plied cord was then laid across the top of each strip and stitched with linen thread to the textile backing cloth through the upper pairs of holes. The next row of scales was then attached above in similar fashion, each scale being offset by half a scale to form a brickwork pattern (like roofing tiles), the lower parts of the scales covering the cord that had been stitched above the lower row, which then served as a buffer to prevent one row abrading the row beneath and to help absorb the force of any impact. Two sections of leather were also found, 128 mm by 220 mm, which had been folded lengthways and attached for either neck or underarm edging, using leather thonging (Coulston, 1992, 21–2; Feugère, 2002, 98).

At Carnuntum, as previously mentioned, von Groller catalogued thirty-six different kinds of scale, some of bronze but mostly of iron, ranging in size from the smallest bronze (2.8 by 1.4 cm) to the largest iron (8 cm by 5.4 cm), with one iron example made of double-thickness folded metal. Variety was also seen in both shapes and perforation patterns, indicating slightly different methods of lacing together (in much the same way as the previously described examples from Newstead and Carpow), but nevertheless with a basic level of similarity overall, mostly using two holes on each side, usually about halfway down, for lateral linking. Some were found to be still attached to each other, simplifying the determination of construction, indicating that most, if not all, had been overlapped and wired to their lateral neighbour through side holes, using top holes to tie or lace to a backing garment, again similar to on the Newstead and Carpow examples (von Groller, 1901a, 85; Russell-Robinson, 1975, 154).

Von Groller noted a variety of top hole sizes and patterns which he separated into six distinct categories (von Groller, 1901a, 85):

i)   Large single hole (e.g. Newstead style).
ii)   Two holes – one at each corner.
iii)   Two horizontal holes, near to top centre.
iv)   Two vertical holes near to top centre.
v)   Two pairs of two vertical holes near to top centre (four holes in total).
vi)   Three pairs of two vertical holes, one pair in middle, one each side (six holes in total).

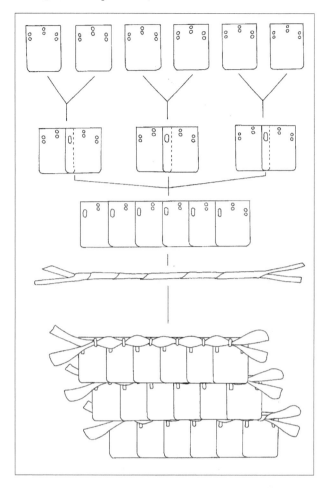

Fig. 53 Carpow scale construction
(from Coulston, 1992).
(*Redrawn by J. R. Travis*)

Some scales also retained traces of top lacing, from which von Groller proposed two methods of attachment of each horizontal strip to the bodice (von Groller, 1901a, 85):

1) Using leather thongs, lacing through large top holes (as with Newstead examples).
2) Stitching with threads through small holes (as at Carpow), although within this method he proposed three further possibilities. Either:
   i) Single row of stitching.
   ii) Double row of single stitches.
   iii) Double row of double stitches.

Most of the scales were of the round-bottomed type, similar to those from Newstead (the most common being those 2–3 cm long by 1–2 cm wide), others were pointed, and others square with rounded/clipped corners, as on the examples from Carpow. Clemetson in his study identified four similar examples from three British sites at Corbridge, Great Chesters and Caerleon, of small-sized, pointed bottomed, copper-alloy scales (brass – 2 per cent tin and 13 per cent zinc), with a common pattern of six holes in vertical pairs at the top, with similarities to examples from elsewhere in the Empire (Vindobona, Carnuntum and Dura-Europos), estimating the quantity of scales required for the construction of an average scale coat (Clemetson, 1993, 8–10; Curle, 1911, 160).

The scales overlapped their neighbour to the left by a third of their width, with a vertical overlap so that the point would reach to halfway down the left-hand edge of the scale below. In the first Corbridge example, the lateral fastenings were executed using wire clips 12.7

mm long, cut from sheet 0.5 mm thick, in strips 0.76 mm wide, the side holes being 1.5 mm diameter. These holes were similarly sized on the second Corbridge example and closely sized (at 1.3 mm) on those from Great Chesters, suggesting a similar wiring method to be probable (Clemetson, 1993, 8–10).

Clemetson notes that the metal shows no signs of annealing (as would have been necessary at regular intervals if copper-alloy bar had been worked into sheet metal). He proposed that this factor, combined with the uniform thickness of the plates, indicates the possible use of rolled sheet (Clemetson, 1993, 10).

In his study of scale armour, Russell-Robinson also remarked on similarities of size and shape between scales from different find sites, which he suggested in some cases could be indicative of the work of the same workshop. He also suggested that the standardisation of size and shape, along with standardisation of hole pattern and distances apart, hole sizes and wire width, as reported by von Groller, could be for the deliberate purpose of speeding production and ease of repair in workshops, in order that component parts of correct dimensions could be readily obtained (Russell-Robinson, 1975, 154).

Although some scale appeared to have been simply cut (or perhaps pressed, for uniformity of size and speed of production), others had been deliberately given a convex shape to give added rigidity, as seen on some of the scales in Clemetson's study, and on many of the Carnuntum examples (Clemetson, 1993, 8–10; von Groller, 1901a, 85). As an extension of this practice, many bronze scales were found to have been embossed with a vertical medial ridge, to strengthen and minimise bending of the plate. This medial ridge is also seen in cruder forms on the early Hittite and Egyptian examples discussed earlier, and can also be seen on some sculptural representations, such as that of the mid-first-century AD centurion, Q. Sertorius Festus, at Verona (Russell-Robinson, 1975, 156). On some scales it may be more finely executed to the extent that they take on the appearance of fine feathers (with such examples found at Newstead, Ouddorp, Augsburg and Becançon, some of which have been found attached to mail shirts), which Russell-Robinson (1975, 154) named as *Lorica Plumata* (Curle, 1911, plate 38). Curle quotes Ammianus Marcellinus (XXIV.4.12), who described the Parthians' armour as being 'of tongues of iron like feathers' (Curle, 1911, 160).

The example from Augsburg is of particular interest as the tiny scales (10 mm by 7 mm) are made in alternating iron and copper-alloy metal, to give a varied effect (Feugère, 2002, 100; Stephenson and Dixon, 2003, 49). A similar effect can also be seen on examples of larger scale, for example on forty-seven scales found at Ham Hill, Somerset, where tinned or silvered bronze scales alternate with plain bronze ones, producing a chequerboard effect (Curle, 1911, 160; Russell-Robinson, 1975, 156). Other scales have also been found elsewhere with evidence of surface tinning with white metal (for example, the two large scales 2.6 cm long from Hod Hill) which Russell-Robinson suggested may have served as much for purposes of protection from corrosion as for its aesthetic visual effect, citing by example the medieval practice of tinning brigandine plates to protect the surface fabric (Russell-Robinson, 1975, 156).

This effect of using differently coloured scales can also be seen at Masada, on the lowest terrace of the Northern Palace, where 340 scales which appear to originate from a single garment were found using a mixture of colours (silver, red and gold colourations produced by varying proportions of inclusions in their copper-alloy base), and also using a mixture of different shapes and sizes (long and short scales in both narrow and wide forms). If these had in fact come from the same garment, it may have used differently sized and shaped pieces in different parts of the garment, with the majority from the main body part being of the long and narrow form (Steibel and Magness, 2007, plates 1 and 2).

Stiebel proposed that this variation in size, shape and colouration suggests a higher status garment, possibly being parade armour, whereas a further deposit of 650 similarly designed but monotone scales found in a rock-cut cistern in the small bathhouse, he described as from a 'utilitarian', lower-status cuirass (Stiebel and Magness, 2007, 1–2). Again, these probably all belong to the one single garment, being found sealed under a burnt layer of debris in close association with a male body, suggested by Yadin to have been one of the defending Zealots (Yadin, 1966, 54).

This attribution to the defending side by Yadin is feasible, in that both sets of scale found bear striking similarities of design to each other, and also to bronze scales from the site of Gamla, also in Israel (with raised medial and circumference ridges and a similar method of attachment using four pierced holes set in a square at the top of each scale), but without similar examples from known Roman contexts. As the ridged design of these scales is unlike any Roman types (including those catalogued from Carnuntum by von Groller, or from Dura catalogued by James), they are unlikely to have belonged to any member of the 10th Legion, although use by auxiliary troops cannot be entirely ruled out. The finds associated with the body in the small bathhouse, however, being also found close to that of a female and a child, concealed under burnt debris, in all probability belonged to a member of the defending side (Yadin, 1966, 54). However, with this assignment, the garment could have originated from the earlier Herodian stockpiled equipment, or may have been brought to the site much later by Zealot or Siccarian rebels. With the probability, therefore, that these scales did not belong to any Roman forces, legionary or auxiliary, they are included here in this discussion for reasons of completeness and comparison, and in the event of any similar finds elsewhere from known Roman contexts which may permit a revision of this viewpoint.

Von Groller had noted, on all of the examples of scale catalogued from Carnuntum, that the side perforations would be a uniform distance from the edges of any plate, regardless of its size, so as not to weaken the metal, which therefore causes smaller plates to overlap a greater percentage of their neighbour than would larger plates, and which he thought would

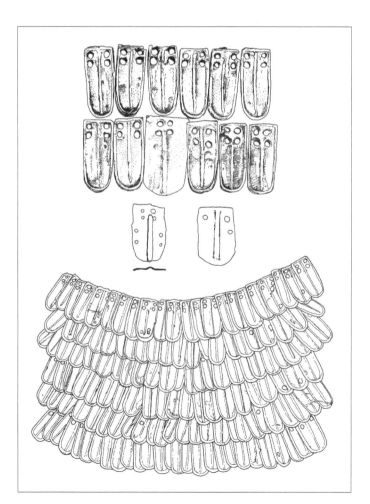

Fig. 54 Group of 650 scales from rock-cut cistern in small bathhouse at Masada: one showing offset stamping and one probable crude repair plate (from Yadin, 1966, 55, and Stiebel & Magness, 2007, plate 2). (*Drawn by J. R. Travis*)

cause the former to be heavier (von Groller, 1901a, 85). Russell-Robinson disagreed with
this opinion, considering that, in view of the smaller scales being produced in thinner metal,
there would be no difference. Von Groller also had thought that the smaller scales would
have been only suitable for children's armour, whereas Russell-Robinson thought them 'too
delicate' for war use, but probably acceptable for cavalry sports or ceremonial wear (Russell-
Robinson, 1975, 156). Clemetson, however, disputes this view, along with the existence of
parade armour in general. He considers that, although the scales are delicate and thinner, the
greater horizontal and vertical overlap means that a greater percentage of the surface of the
shirt would be double thickness, increasing its strength (Clemetson, 1993, 10).

In addition to the categorisations of side and top perforations, as described by von Groller,
there is a further feature distinguishing a small number of examples found, in that some
scales also have an additional hole, or pair of holes, at the bottom edge, which would have
been used to wire each row to the row above, producing a much more rigid lattice (von
Groller, 1901a, 85; Russell-Robinson, 1975, 154). This semi-rigid 'solid scale' is mostly seen
as a development from the Antonine period, using relatively small, long and slender scales,
with examples from Mušov and at Corbridge (and which has been suggested to indicate the
presence of auxiliary troops of eastern origin). However, some similar but larger semi-rigid
scales have also been found in the pre-Antonine context of Carnuntum, which Russell-
Robinson suggested may represent an early stage in its development (Stephenson and Dixon,
2003, 48; Russell-Robinson, 1975, 154).

These rigid armours would have given increased protection from missiles and thrusting
weapons, but would have been much less flexible than conventional scale. Russell-Robinson

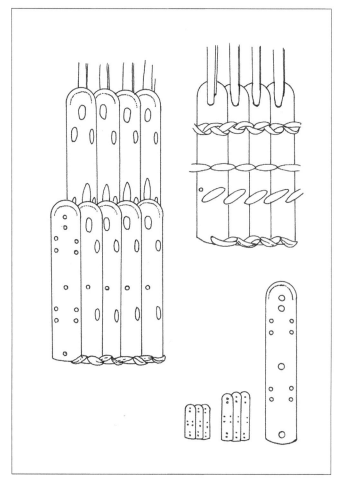

Fig. 55 Lamellar armour from
Corbridge (after Russell-Robinson,
1975). (*Redrawn by J. R. Travis*)

therefore suggested that it may have been used for short, waist-length cuirasses, perhaps worn over mail, for additional protection. Its rigid construction would not have needed a backing garment to hold the rows together, as with conventional scale, although this would probably still have been necessary to prevent the sharp ends of the wire links, bent over on the reverse side, cutting the wearer. This, Russell-Robinson considered, would probably be of leather for extra resilience, although examples from Carnuntum show traces of what may be straw padding, presumably for this purpose (Russell-Robinson, 1975, 156).

DESIGN

Although scale armour remained in use by the Roman army throughout its existence, its appearance, function and status was by no means static, its changing design showing the same developmental progression of body shape. This trend can also be seen in contemporary mail cuirasses, within the two distinct models for infantry and cavalry use (although incidence of infantry use did reduce in the later Imperial periods), these changing designs being reflected in sculptural representations (Feugère, 2002, 98).

For example, from the Republican period (as described by Polybius, writing in the mid-second century BC) through to the start of the first century AD, mail and scale cuirasses were used by both legionary and cavalry troops, following a simple, loose-fitting, sleeveless body shape. The shoulder areas on some examples are reinforced, on mail shirts at least, by wide straps passing over the shoulder from the back (where they may have been permanently fixed), drawing across to protect the neck area, and fastened on the front, either by tying to rings (as can be seen on infantrymen in the Augustan-period relief from the Palazzo Ducale, Mantua, which depicts both Roman and Gallic combatants) or using S-shaped hooks attached to a disc at the front centre (as used by cavalrymen in the same sculptural representation; Russell-Robinson, 1975, 157). The cavalry cuirass appears to be of the same loose-fitting design as that of the infantrymen, with its fullness drawn in by use of a belt (as also seen on that of a cavalry officer on the Arch of Orange), which also draws it up to a shorter length, so as not to inhibit movement on horseback, while transferring part of the weight of the cuirass from the shoulders to the hips (Russell-Robinson, 1975, 157).

In the second quarter of the first century AD, an increase is seen in the use of scale for auxiliary troops, mostly cavalry, which, as suggested by Russell-Robinson and Feugère, may be symptomatic of an influx of eastern auxiliaries (Feugère, 2002, 74; Russell-Robinson, 1975, 158). An example of a cuirass of this period can be seen on the stela of the cavalryman Vonatorix, of the ala Longiniana (at Bonn), which appears to reach to the upper thighs, but now with the additional feature of a short side slit for ease of use when riding (Russell-Robinson, 1975, 158). The cuirass is still sleeveless, but with *pteruges* providing additional protection for the upper arm, and using wide shoulder straps to provide a close neck fitting.

Almost contemporary with the previous example but possibly slightly later, dating to between AD 43 and 60, the stela of another cavalryman (a Thracian *dupicarius*), Longinus, from Colchester (Russell-Robinson, 1975, 106 and 158, plate 306), wears a scale shirt following a design which remains in vogue throughout the second to third centuries AD, of simple design, hip-length, with short sleeves, but without any additional shoulder doubling, a similar design to which can also be seen on a cavalryman on the Arch of Galerius, dating to AD 297 to 311 (Feugère, 2002, 143; Russell-Robinson, 1975, 158).

Further sculptural examples of this style of cuirass, some indicating non-cavalry use, are seen on the reliefs of the metopes of the Tropaeum Trajani and Adamklissi, depicting legionaries, auxiliaries and cavalrymen as combatants in Trajanic campaigns against the Dacians (some also featuring use of laminated sword arm vambrace protections, or *manicae*), and including one 'officer' figure in scale cuirass and double pteruged skirt which has been possibly identified as Trajan (suggesting the maximum of high-status use for scale armour; Russell-Robinson, 1975, 158). Other sculptural representations showing higher status, non-

Fig. 56 Cavalryman on the Arch of Galerius in belted, loose-fitting scale coat, wearing spangenhelm-type helmet (from Russell-Robinson, 1975, 93, fig. 123). (*Drawn by J. R. Travis*)

cavalry use of scale are mostly centurion in rank (for example the stela of Q. Sertorius Festus, at Verona; Russell-Robinson, 1975, 156, plate 442) with some 'other' officer ranks (such as that of the *aquilifer*, or eagle standard bearer, L. Sertorius Firmus, of the Legio XI Claudia Pia Fidelis, also at Verona, and presumably related to the former; Russell-Robinson, 1975, 157, plate 443).

However, despite the apparent legionary and cavalry use of scale on the Tropaeum Trajani and Adamklissi monuments, it does not feature on Trajan's Column other than for Syrian auxiliary archers and for Sarmatian cavalry fighting on the opposing Dacian side (Russell-Robinson, 1975, 160). This may suggest that its use at that time was not widespread, or that its omission could be symptomatic of the stylisation of the imagery on the monument, and it has been suggested that the sculptors of the Column may not have been totally familiar with all contemporary armour types, perhaps only reproducing those which were commonly seen in and around the capital.

By the third century AD, the cuirass shape had changed once more into a style which then continues down to the sixth century, now being provided with sleeves of varying lengths, and becoming longer, mostly knee-length but occasionally even ankle-length, the side slits being replaced by longer ones, centrally placed, front and back (Stephenson and Dixon, 2003, 44). This would have permitted the wearer to walk unimpeded, with the additional benefit of spreading across to provide leg cover on horseback. Quite when this change came about is unclear. Tombstones of the period usually show the deceased unarmoured (with the exception of one unnamed and undated legionary stela from Brigetio, Hungary), and monumental propaganda sculptures fall out of fashion during the years between the reign of Severus and the rise of Diocletian around AD 284 (Stephenson, 2001, 32). However, the style is clearly well developed by the time of an early fourth-century relief on the Arch of Diocletian,

Fig. 57
Sarmatian
cataphracts on
Trajan's Column
depicted in
closely fitted,
figure-hugging
mail suits, their
horses similarly
scale-clad. (*From
Cichorius, 1896,
Die Reliefs der
Traianssäule, 28*)

depicting two soldiers in conical helmets, wearing long-sleeved, loose-fitting cuirasses (one in scale, and the other possibly either in mail or lamellar), with similar armour appearing in the Brigetio legionary (Stephenson, 2001, 32). Images of this style of armour are also known, however, from the third-century context of Dura-Europos, with depictions of armoured men in the synagogue frescos representing the Battle of Ebenezer (Stephenson, 2001, 32; James, 2004, xxvi, plate 4). These figures are shown wearing knee-length, long-sleeved, loose-fitting armour, some bare-headed, some wearing coifs, although it is not possible from the stylised nature to determine whether these are of scale or mail.

METHOD OF OPENING/CLOSURE

Although archaeological evidence can provide information about how the scales were attached to each other and to the backing garment, and artistic representations (including both sculptural and painted mediums) can show the overall designs and shapes of the cuirass, their method of opening/closure is still unclear, with a variety of possibilities suggested, some dependent on whether or not a close fitting was required (and this requirement may not have been consistent throughout the entire history of its use). Von Groller, for example, proposed an opening down the back, Joseph Alf proposing opening down the left side, these methods and others being discussed by authors including Russell-Robinson, Feugère and Stephenson (von Groller, 1901a, 85; Feugère, 2002, 100, Russell-Robinson, 1975, 156; Stephenson, 2001, 39).

According to Russell-Robinson, if a close fitting had been required, this would have required the use of hooks or laces, the lack of archaeological evidence for such hooks suggesting laces as the most likely method. Both he and Feugère thought that the option of back closure, as proposed by von Groller, was unlikely, as this would have necessitated the

Fig. 58 Late third- to early fourth-century AD armoured infantrymen from the Arch of Diocletian, Rome, wearing long-bodied, long-sleeved, loose-fitting mail and scale coats (from Stephenson, 2001, 35, fig. 9). (*Redrawn by J. R. Travis*)

Fig. 59 Part schematic of the 'Battle of Ebenezer' fresco from the Synagogue, Dura-Europos, depicting infantry soldiers in loose-fitting, long-sleeved, knee-length mail or scale coats, some bare-headed and some wearing coifs (from James, 2004, xxvi, plate 4). (*Artwork by J. R. Travis*)

assistance of a companion, the wearer being unable to dress himself alone (a view upheld by Stephenson).

All three considered that a shoulder opening would be feasible on earlier-period cuirasses, permitting the neck to open sufficiently for the head to pass through, with additional side opening for close-fitting bodices, which would probably have been on the left-hand side for any weaknesses to be covered by the wearer's shield (Feugère, 2002, 100; Russell-Robinson, 1975, 156; Stephenson, 2001, 39). However, this would not have been necessary if a fuller, looser body were used, drawing in the excess fullness by use of a belt (as is borne out by several of the sculptural representations, including those on the Arch of Diocletian which appears to show pouching of the upper body, as if a loose-fitting bodice had been drawn up over a belt; Stephenson, 2001, 35). On such a loose-fitting body there may have been no need for any additional vertical closure, the armour being pulled on over the head, as with mail shirts, the only opening necessary, if any, being to widen the neck for the head to pass through.

Stephenson, however, in his discussion also considers methods of attachment of the sleeves seen from the third century onwards, citing experiments by the Arbeia Society which suggest that sleeves may have been made separately and tied to the body with laces, any gaps being covered by the use of *pteruges* (Stephenson, 2001, 39). He suggested that if back opening had been used, the rectangular plates used on both mail and scale coats of the period would not have needed to exist, so that their very existence argues against back opening. Similarly, front fastening he considers as a possibility, citing the existence of Chinese front-fastening examples, although these would not then have required the rectangular neck plates (the existence of which again argues against this method being used). Side opening he considers again as a possibility, but which would have only been necessary if a close fitting were required. However, his preferred option was for a loose-bodied coat, a close fit at the neck being achieved by used of plates similar to those used on mail coats, negating the need for any shoulder or side opening (ibid.).

These neck closure plates, embossed from copper-alloy, have been proposed for use on both mail and scale coats. They are found in two different forms, both of which are curved at the neck edge to provide a close fit (Stephenson, 2001, 35):

> The most common type found consists of two equal-sized plates (around 15 cm by 7.9 cm). They were fastened using a square-headed pin with a central perforation, passed through a slot in each plate, and held by a rod passing through the hole in the pin.
>
> In the second form (an example of which is known from Bertoldsheim), two asymmetrical plates are used, which together form a trapezoid shape (the larger plate being around 14 cm long, by 6.4 cm across the base and 5 cm across the top, and the smaller plate being 1.1 cm wide for its full length), the larger left-hand plate extending at the centre to form a hook to catch on a slot provided in the smaller plate.

CAVALRY AND HORSE ARMOUR

Throughout the Republican period, the Roman army had made use of the service of mercenary troops, drawn from allied states (*socii*), or from kingdoms defeated in previous conflicts. Further, in addition to its legionary infantry troops, whose armour, weaponry and rank were dependent on property qualifications, it also fielded units of legionary cavalry, drawn from the elite knightly class of *equites*. Marius' reforms at the end of the second century BC brought about radical changes to the organisational structure of the army, however, part of which included the disbandment of this legionary cavalry, its function being replaced by an exclusive use of mounted auxiliaries from a variety of sources, using armour derived from their own ethnic traditions, including (as described by Caesar in his *Gallic Wars*) Gauls (fighting in their native mail), Numidians (who preferred to fight as light cavalry, without helmet or armour) and Germans (again probably using mail; Caesar, *Bell. Gall.* II.7; VII.65; Feugère, 2002, 142).

Fig. 60 Type 1 breastplate from Manching (from Russell-Robinson, 1975, plate 454).
(*Drawn by J. R. Travis*)

Fig. 61 Type 2 breastplate from Bertoldsheim (from
Stephenson, 2001, 38, fig. 12).
(*Redrawn by J. R. Travis*)

As had been the case during the pan-Italic wars of the fourth century BC described previously, the Roman army again made use of those elements of cavalry equipment which had impressed them the most (Burns, 2003, 62). For example, Tacitus tells of the invasion of Moesia in AD 69 by 9,000 Sarmatian horsemen (*cataphracti*) of the Rhoxolani tribe, defeating two cohorts of Roman troops, describing the armour of their 'chiefs and nobles' as being 'made of tough leather and iron strips', covering their bodies, arms and legs, and which were 'impervious to blows' (Tacitus, *Hist.* 1.79; Feugère, 2002, 142; Negin, 1998, 65).

Negin (1998, 65) reports that the Sarmatians had not always used heavily armoured cavalry (although from an equestrian background), but developed its use as a result of overwhelming defeat at the end of the first century BC at the hands of Mithridates VI Eupator (when 6,000 of his armoured, phalanx formation warriors defeated 50,000 lightly armoured Rhoxolani horsemen). In answer to these events, they then redeveloped their riders into heavily armoured *cataphracti*, their style of armour assemblage then being taken up first by other Sarmatian tribes by the end of the first century AD, closely followed by a number of other eastern peoples, such as Bosporans, Bactrians, Parthians and Scythians (as evidenced in various artistic and archaeological sources).

The Romans were so impressed with the success of their opponents' armour type and fighting style, despite its obvious disadvantages when wet (Tacitus describing wet riders being 'weighed down' by their armour, making it 'impossible for any fallen warrior to regain his feet') that they had developed units of their own *equites cataphractarii* by the time of Hadrian. The Roman cataphract equipment was, however, more uniform, avoiding the disadvantages of leather scales (as had been described by Tacitus, Arrian and Ammianus), in favour of metallic plate (Feugère, 2002, 142). By the third and fourth centuries these cataphract units had increased in number, with the Emperor Galerius using them for his personal protection during his Persian campaigns, and as depicted for his guard on the Arch of Galerius (Negin, 1998, 74).

Actual examples of Sarmatian cataphract armour do not exist, although some remains of possibly similar Scythian armour have been found in barrow deposits (Negin, 1998, 68). Scales of varying lengths have been found which may suggest different length scales within one garment, possibly with longer scales being used at the waist to prevent entanglement with an overlying belt. Representational views of Sarmatian *cataphracti*, however, are known from a number of sources, along with those of other peoples. Sarmatian *cataphracti* are seen

Fig. 62 Funerary stela from the Bosporan centre of Tanais, of third-century Sarmatian lancer wearing scale armour and conical helmet.
(*Drawn by J. R. Travis*)

on Trajan's Column, although representing enemy forces fighting with Decabalus, but these views are thought to be rather too stylised to be accurate, their closely moulded figure-hugging scale armour on both man and horse considered to be unfeasible (Feugère, 2002, 142). It is even disputed, from references to other depictions, whether the horses ('cataphracts') were ever provided with armour at all, perhaps it being the rider alone who was heavily encased in scale body protection. This view is supported by the lack of references to horse armour in descriptions by Tacitus, along with the lack of physical evidence (Negin, 1998, 74).

From the views available, two versions of Sarmatian-style cavalry armour can be determined, these being:

i) A long, knee length shirt, with short sleeves, as seen on the Triphon relief (Negin, 1998, 68, plate 1.1) and the Arch of Galerius (Stephenson and Dixon, 2003, 28, fig. 14).
ii) A coat with two 'laps' beneath, and with either long or short sleeves, as seen on Borporus crypt paintings (Negin, 1998, 68).

Sarmatian full-length armour is not known, but some has been found in Scythian barrow burials. It has been suggested, therefore, that where depicted on Trajan's Column, this may represent Parthian riders serving similar functions. By the beginning of the first century AD, scale began to be replaced by composite forms, with finds in barrow contexts near Kazanskaya Stanitsa of composite armours, consisting of a mixture of iron scales, plates and mail binding, some with scale protecting the more vulnerable areas (such as the shoulders), or which could have formed some kind of horse armour (although again, this is unproven; Negin, 1998, 68).

By the late third and fourth centuries AD, a new form of heavily armoured cavalry unit appeared with the Roman army, the *clibanarii*. Ammianus Marcellinus (XVI.8) describes the appearance of *clibinarii* as 'faces masked by their visors', 'chainmail coats on their chests', with arms, legs and bodies 'sheathed in fine chainmail', like 'statues polished by the hand of Praxiteles'. These again derived from eastern auxiliary influences, but with better-developed armour from a probable Iranian prototype, although which Negin proposed may have been manufactured in Imperial *fabricae* (as suggested by images of articulated arm and leg protection seen on the *Notitia Dignitatum*; Feugère, 2002, 143; Negin, 1998, 74). The *clibanarii* armour, however, did extend to protection for both horse and rider, and it is this type of unit that is thought to be depicted on the graffito image from Dura-Europos of a heavily armoured horse and rider (James, 2004, 43, fig. 23). The rider is shown to be wearing a tightly fitting suit, with mail or scale on the upper body and thighs, and larger vertical plates on the abdomen, along with articulated arm and leg protectors (*manicae*), the horse also being provided with similarly armoured scale covering (Feugère, 2002, 143).

Examples of three such armoured horse coverings ('trappers') were found at Dura, dating to the mid-third century AD, one of which was fragmentary, but two of which were complete (sufficiently so to be modelled by a modern-day horse), one being formed from copper-alloy scales, the other from iron (James, 2004, 129–33; Stephenson and Dixon, 116). The copper-alloy scales (35 mm by 25 mm) were fixed to each other with copper wire, then sewn to the textile backing with linen thread, in thirty-one rows per side, with an oval opening for the saddle and an additional triangular section for the tail (the spine and edgings being trimmed in red leather).

The iron example was slightly different in both style and construction, with larger scales (60 mm by 45 mm) set in nineteen rows per side, attached to the textile backing using leather thongs. Again, an oval section was left open for the saddle and a triangular cover provided for the tail area, but also two extra curved extensions reached around the neck to fasten at the front chest for additional protection.

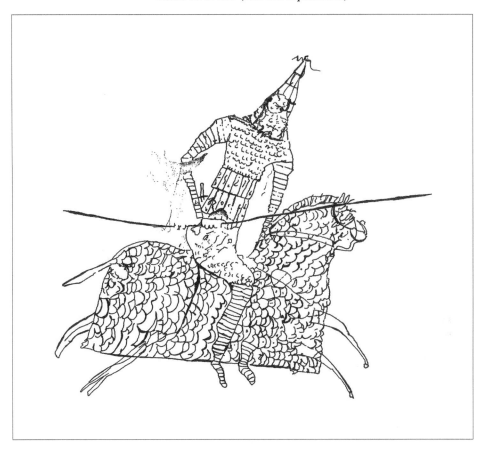

Fig. 63 Graffito image from Dura-Europos of a heavily armoured horse and rider (*clibinarius*). (*Redrawn by J. R. Travis*)

LAMELLAR ARMOUR

Among the many variations of scale armours and composite armours (for example *lorica plumata*) as detailed above, lamellar is distinct enough to merit discussion as a separate type. Again, not strictly speaking of Roman origin (but then again, as has been shown, very little armour has been found to have been of exclusively Roman invention), lamellar saw a long use, making brief intermittent appearances in the history of Roman armour, mostly from the first century onwards and more commonly from the early Byzantine period, and where found is generally accepted to indicate the presence or influence of eastern auxiliary troops or allies.

It was reportedly developed by the Assyrians, the influence then passing to the Persians and across into Asia, and with some fragmented examples dating to the seventh and sixth centuries being found in Cyprus (Russell-Robinson, 1975, 162). Its existence was known to both the Etruscans and neighbouring Italic peoples, either by contact through southern regions or through Greece, as evidenced by a Greek-style thorax from Todi (formed from vertical lamellae, attached by herringbone lacing to a linen backing) and a fifth-century BC bronze statue of Mars in the Vatican Museum (Russell-Robinson, 1975, 162). It then fell out of use in the Italic regions but continued in the east, spreading across into Asia and further north into the steppe regions (Stephenson and Dixon, 2003, 48). The tradition also continues in areas of Persian influence, where it was developed for use with heavily armoured cavalry from the first century BC (Russell-Robinson, 1975, 162). Its use then reappears in Roman contexts, albeit rarely, as seen in the first-century AD relief of three Palmyrene gods, depicted wearing a mixture of Roman and Greek armour styles, with Roman-style swords (*gladii*) and Greek-style lamellar cuirasses (Russell-Robinson, 1975, 162; Stephenson and Dixon, 2003, 48).

Examples of bronze lamellae have been found at Corbridge, with some very small plates (some 2.5 cm by 0.7 cm, and others 1.8 cm by 0.5 cm; Russell-Robinson, 1975, 162), and Newstead, which have been suggested to indicate the presence of eastern auxiliaries, and also at Dura-Europos, where two thigh defences ('cuisses') were found deposited awaiting repair in Tower 19 (possibly belonging to *clibanarii*, described previously), and which were in sufficiently preserved condition to show the method of lacing employed in their construction (James, 2004, 122–7).

Lamellae may be fashioned from almost any rigid material, such as wood, bone, rawhide, bronze or iron, although bronze and iron are the most likely in Roman contexts. Within the same cuirass, different sizes of lamellae appear possibly to have been utilised for different parts of the body, using shorter plates for those areas that would require the most flexibility and shaping, such as the shoulders and upper arms. Plates were pierced with three sets of holes. As with conventional scale, double holes would be placed down the sides, but as the scales (or *laminae*) are formed of long and thin plates, these can accommodate two lacing positions, one pair at the centre and the other pair towards the bottom. The individual scales would then be laced horizontally to each other across the rear of the plate, using rawhide, oil-dressed leather, cord or fabric thread. The rows of lamellae would then be laced vertically from the front, their plates aligned with those above and below, using double or single holes pierced in the centre of the plates, forming a rigid structure (similar to the semi-rigid scale described previously) without need for a textile backing (Russell-Robinson, 1975, 162).

Lamellar then slips from use in Roman representations, but continues to develop in the East, reaching Japan around the fifth century AD and re-emerging in the eastern Empire under Avar influence in the sixth century, superseding mail by the middle Byzantine period, as seen on the Isola Rizza dish, depicting a Byzantine cavalryman in a long lamellar cuirass, with centre front opening, worn over a long sleeved tunic (Russell-Robinson, 1975, 153; Stephenson and Dixon, 2003, 48).

BODY ARMOUR – DISCUSSION

It would appear that over the course of its history the Roman military repeatedly absorbed and integrated the best examples of armour, weaponry and fighting techniques that it had observed in use by other peoples (frequently from the viewpoint of being on the receiving end, an ideal position from which to best measure their success). As a result of this process, its basic armour and weapon assemblage had been subject to constant improvement and modification (some of quite radical nature). This manifested itself in the development of the forms of body protection discussed previously – the retro Greek-style muscle cuirass, the Gallic-style mails, and the more exotic 'eastern' scale, both of the latter following similar design progressions over the centuries of their use.

As many of the sculptural representations are of a somewhat stylised nature, further complicated by years of erosion and accidental damage to the surfaces, it is not always possible to determine with accuracy, in some cases, whether the intended representation was to be of scale or mail (with the further possibility of some of the diagnostic features of scale or mail having been painted on rather than carved/incised into the stone).

Certainly scale finds are perhaps more frequent than mail in archaeological contexts, but this could be due to the slightly larger component parts faring better against the elements, all other literary evidence suggesting a greater use of mail than scale. However, this also suggests that perhaps the scale cuirasses were more susceptible to accidental loss of their component parts, scales being easily dislodged, each of which would as consequence have produced a more significantly sized hole than the loss of a couple of rings from an equivalent mail shirt. Scale, therefore, would probably have required more regular, if not constant, repair than mail in order for it to remain effective.

In some sense, mail does appear to have notable advantages over scale in its greater flexibility and durability. Scale in contrast is more rigid. Its construction also necessitates attachment to a leather or fabric backing garment, which then adds to its weight and makes it more susceptible to soaking up water in damp or wet conditions (further adding to its weight), as Tacitus described having a detrimental effect on the Sarmatian *cataphracti* (Feugère, 2002, 142). This lack of flexibility became more marked with the transition to sleeved bodices, the scale versions requiring separately formed sleeves, necessitating the addition of leather strips (*pteruges*) to try to protect the gap where these components meet, although the underarm area would still have remained an area of particular weakness (Stephenson, 2001, 39).

However, it should be remembered that body armour is just one component of a greater assemblage of protective equipment (the most significant piece of this protective equipment being the body of men also fighting with the wearer as fellow combatants), representing the defence of last resort. By comparison with the simple *cardiophylax* breastplates of earlier periods, scale cuirasses would still represent an improvement of monumental proportions, although its aesthetically pleasing appearance when polished lends itself more towards officer use than that of lower ranks, the former being less likely to see the heaviest combat conditions (Burns, 2003, 70).

Nevertheless, scale does offer as effective a protection against most forms of attack as mail, possibly even better against close-quarter attack, which may be better deflected by its smoother surface. Its tendency to shed scales may not, however, necessarily have been a disadvantage, as this process may also be intentional to absorb and dissipate the force of an impact, in much the same manner as modern-day motorway barriers are intended to crumple and absorb vehicular impacts. Any scales dislodged could have been easily replaced with a small amount of thread or wire and using any available small scraps of metal, the attachment holes being pierced using any pointed implement, such as a standard nail (Russell-Robinson, 1975, 153).

The lack of flexibility would have become less of an issue in the case of the composite armour types of the later periods, when shorter-length torso protectors in scale were combined over conventional mail shirts, offering an additional layer of protection (Stephenson, 2001, 40). However, even with this double layer of armour, the wearer was not guaranteed total body protection. Any armour is obviously better than no armour at all (hence the use of the minimal *cardiophylax* in earlier periods).

	Number found	Length (mm)	Width (mm)	Thick (mm)	Point angle	Estimated number for shirt
Corbridge 1		14.2	9.9	1.5	110°	14,000
Corbridge 2	25	13.6	7.3	0.5	110°	
Great Chesters	276	12	7	0.25	90-110°	28,500
Caerleon		17	9.5	-	-	
Vindobona	1	14	10	-	-	
Carnuntum	1200	14	8	-	-	
Dura Europos	Many	9	6.5	0.25		47,000

Table 6-1 Comparison of small, pointed copper-alloy scales with six vertically paired holes at the top (after Clemetson, 1993, 8–10).

VII

PROTECTIVE UNDERGARMENTS (*THORACOMACHUS* OR *SUBARMALIS*)

THE EXISTENCE OF PROTECTIVE UNDERGARMENTS

The innovations of the introduction of mail and scale cuirasses indeed would have covered a larger proportion of the body area, and would have offered greater resilience against slashing and some stabbing attacks. However, some penetration wounds would still have been possible, particularly from missile attack, with potentially fatal results from deep or infected injuries. Injury could also still have been sustained with non-penetration attacks, even against the most heavily protected segmented plate armour, causing blunt force impact damage, such as broken bones and internal injuries (Stephenson, 2001, 29). This type of injury, potentially as fatal as stabbing and slashing injuries, could be minimised by use of some form of densely padded undergarment to absorb the impact. Similarly, a padded undergarment could act as an additional layer of defence against the slashing and penetration injuries, each layer of armour, padding and clothing dissipating the impact force or acting as barriers to penetration, reducing, if not eliminating, damage to the wearer.

Although such a garment, had it existed, would probably not survive in the archaeological record, there are some written references that indicate the possibility of its existence. For example, there are references to an item called a *thoracomachus* in the *De Rebus Bellicis* that may be some form of padded undergarment, although there are some conflicting translations describing the material of its construction (*De Rebus Bellicis*, XV.6; Stephenson, 2001, 29).

Two references describing the use of a protective undergarment and the materials used in its construction can be found in *De Rebus Bellicis*:

> *Inter omnia, quae ad usum bellicum provida posteritatis cogitavit antiquitas, thoracomachum quoque mira utilitate ad levamen corporis armorum ponderi et asperitati subiecit ...*

> The ancients, among the many things which ... they devised for use in war, prescribed also the thoracomachus to counteract the weight and friction of armour ...

> *Hoc enim vestimenti genus, quod de coactili ad mensuram et tutelam pectoris humani conficitur, de mollibus lanis timoris sollicitudo sollertia magistra composuit ...*

> This type of garment is made of thick sheep's wool felt to the measure ... of the upper part of the human frame ...

In the above, *de coactili* is probably used in this context meaning 'felt'. (Anonymous, *De Rebus Bellicis*, XV.1–2)

The *De Rebus Bellicis* (XV.1–2), therefore, describes the *thoracomachus* as a garment of thick cloth (in some translations this appears as 'sheep's wool', in others as 'felt'), designed to serve a three-fold purpose: to protect the body of the wearer, to counteract the weight and friction of the armour (and anyone who attempts to wear armour without padding, particularly the plate varieties, will attest to the results of friction damage after only a few short hours) and to allow the wearer to function in cold weather (i.e. to keep him warm).

There has been much debate as to the constructional methods and materials used to make such a garment (*thoracomachus*) and even as to the possibility of its existence at all. It is possible that the Romans were aware of the use of felt (the term *coactili* being possibly interpreted as 'felt') with *coactiliarius* or 'felt maker' being a recognised vocation. Although an organic material, felt has been found in graves of Scythian contexts, and a felt cap was found at Dura-Europos that has been interpreted as being for wear under the helmet. The remains of a possible felt (unwoven) 'arming doublet' of a light-brown fibrous material was also reported by James (2004, 116), as having been found at Dura-Europos worn under a mail shirt, of a simple pullover design, by one of the bodies in the Tower 19 countermine. It was also suggested by Kimmig that the surface of the Fayum shield may have been covered with a layer of sheep's wool or felt. Felt, however, is not a good material for use in garments as, having no proper structure, it would tend to fall to pieces under stress, or on any attempt to launder it. As the garment would tend to make the wearer hot (a disadvantage offset against the greater peril of fatal injury), it would quickly become soaked in perspiration with the exertion of combat, requiring no doubt periodical, if not frequent, laundering.

As an alternative, it is possible that an undergarment could have been made of linen or hemp fabric, in two layers, with a quantity of sheep's wool in between, or of multiple fabric layers, quilted to prevent slippage of the filling. It was also suggested that a thin leather, such as goatskin, could have been used instead of fabric, (the *De Rebus Bellicis* referring also to the use of 'Libyan Hide'), but although leather is resilient, it is unlikely to have been used as it would have been difficult to clean. Fabric, therefore, would be a more likely medium to use, and would not be without precedent, this being the method of construction used for the medieval 'gambeson', or 'jack', a garment serving an almost identical purpose, and probably exhibiting a continuity of tradition (Stephenson, 2001, 29–31).

Again, although only suitable for higher-status garments, another possible fabric that can not be entirely discounted may have been silk, but without precendent. Silks were accessible through trading links with the East, but were very costly. It produces, however, a very strong, dense but lightweight fabric which could have produced a far less bulky protective garment, and was used with noted success in the prototype 'bullet-proof vests' of the early twentieth century.

It has also been suggested by Stephenson that the 'Libyan Hide' described in the *De Rebus Bellicis* may have been an additional protective overgarment, worn over the armour in the same way as a medieval surcoat (and would have been a loose fit, of similar shape to the *thoracomachus* but slightly larger) providing both an additional protective layer against penetration weapons, and also protecting the armour from corrosion while keeping any padded undergarment (*thoracomachus* or *subarmalis*) from soaking up water in wet conditions (Stephenson, 2001, 29–31).

Stephenson also suggested that the *De Rebus Bellicis* may not actually represent a true impression of real armour in use at the time. It was written in the late fourth to early fifth centuries AD, by an anonymous author, reputedly as a suggested list of reforms and improvements, which may not have been actual practices currently employed. One of the references to the *thoracomachus* describes it as being 'devised for use in war' by the 'ancients', and Stephenson proposed that this may therefore have been an imaginary item from a previous 'better' age, to which the author would wish to return.

However, anyone who has attempted to wear any of the forms of body armour described above (whether mail, scale or plate) for even a short period will attest the need for some form of sub-armour protection, so any such suggestion may be discounted, with the probability that armour had always been used in conjunction with under-armour protection, however flimsy or makeshift. During the medieval period a variety of names were used contemporaneously, and often interchangeably, for padded undergarments (including jack, pourpoint, heuk, brigandine, haubergeon, gambeson, hacketon, aketon, jupon and arming coat). Artistic representations of a range of such medieval period garments are known from a variety of sources, including the Maciejowski Bible (*c.* 1250), the Reliquary of St Ursula (*c.* 1489) and the Passion (*c.* 1480s), both of the latter being the work of the Flemish artist, Memling (Embleton, 2000, 64–6). Some of these garments were simply padded; some featured attachment points for fitting

Fig. 64 Funerary stela from St Petersburg of first-century AD Bosphoran, Rhodon son of Helios. As shown in semi-domestic setting with his wife and child, he is depicted without armour, but wearing a tunic with diamond-shaped quilting, possibly some form of protective padded *subarmalis*. (*Drawn by J. R. Travis*)

Fig. 65 Funerary stela of second-century Bosphoran noble on horseback, his bow suspended from the left side of his horse. A heavy armoured cavalryman in scale or mail cuirass and conical helmet can be seen behind him. (*Drawn by J. R. Travis*)

mail, or plate armour sections; some had integral mail, horn or plates fixed to the inside of the garment. Styles of garment also varied (from long or short-bodied, long or short-sleeved, close or loose-fitting), variations that may have been reflected in the range of names used. The different names used may also have designated whether the garment was intended to be worn under or over the chosen armour. Likewise, similar variety in style, material construction and thickness of padding may have existed in their Roman-period counterparts, dependent perhaps on the type of armour they were intended to accompany.

As most sculptural representations depict men either in full armour (as on Trajan's Column), or in unarmoured 'dress-down' civilian clothes (as on many many funerary stelae), protective undergarments are not often visible. One possible exception may be on the funerary stela from St Petersburg of the first-century AD Bosphoran, Rhodon son of Helios. He is shown in a semi-domestic setting with his wife and child, and although depicted without armour, he appears to wear a tunic with diamond-shaped quilting, in the Scythio-Sarmationa crossover style, which may be some form of protective padded *subarmalis*. A similarly dated funerary stela of a second-century Bosphoran noble on horseback, although unarmoured, may depict the type of equipment which he would have carried (his bow shown suspended from the left side of his horse), with a heavy armoured cavalryman in scale or mail cuirass and conical helmet visible behind him.

REPRODUCTION OF A RANGE OF PROTECTIVE UNDERGARMENTS

In order to test the optimal level of padding under each of the respective armour types, a number of possible undergarments were constructed by the author and field-tested under the reconstructed armour: these being a simple, leather under-tunic (2 mm thickness), a lightly padded bodice (4 mm thickness), and, for comparative purposes, a full-thickness, fifteenth-century medieval-style padded arming doublet/jack/gambeson (18 mm thick, constructed of twenty-five layers of linen). In the case of the minimal leather under-tunic, further consideration was given to the suggestion of additional shoulder protection, as promoted by one re-enactment group in their interpretation (without provenance) of some leather finds from the Flavian-period fort at Carlisle (Luguvallium). In this particular 'reconstruction', two shaped fragments of leather, pierced for the addition of decorative top-stitching, or appliqué (now missing), which were reputedly found in workshop contexts, and had been previously identified as being saddle horn coverings (by merit of their shape and proximity to other 'cavalry' artefacts), were re-assigned by this group as shoulder protections for a leather under-tunic. Although an unlikely interpretation, I therefore reproduced a similar leather garment, as a means to test the efficacy of additional light shoulder protection.

With regard to the reconstruction of the padded fabric undergarments, for the more lightly padded garment, consideration was given to the description in *De Rebus Bellicis*, to give protection to 'the upper part of the human frame' (XV.1–2), producing a garment protecting the upper torso area alone (the area of body which would have been protected by a *lorica segmentata* or *musculata*). For this garment, the outer layers were formed from a strong, densely woven linen, with a cottonwool stuffing, following Edward II's orders to the Armourer's Company of London (*c.* 1322) to stuff similar garments with 'old (soft) lynnen and of cottone' (Embleton, 2000, 64). This method of construction can also be seen in use on the coat-armour ('jupon') of King Charles VI of France, now in Chartres Cathedral, dating to the end of the fourteenth century, where a quilted white linen body was stuffed with cotton wool and covered with a crimson silk damask (Embleton, 2000, 26–7, fig. H). For the more heavily protected garment, however, the ordinance of King Louis XI of France was considered, which described construction using '30, or at least 25 folds of cloth, and a stag's skin' (although with the omission of the stag's skin), producing a deeply layered effect, with the quilting/stitching passing through all layers. This then produces a garment with a consistent thickness throughout, unlike many modern reconstructions, whereby the inner and outer layers are quilted, with the resulting 'tubes' stuffed with rolled cloth or padding (as this will produce weak areas of only two-layer thickness at the stitching points).

FIELD-TESTING ARMOUR WITH A RANGE OF PROTECTIVE UNDERGARMENTS

The reconstructed garments above were then subjected to field-testing, used under both mail and *segmentata* armour reconstructions described in previous chapters, in order to consider their practicalities of use. They were then (similarly combined with both armour types) subjected to test assaults with both sword and arrow strikes (although in these incidences, for health and safety reasons, without the use of a human test subject).

LIMITATIONS OF FIELD-TESTING REPRODUCTION EQUIPMENT

Any attempts at field-testing reproduction equipment would need primarily to recognise a multitude of possible limitations, based on a wide range of variables within the test equipment. Within any tests, the accuracy of any results is proportional to the sample size used. However, regardless of sample size, the value of any results produced would be reduced to a far greater extent by any divergence from the accuracy of the test conditions – factors such as materials and equipment used, weather conditions and abilities of the tester. Ideally, therefore, the armour to be tested, the test 'subject' wearing the armour, and the equipment used for the test 'assaults' should be reproduced from materials matched as closely as possible to the originals. The tests should then be performed by a tester of comparable competence to the original users, under a range of possible weather and geographic conditions, and repeated to produce a significantly large bank of test data. It has to be recognised, therefore, that any of the above factors may be manipulated, intentionally or unintentionally, in order to skew test results to favour an anticipated predicted outcome. With these caveats in mind, we may consider each of the main limitations of the 'test':

- Accuracy of the armour materials
- Weather and geographic conditions of the tests
- Ability of the tester and accuracy of the test weaponry: the bow; the arrows

ACCURACY OF THE ARMOUR MATERIALS

Any test of the effectiveness of an item of armour against a weapon strike would be affected by the quality of both the weapon and the armour itself, in constructional details and materials used. Some tests have been carried out by members of the re-enactment community on medieval mail, although as some re-enactor mail is made from pre-formed, square-sectioned split washers, and not from authentic materials, the results may not be conclusive. As discussed in the chapters dealing with the separate armour types and subsequent reconstructions, while the highest level of accuracy can be maintained in constructional features, by close consideration of existing artefacts, it is never possible to totally reproduce the materials used – leather will have been produced from modern tanneries, with hides from animals culled at different life stages; metal will have been smelted from different ore streams, with modern-day background pollution levels.

Provided the nearest equivalent materials are sourced, and that constructional methods are as close as possible to the originals, the performance of test items may still be assessed objectively. As described in earlier chapters, all leather used in the reconstructions was produced using vegetable-based tanning processes; plate armour was produced using mild-steel plate, heated and hammer-forged to shape; mail was produced using hand-wound 'worms' of mild steel wire obtained from a foundry at Templeborough, South Yorkshire (the use of steel wire is known in the manufacture of some Roman-period mail). Where testing the performance of 'naked' mail in comparison to padded mail, any minor inaccuracies within the material properties of the metal will be negligible, as the test will be assessing the effect of the padding, rather than the tensile properties of the mail itself.

WEATHER AND GEOGRAPHIC CONDITIONS OF THE TESTS

As the Roman army operated across a widely varying geographic area, it would no doubt have encountered the full range of weather and geographic conditions, and would have had to contend with any of these. However, it is recognised that heat and humidity will have effects upon the performance of archery equipment; the elasticity of bow limbs is different when warm (with archers, where possible, warming the limbs of the bow before use); the bow string will similarly be susceptible to extremes of temperature and moisture (hence the term 'keep it under your hat', deriving from where archers traditionally kept spare bow strings warm and dry); and arrow shafts and fletchings will also perform differently in the cold and wet. The distances achieved by an archer, using the same bow and the same arrows, will also be greater where shooting downhill rather than uphill, so results in hilly regions will be different to those on a level, flat shoot.

For the purpose of the armour tests, therefore, test shoots were performed at different times of the year, under a range of climatic conditions, with targets at a range of distances, some uphill, some downhill and others as flat shoots, to produce a range of 'average' results for a selection of different arrowhead types.

ABILITY OF THE TESTER AND THE ACCURACY OF THE TEST WEAPONRY: THE BOW; THE ARROWS

We can assume that for the most part the effect of the tester's abilities will be minimal on the test outcomes, provided that the tester is able to hit the target at the required distance. In this respect, the tester (J. R. Travis) is a historical re-enactor, with over ten years' experience in the use of medieval longbow, in addition to representations of both a Roman legionary and auxiliary archer, using a range of bows, including Scythian-style recurved bows. However, due to health and safety constraints, the bows used in modern re-enactment are deliberately restricted to 30–40 lb strength, whereas the exact poundage of Roman-period bows is unknown, with speculation that some may have been more powerful (it is known that the medieval longbows were indeed of considerably higher poundage).

Without intending a full discussion of the function of archers (*sagittarii*) or archery units (*sagittariorum*) within the Roman military, which is too extensive a subject to be discussed in depth in this particular publication, a brief description of archery equipment available will be necessary, in order to consider testing the effects of archery projectiles (arrows) on the armour. This will require a discussion of not only the bow types used, but also the arrows (shaft materials, arrowhead type, weight and hardness).

BOWS

There are two types of bow known to have been in use during the Roman period: self bows (made from a single piece of wood) and composite bows (wooden core, sandwiched between layers of horn on the inside and sinew on the back), first invented by the nomadic peoples of the Asiatic steppes. The sinew and horn stores energy when drawn, delivered to the arrow on release, so that comparable power can be produced by a much shorter bow than an equivalent self bow. Composite bows are generally recurved, storing further energy and producing a greater final draw weight. The ends of the bows would be stiffened by attachment of bone or antler laths, which, being more resistant to decay than the wood or sinew components, are often the only parts found in archaeological contexts.

Vegetius (*Epitoma Rei Militaris*, Lib. I.15) proposed that legionary recruits were trained with 'wooden bows' (*arcubus ligneis*), which may have been self bows, possibly using the European yew (*Taxus baccata*), like the later northern European 'longbow' (although it is not known whether these matched the medieval longbow in strength or performance properties). Vegetius also cited Scipio Africanus, who, describing Numantine opponents, 'did not consider himself superior, unless he had mixed selected archers in all centuries' (ibid.).

The bows in use by auxiliary archers within the Roman army may, however, have been constructed using their own ethnic traditions (possibly composite bows, as were known to have been used by many of the nomadic Central Asian horse archers, including the Scythian, Sakas, Sarmatians and Parthians), with bow laths being frequent finds in many Roman military contexts (Coulston, 1985, 220–366).

While bow laths are found from a number of Roman context sites, including Carnuntum (von Groller, 1901b), complete bows are rare, their component parts being organic and not readily lending themselves to preservation in most soil conditions. A couple of notable exceptions are the Yrzi and the Qum-Darya bows. The Yrzi bow, from a necropolis context at Baghouz, on the Euphrates, has been identified as a Parthian weapon, dated to between the first century BC and the third century AD based on associated finds. Unfortunately, although almost complete, one arm was missing. Various reconstructions have been attempted, but its attribution as a 'horse archer' bow (for warrior or hunting use), of 'Eastern Parthian' or 'Western Parthian' origin, hinges on whether it should be reconstructed with a symmetrical or asymmetrical shape (with limbs of different lengths). This, then, has a direct bearing on its estimated draw weight, with Coulston (1985, 240) proposing 60–70 lb draw weight symmetrical reconstruction, while James (2004, 19) proposed a greater strength of 80 lb, with an asymmetrical shape better suited to horse archer use.

The Qum-Darya bow was found in a mass grave associated with a Chinese–Turkistan frontier post (the Tibetan fortress of Mazar-tagh at Khotan-darya, in the Lop-nor region of Sinkiang). Like the Yrzi example, it was a recurved composite bow, similarly dated from the first century BC to the third century AD, although styled in 'Hunnic' tradition, with straighter shaped ears, and using a greater number of ear and grip laths – up to seven, compared to only four on the Yrzi bow, although this may be due to the latter being considered of poorer quality manufacture (Bergman, 1939, 121–4). Again, unfortunately the bow was poorly preserved, with only a quarter remaining, so estimations of its poundage would be speculative, other than that it may be comparable to the similar Yrzi example above.

ARROWHEADS

Literary sources suggest the efficiency of arrowheads in use during the Republican period in armour penetration, for example in both Plutarch's and Cassius Dio's reports of Crassus' experience of Parthian arrows at Carrhae:

> When Crassus ordered his light-armed troops to make a charge, they did not advance far, but encountering a multitude of arrows, abandoned their undertaking and ran back for shelter among the men-at-arms, among whom they caused the beginning of disorder and fear, for these now saw the velocity and force of the arrows, which fractured armour, and tore their way through every covering alike, whether hard or soft. (Plutarch, *Crassus*, 24)

> The missiles falling thick upon them from all sides at once struck down many by a mortal blow, rendered many useless for battle, and caused distress to all. They flew into their eyes and pierced their hands and all the other parts of their body and, penetrating their armour, deprived them of their protection and compelled them to expose themselves to each new missile. (Cassius Dio, XL.22)

However, in consideration of the above reports, it should be remembered that, at this time, not all combatants would be wearing the same level of armour as in later periods (mail was not universally used, some still using the less efficient simple breastplates, offering only minimal protection, and *segmentata* was not yet developed for heavy infantry), the quotation above from Cassius Dio describing a range of soft-tissue injuries to unprotected parts of the body.

Further, we are unable to determine the accuracy of these reports in the ratio of arrow injuries sustained compared to those received in hand-to-hand combat or from cavalry assault, which would also have featured in this particular event. In addition, the sources do not relate the types or range of arrowheads in use, in that archers may have made use of untipped or lightweight-headed arrows, to wear down an opponent in an initial 'arrow storm', before using heavier, weighted specialist arrowheads for specific targeting of armoured opponents at closer range.

The most common form of Roman arrowhead was trilobate shaped (mostly made of iron and tanged, although with some earlier forms in copper-alloy and socketed), with average blade length of around 2.5 to 6.5 cm, not including tang, although bilobate and leaf-shaped forms are also known. Although it is not proven which shapes, if any, were intended specifically for war or hunting, the trilobate forms were probably well suited to both purposes, being more aerodynamic and more accurate. They also caused greater injury and would have been more difficult to remove from an unarmoured target. However there were other 'eastern' types of arrowhead forms in use, in addition to some not dissimilar to London Museum types 7, 8 and 10 medieval period 'bodkins', and some other heavy piled forms, which appear in later period contexts, any of which could have been used for armour-piercing purposes.

A comprehensive discussion of Roman archery equipment can be found in James's report on the arms and armour at Dura-Europos (2004, 191–208), where remains of both bows and arrows were found. Although no complete arrows were found, the site produced fragments of all component parts of numerous arrows, some iron or copper-alloy tipped, others wooden tipped, and with one example still retaining its fletchings. The large number of copper-alloy socketed arrowheads found James discounted as probably being 'residual' deposits, pre-dating the Roman occupation by several centuries (2004, 195). He similarly discounted the two flat-type iron arrowheads as being later period 'surface finds' (2004, 195), identifying the remaining tanged iron arrowheads with three barbed, triangular blades as being from the Roman period, although probably in use by both attacking and defending sides.

James (2004, 195) also proposed that many of the arrows found at Dura-Europos were more simply constructed with wooden tips rather than metal arrowheads, as these had been 'very common in the ancient world', either for training purposes (citing Arrian's description of wooden training javelins, in *Ars Tactica* 34.8, 40.1), or for general use, where he considered them 'adequate' against unarmoured men. In support of this suggestion, he noted that a number of these wooden-tipped arrows exhibit signs of decoration, so should not be considered as emergency replacements which had been pressed into service before time was found to finish them off by the addition of metal arrowheads.

Although discussing medieval-period equipment, *De Re Metallica: The Uses of Metal in the Middle Ages* (whose title 'about metallic things' is taken from the sixteenth-century treatise by Georgius Agricola), is a collection of twenty-three papers, including that by David Starley (ed. Robert Bork, 2005). Starley, using metallography based on a very small sample of four Type 16 broadheads and two bodkin heads, proposed that late medieval arrowmakers developed 'high-tech' steel-enhanced broadhead arrows in order to counter the advance from mail to plate armour. He cited Jessop's typology of medieval arrowheads (1996, 192–205) to suggest that bodkin heads were intended for use against mail.

However, it is equally possible, based on Halpin's study of medieval arrowheads from Ireland (Halpin, 1997), that heavier-weighted bodkins may have been introduced in the medieval period for the purpose of piercing plate armour, and that these may not necessarily have been hardened, with weight and diameter of the projectile being more significant than its hardness. Test shooting of Type 8 bodkins and Type 16 broadheads of the same weight, using the same bow, has found that the former, being more aerodynamically shaped, exceeded the latter in distance. In terms of piercing plate armour, however, the heavier, Type 7 bodkins performed best, but would have only been intended for short-range shooting.

Although hardened arrowheads may be preferable for armour piercing, it is not proven that all non-hardened arrowheads were not so intended. Further, as the sample range of tested arrowheads is so small, it is not possible to say with any certainty that the medieval broadheads were the first and only arrowheads to be hardened. Certainly the technology to produce hardened heads was not unknown to Roman blacksmiths, so until a comprehensive metallurgical study is carried out of Roman-period artefacts, this can not be proven either way. However, it is equally possible that when producing large numbers of arrowheads at short notice, time constraints may have lent more towards the majority of points being unhardened in both Roman and medieval periods, with the additional possibility of some untipped arrows in combat use.

FIELD-TESTING EQUIPMENT USED

For the purposes of testing the reconstructed equipment above, therefore, both tipped and untipped arrows were used, test shooting from distances of 30 feet and 60 feet from the target. For the test archery assaults, a replica first-century AD Scythian-style recurved bow of draw weight 35 lb was used, with arrows spined to 30–35 lb (this being close to that which may have been available to horse archers of the Roman period, although possibly not as powerful as the Yrzi example above, but limited by modern re-enactment health and safety regulations). The fletchings observed on the arrows from Dura-Europos were approximately 6 inches long (15.5 cm), but were of a very low, rounded profile (only approximately 1 cm in height), which would have projected a fast, straight course, with maximum penetration. For the test shooting purposes, arrows were used using a range of possible arrowhead types, with similar fletching length to those from Dura-Europos, although with fletchings set further from the nock, for conventional 'standard' release, rather than 'thumb ring' release (as had been the case with the Dura examples).

When an arrow is shot from a bow, the stored energy in the bow transfers to kinetic energy in the arrow and the bow. This can be shown using the following mathematical calculations (Rees, 1995), where:

F = force required to draw bow
x = distance bow is drawn
e = estimated efficiency of bow = 0.9
M = mass of the bow
k = factor representing the kinetic energy of the bow (0.03 to 0.07, depending on bow)
m = mass of arrow
v = speed of arrow
g = acceleration due to gravity
d = maximum distance achievable

Stored energy in bow = $eFx/2$ (using Hooke's Law)
Kinetic energy in arrow = $(mv^2)/2$
Kinetic energy of the bow = $(k\,Mv^2)/2$

Thus:

Kinetic energy in arrow + Kinetic energy of the bow = Stored energy in bow
$(mv^2)/2 + (k\,Mv^2)/2 = eFx/2$
$(mv^2) + (k\,Mv^2) = eFx$
$v^2\,(m + (k\,M)) = eFx$
$v^2 = (eFx/m + (k\,M))$
$v = (\,eFx\,/\,(m + kM))\text{-}2$
$d = v^2/g$

The maximum range (d) that can be achieved (by aiming at 45° to the horizontal) depends on the initial speed of the arrow (v), and the acceleration due to gravity (g). The true maximum distances achieved will, however, be less, due to the drag caused by air resistance on the arrow, although for purposes of calculating equivalent distances between different poundage bows, the discrepancy can be ignored.

The calculations above were derived by Rees (1995) to gauge comparitive capabilities of English longbows, using an estimated 154 lb strength. It can, however, be used to extrapolate values for other weights of bows. The Yrzi bow is described as being in the range of 60–70 lb (Coulston, 1985) and 80 lb (James, 2004); from the above calculations it can be seen that for the test bow of 35 lb to produce an equivalent impact, its distances to the target would need to be decreased by 50 per cent. The results then shown in Table 7.1 would represent those given by an equivalent bow to that from Yrzi at double the distances indicated.

For purposes of the tests, a piece of pork was employed as the willing 'subject', to provide a simulated body texture behind the mail and underpadding, although it is known that the properties of the subject body would differ dependent on the ratio of fat to muscle, and on whether the muscle is tensed or relaxed on impact. However, as this would only provide a measure of arrow penetration, the tests were then repeated using a block of clay behind the layers of mail and padding, in order to gauge the level of impact compression, as even in impacts without penetration, fatalities could still be caused through soft tissue impact injury.

FIELD TEST RESULTS

A breakdown of average test results using a range of arrowheads against both wooden shield and mail, using varying depths of padded undergarment, is provided in Table 7.2 below. For example, it was found that the metal-tipped ('bodkin'-headed) arrows, flat shot at a distance of 9.23 m (30 feet) were able to easily penetrate a 10 mm thick, 3-ply wooden shield, the arrow totally clearing the shield, although penetrating the shield by a depth of only 24 cm from a distance of 18.28 m (60 feet). At the same distances, even the wooden-tipped arrows penetrated the same shield by 45 cm and 15 cm respectively, although some arrows striking the curve of the shield at a tangent were deflected to the side. Clearly, the main function of the shield would have been in its use as a weapon, and in its ability to deflect weapon strikes in hand-to-hand combat, or to collect untipped arrows from an 'arrow storm', the energy of which were almost spent. They would have offered little protection against a close, flat-shot direct arrow strike, other than as a first line of defence, to slow the arrow before it struck the mailed, padded body behind it.

When not used in conjunction with any form of undergarment, the 'naked' mail also yielded to both arrow types, although faring worse against the metal-tipped arrows, and riveted mail faring better than butted mail, where the shafts of the arrows were able to force apart the weaker links. However, in combination with the fully padded medieval-style gambeson/jack, it was found that, although resistant to the untipped arrows, at 18.28 m (60 feet) the metal arrows were either resisted or unable to penetrate fully through the padding, and at the closer distance of 9.23 m (30 feet) these only penetrated by a short distance, sufficient as to have caused minor injury, but not necessarily to have caused a fatality. However, close shots with the broader-tipped arrowheads did prove to cause some compression to the underlying body tissue, although again, with the more substantial level of padding, this was unlikely to cause fatalities.

Subjecting the 'naked' mail, and that used in conjunction with the various undergarments, to thrusting and slashing assaults with a Roman short sword (*gladius*) yielded similar results. Although in a slashing assault some damage to the unpadded mail was sustained, and the blow transmitted to the 'body' below, when used in conjunction with the padding the force of the impact was cushioned and dissipated through the padding, resulting in probable severe bruising, but not necessarily in maiming the recipient. However, a thrusting blow would penetrate the mail, with the level of damage therefore depending upon the density of the underlying garment. Obviously, in these circumstances the more densely constructed gambeson/jack fared best, whereas the simple leather tunic was easily compromised. These findings were, therefore, in agreement with the literary descriptions of padded jacks of the Duke of Gloucester's men (c. 1483), which record that the 'softer the tunics, the better do they withstand the blows of arrows and swords', and in Louis XI of France's ordinance (c. 1470), which claims that 'never have been seen half-a-dozen men killed by stabs or arrow wounds in such jacks, particularly if they be troops accustomed to fighting' (Embleton, 2000, 64, 67).

It has been suggested that the use of heavy padding under mail was only a medieval innovation, and that Roman period mail would have been used without underpadding, citing the figure-hugging appearance of mail cuirasses depicted in sculptural representations (which is in all probability an artistic convention). As detailed above, there is little by way of artefactual evidence for the use of padding, and only vague literary references to garments that may have served that purpose. Mail used on its own, without underpadding, would have been a distinct improvement over no armour at all or the very basic metal discs strapped to the chest, as was the case for less wealthy combatants under the early Republic. It is most unlikely that mail would have been used without substantial clothing underneath, or with mail worn under clothing, as any weapon strike would then drive the metal fragments deep into the flesh of the target.

However, mail was in use by the Romans for many centuries, with a further millenium of use before the above medieval 'innovation'. It seems highly unlikely that a militaristic society such as that of the Romans, with a proven track record for innovation in armour and weaponry designs, would have failed to recognise the efficacy of padded undergarments (which are cheap and easy to produce, using readily available scrap materials). Indeed, the looser-fitting style of mail shirts, as seen on the Battle of Ebenezer depictions from Dura, may suggest a progressively higher level of underpadding being used by that time. The appearance under the later Empire of combatants seemingly clad only in heavy, unarmoured tunics, may then represent an additional overgarment, with the mail and underpadding beneath.

What the above suggests, in addition to the efficacy of using padding under mail armour to absorb and dissipate impact forces (gauging the optimum maximum level of padding against the disadvantages this may cause by overheating and restriction of movement), is the need to reconsider the way in which archers were utilised in combat situations. Clearly some arrowheads (particularly bodkin types) were more efficient at armour penetration, others were better at causing soft tissue injuries (broad head and barbed types), whereas the lightweight untipped arrows were best suited to arrow storms, where they may cause ad hoc injuries to exposed areas of flesh (face, arms, legs, hands, feet, etc.) or may render a shield an unwieldy encumbrance. The untipped arrows were, however, virtually useless against any level of body protection. They would also have been of little use by heavier poundage bows, as they would in all likelihood disintegrate under the stresses of release.

The existence of these different arrow types would suggest, therefore, that both lightweight and heavyweight bows were in use, with arrow storm assaults being used to cause the opposition to raise their shields, exposing unprotected or lesser armoured body parts (such as underarms) to more direct shots by more substantial arrow types. Alternately, longer distance arrow storm assaults by heavier poundage bows would similarly cause the enemy to raise their shields, exposing the less armoured areas to lightweight arrows from waves of horse archers with smaller, lighter bows. It would then follow that the use of this variety of arrow types and bow weights suggests that padding was probably in use to some level to combat the efficiency of the armour (which, as can be seen from the tests above, is easily compromised when used without padding).

DISCUSSION

Experimental use of reconstructed armour found that mail and scale coats subjected to simulated attack will be more easily penetrated if used without any form of padded garment underneath, whereas those used with the padding will absorb the force of a blow, often with minimal or no damage. The balance of probabilities, therefore, would lend itself more towards the use of some form of underpadding, at least in conjunction wth mail and scale (plate armour faring better against all but very close-distance strikes from heavyweight, narrow-diameter arrowheads).

However, any undergarments used may not necessarily be uniform in appearance. As styles of bodice varied over time, it would be logical to assume that any undergarment would vary similarly, and may also vary to accommodate differences across armour types and functions. For example, armour under *segmentata* cuirasses may have been shorter-bodied and may have been provided with additional padding in the shoulder regions to combat the extra weight of the shoulder guards, with less in the body and abdomen areas to allow for a closer fit of the girdle plates. In contrast, any undergarment used with scale or mail would have required a more uniform thickness with a longer body, matching in shape the overlying cuirass, and any used with a muscle cuirass (if these indeed had existed) could have been simply a thin leather jerkin to which arm and skirt *pteruges* could be attached.

Whereas a thin leather jerkin/tunic may have been sufficient to prevent abrasion under plate armour, it would not be able to dissipate the force of any substantial blows and, in consequence, some level of padding would have been preferable (which would have to be offset against the closeness of the fit, in the case of *segmentata*). On consideration, however, of the reconstructed Carlisle 'shoulder protections', when added to such a leather garment, some functional disadvantages were noted: the 'patches' were found to be too large for this purpose. They caught on the overlying plates when the wearer attempted to put on his armour. They also had a tendency to become trapped between the plates when the wearer lifted his arms. They then protruded too far beyond the shoulder, lifting the shoulder guard plates into a more horizontal angle, separating the plates and producing points of vulnerability where a sword blade could pass. This lifting of the shoulder guard plates then had the result that, when struck from above by a sword, the blade would not slide off along the slope of the shoulder, but would instead dent the plate or cut into the plate, with the shoulder taking the full force of the impact.

Although the garment is an attractive proposal for a re-enactor wishing to look decorative in a simulated 'dress down kit', it would therefore appear to be an impractical interpretation of these fragments, which should perhaps be more plausibly interpreted by their original proposed use as saddle horn covers (particularly in view of their find context, in association with workshops and other cavalry equipment).

It is clear, therefore, that personal protection was not confined to body armour alone (in whatever format that was used – whether *segmentata*, mail, muscle cuirass or scale), but that this formed just part of a bigger picture, of an ensemble of protective units all serving an individual need, but operating as part of a whole. All forms of body armour would have been

Bow strength (lbs)		154	80	70	60	40	35
Force required to draw bow (Ns)	F	700	364	318	273	182	159
distance bow is drawn (m)	x	0.58	0.58	0.58	0.58	0.58	0.58
estimated efficiency of bow = 0.9	e	0.9	0.9	0.9	0.9	0.9	0.9
mass of the bow (kg)	M	1.0	1.0	1.0	1.0	1.0	1.0
factor representing the kinetic energy of the bow (estimated)	k	0.07	0.07	0.07	0.07	0.07	0.07
mass of arrow (kg)	m	0.06	0.06	0.06	0.06	0.06	0.06
acceleration due to gravity (ms2)	g	9.81	9.81	9.81	9.81	9.81	9.81
speed of arrow (ms) (eFx/(m + kM))-2	v	53	38	36	33	27	25
max distance at 45° (m) (v2/g)	d	287	149	130	112	74	65

Table 7.1 Comparative calculations of arrow speed and maximum distances for a range of bow strengths (based on Rees, 1995).

	Padding alone		Un-padded mail		Lightly padded mail (leather) (2 mm)		Medium padded mail (4 mm)		Heavily padded mail 18 mm)		Wooden shield 3ply 10 mm)
Arrow	Short range – 9.23 m (30 feet)										
Penetration Compression	P	C	P	C	P	C	P	C	P	C	P
1 (untipped)	0.0	0.0	0.0	0.0	0.0	0.0	0.0	0.0	0.0	0.0	45.0
2 (needle bodkin)	9.4	0.0	10.7	0.0	10.7	0.0	7.1	3.0	3.0	0.0	full
3 (light bodkin)	0.0	3.6	4.8	0.0	4.3	0.0	0.0	4.6	0.0	0.0	full
4 (heavy bodkin)	9.4	0.0	9.7	0.0	9.7	0.0	7.1	3.0	2.5	1.0	full
5 (leaf bladed)	3.3	2.0	6.6	0.0	4.3	0.0	3.3	2.5	3.3	1.5	full
6 (trilobate)	9.7	0.0	8.1	0.0	7.1	0.0	7.6	0.0	3.6	0.0	full
	Longer range – 18.28 m (60 feet)										
Penetration Compression	P	C	P	C	P	C	P	C	P	C	P
1 (untipped)	0.0	0.0	0.0	0.0	0.0	0.0	0.0	0.0	0.0	0.0	15.0
2 (needle bodkin)	2.3	0.0	2.7	0.0	2.7	0.0	1.8	0.8	0.8	0.0	24.0
3 (light bodkin)	0.0	0.9	1.2	0.0	1.1	0.0	0.0	1.1	0.0	0.0	22.5
4 (heavy bodkin)	2.3	0.0	2.4	0.0	2.4	0.0	1.8	0.8	0.6	0.3	24.0
5 (leaf bladed)	0.8	0.5	1.7	0.0	1.1	0.0	0.8	0.6	0.8	0.4	21.0
6 (trilobate)	2.4	0.0	2.0	0.0	1.8	0.0	1.9	0.0	0.9	0.0	22.0

Table 7.2 Penetration test – shooting a selection of arrow types at reproduction mail, using varying levels of underpadding, at a range of distances (average penetration and compression in cm).

more effective when used in combination with a protective undergarment to dissipate any blows and mitigate against abrasion of the wearer's body from the hard outer surface. The protective qualities derive not from hardness of the material but from the ability to absorb the power of a strike from an opponent's weapon and minimise the damage it inflicts. The body armour, therefore, is the last line of defence, as some damage could still be sustained from heavy sword or projectile strikes. Ideally, the wearer would prefer to avoid contact with the opponent's weapon at all, and for this reason body armour would be combined with a helmet (to deflect from projectiles and heavy object strikes from above) and a shield (to deflect projectile weapons, such as arrows, *pila* and javelins).

VIII

THE ARMOUR IN USE

As outlined in Chapter I, this study is intended to assess current views of the history of the Roman army, relative to the development of its equipment, and to meld these with the archaeological evidence available. There have been several works on Roman military equipment with a similar remit but, with the exception of that by Russell-Robinson in 1975, all have been desk-based assessments. Even the still definitive work of Russell-Robinson is now over thirty years old, and during the years since its publication much new information has come to light to add to the jigsaw of our current knowledge. Furthermore, much of the earlier material upon which Russell-Robinson was compelled to rely was poorly reported/published, inefficiently conserved and is now either no longer in existence or difficult to access.

This study, therefore, differs from those preceding in that it has drawn together the streams of published information (of historical events and economic situations, their effects on developmental progression of armour, weaponry and the structure of the army itself), of sculptural imagery and archaeological 'hard' evidence, while also looking at the component parts, how these came to exist (the economy and technology involved in production) and how they are physically put together. This has involved a 'return to basics', in examining wherever possible the original material (as opposed to the published 2-D photographic images, or even line drawings) and attempting to reproduce the aspects of the artefacts observed through physical reconstruction, using materials and techniques as close as possible to the originals. The reconstructions thus produced were then subjected to low-level, simulated wear, over several years, to view how the component parts interacted, which parts were more susceptible to wear damage through regular attrition, and to see what features may be anticipated archaeologically on artefacts as evidence of wear damage and field repairs. It is accepted, however, that fully realistic simulations of potential heavy-use battle damage are unfeasible, as no modern reconstruction is ever likely to be subjected to the conditions of full-on life-threatening combat (for which purpose the original armour was constructed).

Although the study was restricted to body armour types, these were by no means constant in design or use of constructional material throughout the existence of the Roman army. The basic equipment set of the Roman soldier underwent many developmental changes from its earliest hoplite form, through the Republican and Imperial periods to an almost pre-medieval form in the later stages of the Empire. These changes were not only in design features but also in material content, methods of production and even in the level of use, with combatants of both the earliest and latest periods being relatively lightly protected, but using quite different styles of fighting.

In most time periods, innovations in civilian life tend to derive from improvements in weaponry. This then raises the question as to what extent did improvements in Roman metalworking come about because of improvements in Roman armour, and how much of Rome's economy at any time was directed to the production of arms and weapons. Even in the earliest periods, when each combatant was responsible for his own equipment, with sudden increases in demand just before each campaign, a high level of resources and manpower would have been devoted to meeting this need. With expansionist policies and threats from external sources prompting new campaigns, demand at times may have exceeded supply, which stimulated the development of new methods of processing raw materials and of manufacture, such as factory-based mass production. However, in the case of helmets, the quality of mass-produced equipment was not good enough, creating weaknesses in the structure, which then required the introduction of new technology to counter these weaknesses, improvements which would then have disseminated into civilian life with increased metallurgical knowledge and more efficient processing of materials. In order to understand the reasons behind the development of these new features and changes in manufacture for each armour type, it was necessary to also consider the historical events and economic changes running parallel to, and possibly causing, these developments.

PRE-ROMAN ARMOUR DEVELOPMENT

Most Roman defensive equipment can be seen to pre-date Roman use. This is hardly surprising. Man as a social animal has from earliest times been periodically less than sociable to his fellow man. As a natural response, for reasons of self-preservation, he has fashioned body protection from whatever resilient material was close to hand, the head probably being the main area at risk. Where these materials are of organic nature (wood, horn, etc.) they do not survive as well as metallic ones, with the earliest examples of simple copper-alloy helmets found at Ur, in Mesopotamia, dating to 2500 BC (Fagan, 2004, 184).

Of similar date, again from Ur, a sculptural representation (the Vulture Stela) depicts soldiers in early shield-wall formation, wearing simple helmets and carrying large, rectangular shields (Fagan, 2004, 85). Around a millennium later, use of shields, helmets and also body armour (in the form of the Dendra Panoply) can be seen in Greece, with analogies drawn between the latter and both Roman 'muscle cuirasses' and segmented plate armour (Russell-Robinson, 1975, 147).

The history of shields then diverges, with the development of small, round shields (*hoplons*) in Hellenistic regions (for use in phalanx formation) and large, plank-built, wooden or wicker shields in northern European regions (evidenced in Scandinavian bog deposits and later La Tène contexts; Buckland, 1978, 262–3).

Scale armour is also known from pre-Roman contexts (in fact being never distinctly 'Roman' at any time, but generally taken to indicate the presence of non-Roman auxiliary troops; Russell-Robinson, 1975, 153; Feugère, 2002, 74). It is thought to have originated in the East, fashioned again from almost any resilient material (wood, bone, boiled leather or metal) with Hittite and Egyptian examples dating from the fourteenth and thirteenth century BC (Russell-Robinson, 1975, 153; MacQueen, 1986, 63). From the attachment perforations on finds of scale, developments can be attributed to the Egyptians, with improved construction by the tenth century BC, from the introduction of horizontal overlap of scales and vertical offset of rows, creating a double thickness of protection. Wall paintings also provide evidence of how these scales were used, with depictions of rulers wearing long-sleeved, long-bodied garments, sufficiently flexible to permit chariot control, but designed mainly with the intention of the deflection of glancing arrow strikes (Wise, 1987, 20).

In contrast, armour in Hellenistic areas reduced in size to permit greater freedom of movement and was designed to be suited to the close-formation hoplite phalanx system of combat, with helmet, small circular *hoplon* shield, leg protectors (greaves) and body plates covering the ribcage area (as seen on the Argos panoply of *c.* 750 BC), which by the fifth century BC had evolved to linking by use of hinges (the ancestor of the Imperial Roman officer's 'muscle cuirass' of the first century AD; Warry, 1980, 13).

The Hellenistic period also saw the development of features in helmet design of significance to later Roman examples, with the higher status Illyrian and Corinthian styles of the seventh to fifth century BC gradually improving cheek protection, bowl ventilation, overall visibility and hearing, to produce more open styles, such as the Chalcidian (forerunner of the Attic form also seen in later Roman officer use; Warry, 1980, 44). The longer cheek pieces of the later Corinthian styles permitted the wearer to push the helmet up onto the top of the head when not in use, in a feature later mimicked on the Roman officer's Etrusco-Corinthian helmet (with an imitation 'face' on top of the head; Russell-Robinson, 1975, 137).

THE EARLY ROMAN ARMY

This, then, was the basic hoplite equipment assembly in use in Hellenistic regions, which then diffused through trade and cultural links into the Italic peninsula, adopted in the sixth century BC by a number of the Italic peoples including the Romans, the neighbouring Etruscans, and those in coastal colonies with strong links to their Greek neighbours, and as depicted on the Certosa situla (Zotti, 2006). The Italic hoplite, however, differed from the Greek counterpart in his body armour, wearing instead just a simple pair of small discs (*cardiophylax*), linked by a series of rings (Burns, 2003, 62–72). This earliest form of Roman army was organised on an ad hoc basis as need arose, manned by those who satisfied a property qualification. This then determined their level of equipment and status into five classes, some with just shield, others with increasing levels of protection, using next helmet, greaves, then body armour, in order of importance and value (Livy, I.43). The lowest class (the *proletarii*), who could not afford armour, were exempt from military service, those others deemed sufficiently wealthy being responsible for the supply of their own equipment (Paddock, 1985, 143). Armour, therefore, at this time, being privately owned, would have been commissioned from craftsmen operating small-scale workshops, producing superior quality equipment which was as consequence probably handed down to later generations as high-value heirlooms.

At the start of the fourth century BC, the Romans were still using this hoplite assemblage and phalanx tactics. The numerous city-states of the Italic peninsula were at that time engaged in frequent 'war' actions (usually over land and resources), with the Romans and Samnites the main protagonists, the other regions allying on either side (Burns, 2003, 62–3). The Samnites, unlike their Roman counterparts, wore a superior designed triple-disc cuirass, carried long, rectangular shields (*scuta*), fought in more open formation, and used projectile weapons (javelins and prototype *pila*). Each of their allied neighbours had their own, slightly different armour assemblage, reflecting their regional traditions and origins, with different styles of helmets, crests and plumes, and slightly different weaponry and body armour (those people in coastal regions with closer links to Greek culture adapting the triple-disc cuirass and the Greek-style muscle cuirass, to produce a hybrid form of short-bodied, rectangular muscle cuirass with Samnite-style ring fasteners) and during the course of the following century many of these regional variations were merged and modified, assimilating the best features of each (Burns, 2003, 72).

It was during this century that two developments can be seen which are important features of the Roman ethos of armour development, seen throughout their history (and in fact of many aspects of Roman character in general), in the assimilation of ideology and technology, followed by highly successful adaptation and exploitation (as seen also in their exploitation of industries and economies of 'absorbed' regions such as Britain). Firstly, following defeats by Gallic Celts at Allia in 386 BC (Livy, IV.59), the Romans appreciated their opponents' superior body armour (mail cuirasses) and assimilated this into their own assemblage rather than the traditional *cardiophylax*, at least for the more wealthy members, along with the Gallic Montefortino helmet (because of its simplicity and ease of manufacture; Burns, 2003, 70). Secondly, finding the hoplite phalanx method of fighting ineffective against the Samnite open formation fighting, they reorganised the structure of their army into the more flexible manipular legions, abandoning the now obsolete small *hoplon* shields in favour of the Samnite-style long, oval *scuta*, which were more effective against projectile weapons (Burns, 2003, 70).

By the end of the fourth century BC, therefore, a homogenisation of armour can be seen, with almost universal use of Samnite-style oval shields and the Celtic-style Montefortino helmets (although with some higher status use of the Attic and Etrusco-Corinthian helmets for officer and cavalry use), probably due to its simplicity, ease and economy of manufacture, along with its non-contentious, 'neutral' lack of association with any particular Italic city-state (Burns, 2003, 73). However, even by the mid-third century BC, Polybius (VI.23) could report that only the wealthy few were using mail, the majority still using the simple *cardiophylax* plates, and a few, less poor, wearing the rectangular muscle cuirass.

The Punic Wars of the third century BC again brought about change in answer to strained resources. In armour the Carthaginian opposition was closely matched, wearing a similar equipment assemblage (Quesada Sanz, 1997, 155). They differed, however, in the nature of their troops. The Roman forces were at that time still volunteers, equipped from their own resources, recruited ad hoc as necessary, requiring fresh training for each campaign. The opposition, however, were time-served mercenary troops, fighting for financial recompense (Quesada Sanz, 1997, 155).

By the Second Punic War, some Roman troops were similarly time-served, and the army had once more reorganised, reducing the property requirements, to include poorer classes, forming a new light infantry with less armour. The number of legions had been increased, annual selection of temporary conscripts was introduced, and volunteers were encouraged by a small allowance to help man the new legions. Polybius relates that those eligible were called to Rome for selection, then returned home to equip themselves from local craftsmen, then regrouped at predetermined assembly points, their equipment as a consequence reflecting their individuality and regional preferences (Paddock, 1985, 143).

The opposing Carthaginians were similarly equipped with Montefortino-type helmets and oval shields (the Roman-style Fayum shield, for example, potentially being of either Roman or Galatian mercenary ownership), again re-kitting at established assembly points. Finds of helmets of similar date and perhaps similar style of workmanship may reflect the locations of these assembly points, either Roman or Carthaginian mercenary (several of the latter known from the Iberian peninsula; Quesada Sanz, 1997, 155, 162). It was around this time (mid to late third century BC), that the Coolus (Mannheim) style of simply shaped bronze helmets (without crest knobs) also began to appear, these being of Gallic-Celtic origin, rather than the Italic-Celtic Montefortinos, and again may not always represent Roman use, although in both cases the presence of cheek pieces may be indicative of Roman ownership, the Celtic versions being worn with just simple ties instead (Russell-Robinson, 1975, 26).

THE MARIAN REFORMS

The second century BC saw further revisions to the organisation and identity of the Roman army, a variety of modifications initiated by a number of persons, later consolidated into more general use by (and perhaps incorrectly credited to) Marius, with greater relaxation of recruitment restrictions (geographical and financial), an overall increase in manpower, restructuring of the manipular legions into cohorts and some redesign of equipment (such as the 'improved' *pilum*; Campbell, 2000, 6). Many of those newly eligible were unable to afford their own kit, and the quantities required at short notice were beyond the capacity of the small-scale private workshops, this need being answered by the use of mass production 'factories' (probably state-owned). Consequently, many of the innovations seen at this time are improvements to rate of production at the expense of quality, which is particularly evident in helmet construction (Paddock, 1985, 146).

Up to this point there had been little change to the basic shape and quality of the Montefortino and Coolus helmet forms, apart from regional styles of decoration reflecting the work of individual craftsmen. Following these reforms, to meet demand, helmets appear to have been mass-produced by 'spinning', poorly finished, with separately made crest knobs (or none at all), and with little or no decoration (Paddock, 1985, 146). With further relaxation of citizenship following the Social and Civil wars of the early to mid-first century BC, the increase in the number of legions to twelve, and increase in the level of payment to volunteers, quality reduced still further.

The reasons for this mass-production were two-fold. Not only was new equipment required to equip these newly formed additional legions, but also to re-equip existing legions before and after conflicts. For example, Caesar in his Gallic campaigns was reputed to have re-equipped his men using 'friendly' Gallic craftsmen, known for their skills in metalworking and armour production; hence the introduction of Gallic/Celtic features to the military assemblage at that time, seen in the introduction of iron Agen and Port styles of helmet (dating to the siege of Alesia in 52 BC; Russell-Robinson, 1975, 42), and of the Gallic-style round, iron and copper-alloy shield bosses (also found from Alesia, Slovenia and Gaul; Feugère, 2002, 73).

Although the exact locations of these Gallic 'state-owned' factories are unknown, it is suggested that these would have been in regions known to be friendly to Caesar, in particular the Coolus district of Marne, close to the Rhine. Furthermore, Paddock (1985, 146) suggested that the innovation of 'spinning' may have derived from a Greek tradition, reflecting also the activity of Italic workshops, introducing methods for high-capacity production from their own 'historic' traditions (with the possibility of 'spinning' features being visible on Greek, fifth-century BC mass-produced, bell-shaped Pylos helmets).

Metallurgical analysis of copper-alloy helmets also suggests further changes in production methods to increase supply, by speeding up production and reducing failure rates, with a change from the use of the harder bronze (copper and tin) to the addition of zinc, to produce the softer, more easily worked, golden-coloured *oricalchum* (Paddock, 1985, 147). This change to metallic properties may again reflect the actions and influences of different workshops and craftsmen. Some of the regions newly incorporated into Roman territories, or which experienced greater levels of Roman trade and influence, had long-standing metalworking traditions and high mineral wealth, such as parts of Gaul, Germania and Britain. It is possible that the need for mineral wealth, to provide armour for increasingly larger armies, to then power further expansion into regions rich in these necessary minerals, was the basis for a self-generating cyclic process (which may in part explain subsequent expansion into Germania and Britain to access this mineral wealth, and which may here be seen reflected in helmet production). Paddock (1985, 145) then identified a break in production and possible stockpiling of equipment between the death of Caesar (in 44 BC) and the defeat of M. Antonius (in 31 BC), with Augustus introducing further reforms to the military and reducing the number of legions.

THE ARMY OF THE IMPERIAL PERIOD

After a short period of relative peace, around the end of the first century BC and the start of the first century AD, production then recommenced with re-equipping of the legions in advance of the Germanic campaigns. Around this time, new features appear to have been introduced to the military assemblage, possibly in preparation for changing weaponry and tactics of the new opponents. During the Republican (and pre-Republican) period, Rome's enemies had been similarly equipped, using similar fighting styles and tactics. When confronted with different styles or equipment that proved more effective than their own, they quickly assimilated and adapted the best features into their own assemblage and methodology (as witnessed in the movement towards long, oval *scuta*, projectile weapons and manipular formation fighting). Even the Carthaginian armies of the Punic Wars were seen to have been similarly equipped, as obviously would combatants of the Social and Civil wars of the first century BC.

These non-Roman opponents now used different weaponry and fighting style, using long, slashing and hacking swords and axes in open formation fighting, with combatants acting as individuals in guerrilla-style skirmishes, rather than as a solid body of men in regulated, standing battles. Furthermore, many of these conflicts took place in restricted, close, woodland locations or in hilly regions, where the previous Roman strengths of block formations could not be applied, and where opponents could take the opportunity to shower the Romans from above with heavy objects and projectiles.

To combat these new threats, helmet design (unchanged for centuries) can be seen to commence a developmental progression with the introduction of peaks and brow bands to strengthen the helmet bowl, stepping and lengthening of the occipital regions (with ridged 'crumple zones') to better protect the back of the head (and minimise dislodging), and gradual widening and sloping of neck guards (to protect the neck and shoulder areas by deflecting slashing and hacking blows away from the body; Russell-Robinson, 1975, 26). At the same time, ear guards also began to appear (first by simple flanging out directly from the bowl, and later by addition of larger, applied ear guards), while cheek pieces improved (with stronger hinges, more secure, close fastening and, on Gallic examples, with outwardly turned throat flanges).

Shield design also embarked on a progression of minor developmental changes, first with a more widespread use of metallic shield bosses (more resilient against slashing/hacking attack and also permitting greater 'offensive' use, by 'punching' with the boss). Shield shape also changed, firstly by 'squaring-off' the tops, and later similarly 'squaring-off' the sides. This reduced the shield's weight and improved the owner's ability to use it reactively in close-quarter situations without reducing greatly the area of body protection. The new shape also improved the ability to interlock the shields, minimising the tendency towards 'gapping' in shield-wall or testudo formations (the latter being of particular importance under conditions of attack from above from downwardly projected missiles and heavy objects).

This, then, was the atmosphere of innovation and changing armour design which coincided with the earliest appearance of the segmented plate armour usually associated with the typical Roman legionary of the first century AD, the *lorica segmentata*. This may possibly have been in answer to changing enemy fighting styles and weapons, the more robust upper shoulder protection being better suited to defence against close-quarter combat with axe and sword. This being the case, probably only small units of these heavily armoured troops would have been based in each legion initially, with the remainder, and also associated auxiliaries, still wearing mail.

By the time of the defeat in the Teutoberg Forest (AD 9), and even at the time of the conquest of Britain (AD 43), the majority of men in the legions would still have worn mail, possibly even up to the time of the Boudiccan Revolt. However, although later into the Imperial period *lorica segmentata* appears to have become more widespread (if the sculptural relief on Trajan's Column is accurate), the assumed use by all legionary troops may not be correct. *Segmentata* may have been used even then by units of heavily armoured troops and may not exclusively have been restricted to legionary troops alone. Josephus, in his *Jewish Wars*, when describing Vespasian invading Galilee and the order of deployment of troops, refers to 'heavily armed Roman troops mounted and unmounted', as being distinct from ordinary legionary infantry (Josephus, *Bell. Iud.*, III.123). It is probable that here he was referring to a difference in the level and type of armour used by these men, rather than just to their status and function.

Despite the sculptural depictions suggesting that *segmentata* was standard legionary issue, finds have also been frequently found in auxiliary contexts. These could be residual from legionary troops that had since moved on, but could also be evidence of use by auxiliaries, their armour being based on their function as heavy infantry rather than based on status. They also appear to occur mostly in northern Empire frontier situations (such as along the Germanic *limes*, or close to Hadrian's Wall, as at Vindolanda and Corbridge), particularly in hilly or mountainous areas. This may be because of the additional protection afforded against missiles and projectile weapons thrown or fired down on them. They are also found in areas where opponents were known to use heavy, slashing weapons, and weapons which caused substantial damage from overhead assault, such as the long, curved-bladed *falx*, which easily penetrates mail alternatives.

Further finds of *segmentata* have come from forts associated with cavalry, which again are generally auxiliary units. Fragments of *segmentata* have also been found in forts manned by mixed cohorts, as for example by the Tungrians at Vindolanda. *Segmentata* has been found to be unsuitable for use on horseback, for which reason cavalry tended to always be depicted in either mail or scale. However, despite apparent discomfort of use, it is possible that need exceeded comfort at times when extreme measures were required, and it is always possible, however unlikely, that some use may have been made of *segmentata* for heavy cavalry. Alternately, it is also possible that small detachments of heavy infantry troops may have been stationed with cavalry units, but again this is purely speculation, with no basis in fact. Another explanation for the presence of *segmentata* may be that it had been sent to those locations for repair or recycling purposes. Cavalry would by routine have a greater need for blacksmiths than any infantry units. These men would have been specialised craftsmen, and may have performed greater functions than just those of farriers, possibly acting as repair or manufacturing workshops for other, non-cavalry units further afield. The *segmentatas* therefore may have been sent to these cavalry blacksmiths for repair work which required more skill than the simplest running repair, or may have been intended as scrap, sent to the cavalry units for re-use of the metal.

Initially, in the first century AD, body shape of mail and scale cuirasses is seen to be greatly reduced, shortening to hip length and losing the additional shoulder doubling (Russell-Robinson, 1975, 164–9; Feugère, 2002, 75). This would have made the armour much lighter and more flexible to use for soldiers required to combat a fast-moving enemy, fighting in a more individualistic, skirmish-type confrontation, sacrificing body protection slightly in favour of speed and flexibility (of course some units would still be provided with heavy-duty shoulder protection, in the form of *segmentata*-clad heavy infantry). The reduced sized cuirasses would also have been quicker and cheaper to produce, which may have been a deciding factor at times of financial crisis, or when large bodies of men were required to be mobilised at short notice (possibly reflected in the poor quality, mass-produced iron helmets, of Imperial Italic Type C, as found for example in the River Po at Cremona, associated with the civil war of AD 69; Russell-Robinson, 1975, 67).

DEVELOPMENT OF CAVALRY EQUIPMENT

The first century AD also saw the appearance of a new form of cavalry and its associated armour (the *equites cataphractarii*; Negin, 1998, 65). In the Republican period, all Roman legions had associated units of cavalry, drawn from the aristocratic 'knightly' class (the *equites*). This was then disbanded with the Marian reforms of the late Republic, being replaced by units of auxiliary cavalry drawn from native riders from regions with horse-riding traditions, newly incorporated within the expanding areas of Roman control. For example, Caesar described in his *Gallic Wars* the use of lightly armed Numidian cavalry (Caesar, *Bell. Gall.* II.3–4).

In AD 69, the Romans experienced the defeat of two cohorts of their army at the hands of just 9,000 heavily armoured Sarmatian horsemen (*cataphracti*), who invaded the region of Moesia, wearing scale armour which covered virtually all of their bodies (Tacitus, *Hist.* I.79; Negin, 1998, 65; Feugère, 2002, 142). Impressed by the quality of their equipment, the Romans later incorporated units of these heavily armoured cavalry into their own army. The use of these heavy cavalry units increased into the third and fourth centuries, eventually evolving into the later *clibinarii* form (derived from an Iranian origin), whereby both rider and horse were provided with substantial scale, mail or composite armour (as seen both archaeologically and in pictorial depictions from Dura-Europos; Negin, 1998, 74; James, 2004, 129–33).

Again, perhaps in answer to changing tactics and weaponry (with actions in the East against slashing weapons delivered from horseback), the shape of both infantry and cavalry body armour changed once more. From the third century, mail and scale cuirasses are seen to lengthen, becoming looser-fitting and developing sleeves of varying lengths (those for cavalry use developing a central front and rear slit for ease of riding and for added protection to the legs of the rider and flanks of his horse; Stephenson and Dixon, 2003, 44). It is also around this time that the segmented armour appears to fall from use, its function perhaps being no longer necessary against this different type of enemy weaponry, or perhaps due to its higher cost of production (mail and scale being cheaper and easier to make and repair). Helmets again at this time continued to be adapted, developing still larger neck guards, ear guards and cheek pieces to protect against slashing attack from long cavalry swords, and, still later, strengthening crossbars added to the helmet bowl to guard against overhead assault. Shield shapes also can be seen to change once more, with large, wide, oval convex shields (as seen at Dura-Europos, archaeologically and as depicted on the Synagogue images of the Battle of Ebenezer), appearing alongside the conventional rectangular *scutum* (James, 2004).

SCALE ARMOUR

Roman scale types (if any scale can ever be truly described as Roman, being usually attributed to the presence of auxiliary troops of Eastern origin) have been catalogued from Carnuntum by von Groller and from Dura by James. They show a variety of shapes (short or long, pointed or rounded) and perforation patterns for attachment to a backing garment and each other (von Groller, 1901b, plate 15; James, 2004, 136, fig. 82). The perforation patterns suggest two basic forms: loose-ended, or with the end perforated to form a more rigid structure by joining each row to the row beneath. Within the two types, the remaining perforations consist of holes at the top (for lacing together and attachment to the backing garment) present on all scales, and additional perforations on the sides (for lateral attachment to the neighbouring scales) present on almost all scales, with the exception of some smaller examples (where side perforations would be unfeasible and unnecessary). The perforation holes are usually evenly spaced, to a standard design and measurement, allowing for ease of repair and replacement from stock supplies of spare scales. The uniformity of scale shape, metal thickness and hole positioning suggests the probability of production by stamping out using a die from rolled sheet (Clemetson, 1993, 10), and metallurgical analysis of some steel scales from Carlisle and Vindolanda proposing some deliberate hardening through heat treatment (Fulford et al., 2004, 206).

The Masada scales in contrast are cruder and more archaic in appearance, with a raised medial rib (as is also seen on some particularly small Roman scales; Russell-Robinson 1975, 154) and a further raised border around the circumference (Yadin, 1966, 55; Stiebel and Magness, 2007, plate 2). The holes are set only at the top of the scale (with four holes set in a square pattern), with no side holes for lateral attachment to a neighbour. The holes are not uniformly pierced between scales, suggesting that they were individually pierced after the scale body was formed. There is no information provided as to uniformity of thickness, so it is not possible to propose production from rolled sheet or otherwise. The uniformity of measurement does suggest that the blanks were stamped from sheet metal. However, in contrast to the Roman scales (which seem to have been stamped out in a single process, producing a standard shape and perforation pattern), the Masada scales appear to have undergone a three-stage process. First, the basic flat shape would have been stamped from a sheet of metal, then the raised medial and border ridges were added by pressing over a former. This is evidenced on one scale, shown second from the left in the publication by Yadin (1966, 55), where the border ridge is offset from the edge of the plate, having been incorrectly aligned in the press during shaping. Finally, the perforations would have been added in a separate process, resulting in a slightly non-uniform pattern between scales. The oversized scale without border ridging seen on the same photograph (Yadin, 1966, 55) is probably a crudely formed quick repair, suggesting that stocks of standard replacement scales were not available, as would have been the case for Roman equipment.

THE CONTRIBUTION OF MODERN RE-ENACTMENT GROUPS

The study of Roman military equipment has seen increased interest since the work of Russell-Robinson, both from academics and amateur 're-enactor' enthusiasts, in some cases with both working together for mutual increase of knowledge, some making use of internet forums dedicated to Roman military studies for world wide exchange of ideas. Re-enactment groups can be of great value for educational outreach purposes, bringing history alive to the young, who will in their turn become the archaeologists of the future.

Most of the academic works of recent years have consisted of desk-based reassessments of previously published material (with the exception of Russell-Robinson who reconstructed his own material, and Junkelmann who similarly built and tested his own reconstructions under simulated every-day use). The contribution of some of the re-enactment groups (such as Chris Haines' Ermine Street Guard, Len Morgan's XIV Legion and Matthew Amt's XX Legion of America) has been to attempt to test the work of the academics, putting into practice their theoretical reconstructions, in many cases working alongside the academics in combined efforts. Their work has made it possible to test equipment in the field, to try out reconstructions in simulated battle conditions, on occasions to the extreme of total destruction. It is possible, therefore, to see the different types of failure encountered, whether general attrition from everyday use or impact damage from battle situations, and this 'wear damage' can then be compared to archaeological artefacts in order to theorise on similar damage seen. Other work includes endurance tests, such as the route marches of Junkelmann, which have for example permitted estimations to be made on the length of service of footwear and hobnails, or the feasibility of methods of carrying equipment (such as shields) on long marches, although these results may now require some modification in view of the newly published shield material from Masada (Stiebel and Magness, 2007, 16–22), which will be discussed in greater detail in a future publication on Roman shields.

The use of heavier-gauge materials, however, for both body armour and shields, will have a significant effect on the way in which the wearer is able to perform. His endurance capacity will be reduced (which of course has implications for the reconstruction experiments carried out by Junkelmann and others, to look for possible distances marched each day, wear and tear on equipment, etc.), and his flexibility and agility will be reduced (with implications for methods of combat). For example, it is impossible to manoeuvre and march for any length of time while carrying the extremely bulky and overly robust 4-ply shields used by some re-enactment groups without developing 'black hand' from reduced circulation and pressure on the nerves and tendons in the back of the hand. Any such endurance experiments by re-enactors should also consider the disparity between the abilities of the trained Roman soldier (in the prime of life and selected from candidates who met high physical standards), and the average re-enactor (who are in many cases drawn from the more senior members of society, and who normally lead more sedentary lifestyles).

Similar problems are encountered with some of the reproduction *lorica segmentatas* used by re-enactors, in that these are often made oversized so that 'one size fits all', to be able to accommodate an ever-changing line-up of society members. However, an oversized, ill-fitting *lorica* which has not been made to fit an individual owner will hang incorrectly on the wearer, producing areas of 'gapping' between the plates (potentially lethal in combat situations). Furthermore, an oversized *lorica* would require substantial padding to prevent movement of the plates, injuring the man inside. In contrast, the examples of *loricae* from Corbridge were found to have been surprisingly small on examination, and were clearly intended to have been close-fitting, with substantial overlap between girdle plates. Their small size may even possibly have contributed to the reasons for their storage in the hoard, as they may have been awaiting reuse by particularly small recruits (the original recruits possibly having developed physically on maturity and through training, to require larger-sized equipment.

It is clear from the tests carried out using a range of protective undergarments with a variety of different armour types, as described in Chapter VI, that the effectiveness of any armour would have increased with the use of any such protection, the cushioning effect of the padding dissipating the energy of an impact, reducing if not preventing injury to the wearer. However, more is not always better in the case of *lorica segmentata*, where it was found that higher-level protection under close fitting cuirasses could cause an entirely different set of problems for the wearer. The apparent close fitting of the Corbridge material would therefore suggest that only minimal under-protection would have been used to accompany segmentata, and that where the armour is correctly made to fit its wearer, with body-shaped plates, there would be no necessity for substantial padding to prevent gaps.

Furthermore, if *segmentata* is viewed as a form of heavy-duty protection against assault by an overhead barrage of projectile weapons, rather than for use in close-contact skirmishes (where mail would be lighter, more flexible and adequate to most requirements), the potential danger from these perceived 'gaps' would be insignificant compared to its benefits. Consideration, therefore, should perhaps be better directed towards the authenticity of the universal use of *segmentata*-clad legionaries in any context rather than to any minor weaknesses caused by ill-fitting *loricae*.

The re-enactment groups, in common with much mainstream opinion, also tend towards a high level of standardisation, taking their lead from sculptural depictions such as Trajan's Column, where legionaries also appear to have been produced as clones. However, this is accepted as being probably a feature of artistic convention using a standard figure to depict a broad category of men. In reality, it is evident that not all legionary troops wore *segmentata* (with most finds being in the northern regions, particularly in hilly areas) and there is a probability that many continued to wear mail or scale cuirasses (the *segmentata* perhaps being used for 'heavy infantry', as discussed earlier).

There is a tendency to portray an image of regimented military efficiency, with all men dressed identically in the same style of *lorica segmentata* (along with other perceived legionary equipment, such as helmets, *caligae*, and rectangular *scutum*), with a few token auxiliary troops in mail carrying the accepted oval shield. However, grave stelae show a variety of styles between different legions (in much the same way that uniforms may vary between contemporary regiments in armies over the last few centuries), with different shields and weapons (for example using 'pikes' instead of *pila*), use of greaves and *manicae*, and also variety seen according to function (for example for legionary cavalry, legate's guards and higher-status officer equipment).

There is also a distinct possibility of a great level of variation in equipment styles, even within each legion, and among men serving similar functions, as batches of equipment are obtained from different suppliers: either large-scale from 'factory' manufacturing sites, or small-scale from individual craftsmen. Even where recruits were issued with standard, mass-produced stock, they would over time invest their own resources in purchasing better quality replacement 'upgrades', probably from local native civilian craftsmen, their old, mass-produced kit returning to the general stock for re-issue. It is also possible that troops may have replaced their poorer quality equipment by plundering from enemies or allies during campaigns, where this kit was superior to their own. This was also seen in more recent time periods, for example when, in 1915, during the First World War, Canadian troops had attempted to replace their faulty rifles from those of fallen British servicemen (although they were prevented from doing so, as it was deemed to be contrary to the rules of war). However, this did not stop British troops, during the Falklands conflict, replacing their less reliable equipment with that of the opposing Argentinians.

This effect was, however, exhibited to an even greater level during the Napoleonic Peninsular War. In official representations the British combatants are depicted as wearing uniforms that were never issued because of the lack of supplies and poor quality equipment (some fighting in Spain under Wellington were barefoot, due to the lack of boots). Furthermore, the red dye in the fabric used for the jackets was not properly fixed, so that the colours ran into the grey trousers and leatherwork, turning all of the equipment pink. The result, therefore, was a mixture of men in poor-quality, pink-stained clothing, and others wearing backpacks, trousers and boots taken from the enemy, or purchased from local suppliers (pers. comm. from a historian/curator in charge of the Army Museum, Chelsea, October 1986). It is possible, therefore, that a similar situation may have existed within the Roman military, particularly at times where demand may have exhausted supply, or where supplies were obtained from local or native suppliers and craftsmen, and with men replacing Roman equipment for better 'native' equipment where available. If this were the case, the definition between legionary and auxiliary equipment may be far less distinct than currently depicted.

CONCLUSION

Our current knowledge of Roman military equipment is based on over a century of work by antiquarians, historians and archaeologists based on sculptural images, ancient literary sources and, in more recent years, on more tangible artefactual evidence derived from increasingly efficient archaeological investigations. This knowledge base is constantly being refreshed and updated with the addition of new information as new sites and new finds come to light.

When a military installation was abandoned, caches of stored second-hand armour, if it could not feasibly be taken to the next location, may have been deliberately buried or concealed in ditches to prevent its reuse, which may then account for many of the discoveries of recent years. As archaeological techniques improve and more sites are investigated (perhaps through redevelopment of land, road building and other construction work), more such finds may come to light. In addition, projects targeting sites of archaeological interest may similarly produce new finds (as for example with the continued work on the 'battlefield' sites around Kalkriese and along the *limes* in Germany, on the Antonine and Gask forts, on the site of Masada, etc).

Where many of the current reconstructions fall down is that they are not referenced to the primary evidence (the actual artefacts), but are frequently over-engineered copies of modern copies, perpetuating any misidentified features (as with the 'point' on the Corbridge type A upper shoulder assemblies). What is needed for the future is a greater study of the primary evidence. However, in the case of the Corbridge Hoard material, this is a rapidly disappearing resource. The finds have been stored in less than ideal conditions for over forty years due to limited resources, and are now in fragile and crumbling condition and may not survive many more years into the future. The recent reassessment, however, was still able to note several features of the remains that had not been included in the published illustrations. Without this study, therefore, many of these features may never have been seen. As much of the other material, such as that from Newstead and Carnuntum, has been stored for considerably longer periods, and as a consequence, if stored under similar conditions, may have suffered similar attrition, it is imperative that a comprehensive study be made before it is too late, as no doubt there is still much that can be learned from it.

REASSESSMENT OF THE ARMOUR FROM THE CORBRIDGE HOARD

PURPOSE OF THE REASSESSMENT

Before the Kalkriese reconstruction could be carried out, a study was made of the original Corbridge finds. This was because of some inconsistencies found in the published reports which had led to problems with many of the modern reconstructions. The aim of the project was to reconstruct as closely as possible to the original, and not to copy the copies. The inconsistencies in the current reconstructions centre around the materials and methods of construction, apparently due to minor omissions in the published report, and the reassessment aimed to confirm these details, in particular the positions of the upper shoulder guard and mid-collar plates. The particular points of interest, in respect of the reconstruction project, were to confirm the relative thicknesses of the various plates and internal leathers, and answer questions about the rivets used. The use of Roman and Arabic numerals follows the conventions used in the published reports on the Corbridge Hoard, where the Arabic numerals relate to upper body plates (chest, collar and back plates and shoulder guards) while the Roman numerals relate to the girdle plates (from different cuirasses to the upper body assemblies).

WHERE THE FINDS ARE STORED: Finds Stored in Corbridge Museum

As most of the remains of the Corbridge Hoard are presently stored at Newcastle University, the only parts stored at Corbridge Museum are:

CO23085 – Cuirass 1 – Upper shoulder guard, right-hand side.
Box 1215 – Cuirass 1 – Part of upper shoulder guard fused to lesser plates
CO23079/80/81/83 – Cuirass iv – Girdle plates, left-hand side
Box (ref unknown) – Cuirass iv – Fragments of girdle plates
CO23082/84 – Cuirass 5 – Shoulder assembly, left-hand side
All of the above belong to *loricas* categorised as being Corbridge Type A.

Finds Stored in Newcastle University Museum

Most of the sets of girdle plates are stored at Newcastle – some complete, and some in fragmentary condition.

Box 1187 – Cuirass 1 – Breastplate, collar plate, back plates – Corbridge A
Box 2 – Cuirass 2 – Breastplate, collar plate, part of back plate – Corbridge A
Box 2 – Cuirass 3 – Breastplate, collar plate, back plate – Corbridge A
Box 1217 – Cuirass 3 – Upper shoulder guard and lesser shoulder guards
Box 1187 – Cuirass 4 – Breastplate – Corbridge A
Box 1218 – Cuirass 6 – Breastplate, collar plate, back plates – Corbridge B
Box 3 – Cuirass 5 – Upper shoulder guard
Box 3 – Cuirass i – Girth hoops
Box 1210 – Cuirass iii? – Girth hoops – Corbridge A?
Box 1210 – Cuirass v? – Girth hoops – Corbridge B?

FINDS STORED IN CORBRIDGE MUSEUM:

Cuirass 1 – Upper shoulder guard assembly
Box Co23085, Corbridge – Bishop, 1988, fig. 29

The upper shoulder guard assembly consisted of three plates, front plate, mid-plate and back plate, linked by two lobate hinges. In comparison to the published illustrations, part of the back plate was now detached (the plate indicated as being without decorative boss), being now in box 1215, still attached to the remains of the lesser shoulder plates. In its current corrosion expanded state, the average plate thicknesses were: back plate 2.85 mm; mid-plate 3.38 mm; front plate 3.43 mm. Decorative copper/bronze bosses were observed on front plate (2.85 mm diameter, with 0.97 mm diameter dome-headed, copper rivet) and on the mid-plate (2.46 mm diameter, with 0.97 mm diameter dome-headed, copper rivet).

This assembly, in particular, was very much body-shaped, and clearly belonged to a right-hand side. Its side profile was lower and more rounded on one side, and higher, rising to a pointed profile on the other side. This clearly indicated that its rounded side ought to be located over the arm, with its pointed side rising towards the neck, shaped to the contours of the shoulder. The assembly was also not symmetrically shaped front to back, with the back edge of the plate sitting lower than the front, and with the decorated bosses then being located on top and at the front, the plain rivet being to the back. However, on close examination, a faint variance in shade could be distinguished around this rear plain rivet, which could have been the remains of an earlier decorative boss, lost prior to deposition and which would then be evidence of previous damage and repair.

Cuirass 1 – Shoulder plates
Box 1215, Corbridge – Bishop, 1988, figs. 28 and 29

The shoulder plate assembly consisted of two large shoulder plates and two lesser plates, with the remains of (possible) deep back plate and detached fragment of rear upper shoulder guard attached. The assembly had separated into five fragments:

- Part of rear upper shoulder guard attached to two large shoulder plates and remains of two back plates.
- Upper shoulder guard. Average thickness 3.0 mm and width of plate 7.2 cm.
- Large shoulder plate 1 (including curve to shoulder). Average thickness 3.28 mm and width of plate 4.86 cm. Two rivets visible. One round copper rivet and traces of leathering near break at shoulder. Congealed mass around anticipated position of rear rivet.
- Large shoulder plate 2. Average thickness 3.0 mm. Only part of plate visible, between large shoulder plate 1 and the extra plate (see below). One copper rivet visible.
- Extra plate – possible deep back plate. Average thickness 3.0 mm. Two areas of leathering on left-hand side, rear of plate (narrow leather 1.95 cm wide). Small copper rivets are visible, 5 cm apart, 2.2 cm from top and 2.5 cm from bottom edges of plate, although these appears to be the shafts of the rivet, peened over, with traces of a 1.6 cm square washer around the rivet.
- Front part of large shoulder plate 1. No evidence of leather or rivets, but triangular shaped hole visible.
- Two pieces of large shoulder plate 2 (middle and front fragments), with front part of small shoulder piece 1 attached. All three fragments have evidence of leathering and one round, flat copper rivet each (8 mm diameter).
- Small shoulder plate 1 (rear part). Leathering and round, flat, copper rivets visible on rear.
- Small shoulder plate 2 (arm edge). Average thickness 2.08 mm. Evidence of outer edge slightly turned out by 4 mm. Leathering and round, flat, copper rivets on back (approximately 8 mm diameter). Width of plate 4.54 cm at front edge, 4.92 cm centre rivet, 4.6 cm at rear edge.

The lesser shoulder plates of both this assembly, and of those of Cuirass 5, were also similarly shaped to the contours of the body, sloping down sideways towards the arm and reaching further down at the back than the front. Comparison with the illustrations (Bishop and Allason-Jones, 1988, fig. 29) confirmed that these Cuirass 1 lesser plates had indeed been flipped, expanding in the opposite direction to the patterns. In addition, the turned-out neck edges on the upper body assemblies viewed were higher than those on modern reconstructions (with the rivet point on the outer edge of the collar plate rather than the neck edge, as on many), which would deflect and counteract the effect of the plate digging into the neck when the arm was raised.

Another rather curious aspect of these Cuirass 1 lesser shoulder plates, however, came to light when studying their direction of expansion. There appears to be one plate too many. In the one fused piece there appears to be the lower part of the back upper shoulder guard plate (with plain rivet), attached to large shoulder plate 1 (rear part including curve to shoulder); large shoulder plate 2 (lower rear part, broken at the same place as the upper shoulder guard); and the additional plate fused to these (a small part of which is broken off). There are two areas of narrow leathering (1.95 cm wide) on the left-hand side rear of the plate. There are traces of two small copper rivets, approximately 5 cm apart, not rivet heads, but more likely the shafts of rivets, passing through the plate from the other side, through the leather, through a reinforcing washer roughly 1.6 cm square then pinged over. It appears to be a back plate, although it is either wrongly orientated, vertically instead of horizontally, or it is unusually wide. As all the remaining fragments of large shoulder plates, in addition to the smaller shoulder plates, are also present, this additional plate does not belong to this shoulder assembly.

This extra plate does appear on the illustration (Bishop and Allason-Jones, 1988, fig. 28) but is not identified in the text, nor does it appear on any of the pattern drawings of this cuirass (Bishop and Allason-Jones, 1988, fig. 29), or of any other cuirass. If the plate is wrongly orientated, it is possible that it was never attached to this cuirass, and may not actually belong to it. If it is correctly placed, however, then it is much deeper than any of the other back plates found with the Corbridge Hoard. Another similarly deep back plate was found from much earlier deposits at Chichester (Down 1978), originally identified as a shoulder plate, which, it is possible, because of its depth (to maintain a balanced appearance to the back of the *lorica*) may have been one of only two back plates instead of three.

Cuirass 5 – Large shoulder plates
Box CO23082, Corbridge – Bishop, 1988, fig. 42
Two large shoulder plates from a left-hand side shoulder assembly. Both plates are equal length, curved to the shape of the shoulder, so as to be deeper at the rear than at the front. The end edges of the plates are slightly sloping and slightly rounded. Average plate thicknesses are 2.2 mm for the upper plate, 1 and 2.6 mm for the lower plate 2.

Internal leathering is missing from the front attachment positions, but can be seen at the mid-point, where it measures 2.3 cm wide, and at the rear, where it is wider, measuring 3.2 cm. The leather at this rear point appears to be angled downwards towards the back plate. There is no trace of leathering going across to the small plates. Rivets are not distinct, but appear to be round, 8 mm diameter flat-headed, inserted from the inside. Traces of coarse weave textile adhere to the inside front, inner and bottom edges of the plates.

Cuirass 5 – Small shoulder plates
Box CO23084, Corbridge – Bishop, 1988, fig. 42
Two small shoulder plates from a left-hand side shoulder assembly. Both plates are equal length, curved to the shape of the shoulder, so as to be deeper at the rear than at the front. The rear end edges of the plates are angled. The (arm) edge of plate 4 is slightly turned outwards. Average plate thicknesses are 2.1 mm.

Internal leathering can be seen in three places, the top, mid-point and on the two outside edge positions. These measure 3.0 cm wide at the front, 2.9 cm at the midpoint, and 3.0 cm at the rear. Rivets are flat-headed, copper, and inserted from the inside. They do not appear to have been domed on the outside, but simply flattened over.

Cuirass iv Girdle plates
Boxes CO23079/80/81/83/unnumbered, Corbridge – Bishop, 1988, fig. 63
Box CO23079 contained fragments of the rear part of two left-hand side girdle plates of average thickness 1.8 mm (average thickness of 2.5 mm inner/bottom plate, 1.2 mm outer plate), being parts of the bottom two plates – the inner/bottom plate having a turned edge (edge turned to the inside). The leading edge of the plate is angled. On the inside, traces of internal leather can be seen, along with a flat-headed copper rivet. There are no traces of any tie loops having been attached to this plate.

Box CO23080 contained a fragment, 3.5 cm wide, of the rear left-hand side top girdle plate. The average thickness of the plate is 1.7 mm. There is no sign of a turned edge, but the leading edge of the plate is angled. On the inside of the plate a buckle is visible, with a 2 cm iron hinge plate, the hinge pin of which appears to be anchored by being either squared off or bent over. The hinge plate is fixed to the girdle plate by an 8 mm diameter copper rivet, flattened on the outside plate. Internal leathering, 3.5 cm wide, can be seen, partly overlapped by the buckle hinge (1.2 cm of leather being exposed outside of the hinge at this point).

A tie loop can be seen, formed from 1.1 mm thick copper-alloy, fixed close to the leading, bottom edge.

Box CO23081 contained fragments of the rear part of seven left-hand side girdle plates of average thickness 1.7 mm (average thickness of 2.1 mm plate 1, 1.5 mm plate 2, 1.6 mm plate 3, 1.5 mm plate 4, 1.8 mm plate 5, 1.7 mm plate 6, 1.7 mm plate 7). There are no signs of thickening or turned edge for top or bottom plates, suggesting a possible eighth (lowest) plate not here evidenced. Internal leathering can be seen, bent over the top of the plates, 3.5 cm wide. This was attached to the plates using flat-headed (with 8.5 mm diameter head) copper rivets, set 1.5 cm apart. These had been inserted from the back, through the leather before the metal plate. These would have been either domed or peened and flattened on the outer plate surface. This had been obscured by the leathering and the next plates above, although these are more likely to have been flattened than domed, in order to allow a more flush finish with the plate above.

Five copper-alloy tie loops are visible, fixed to the plate by two domed copper rivets with 5.1 mm head. These had been set with their loop against the leading edge, suggesting that this side had been intended to overlap with that from the opposite side.

Only a small fragment remains of the top plate, that being the part with the internal buckle. The loop of the buckle is missing, with only the iron hinge plate and pin remaining, fixed to the girdle plate by a copper rivet.

Box CO23083 contained fragments of the front ends of seven left-hand side girdle plates, of average thickness 1.6 mm (average thickness of 1.5 mm plate 1, 1.6 mm plate 2, 1.3 mm plate 3, 1.5 mm plate 4, plate 5 unmeasurable, 1.6 mm plate 6, 1.9 mm plate 7). There are no visible signs of thickening or of a turned edge on any plates, again suggesting a possible eighth (lowest) plate not here evidenced. Internal leathering can be seen on plates 2 and 4, 3.11 cm and 3.26 cm wide respectively. This was attached to each plate by double sets of copper rivets, with round, flat heads of 8.6 mm diameter, inserted from the back.

Six tie loops are visible, made of very thin copper alloy (3.2 mm at the D-sectioned loop, 1.6 mm at widest, flattened point). These were attached using smaller, domed copper rivets, with 6.7 mm heads, attached from the front.

A hinged buckle plate, 1.73 cm wide by 1.75 cm deep (2.32 cm full depth including hinge loop), is attached to the top girdle plate. This is formed from 1.1 mm thick copper-alloy sheet, folded to form the hinge loop, fixed to the girdle plate by two copper dome-headed rivets, one set vertically above the other.

One box (unnumbered) contained several fragments of up to eight girdle plates which corresponded to parts of Cuirass iv (Bishop, 1988, fig. 63). The plates have been stacked closely before deposition and are now fused, so many features are now hidden by overlying plates. Several of the fragments can be fitted back together like a jigsaw, the remaining fragments also bearing similarities, indicating that all pieces came from the same set of girdle plates, although it is not possible to identify all eight plates in each fragment. The fragments however do not form a complete assembly, and there is no trace of any tie loops or internal/external buckles as these parts in particular are missing.

What can be determined from these fragments is that these were all once part of an eight-plate left-hand side girdle assembly. The top edge of the uppermost, outer plate was turned inwards, at least in the underarm area, close to the centre leathering position. The edge was turned slightly outwards then turned over inward on itself by approximately 5 mm. The bottom edge of the eighth, bottom plate was similarly turned inwards. The plates are approximately 4.9 cm wide, although either the top or the bottom plate may have been wider (approximately 5.8 mm), with an average plate thickness of 1.7 mm.

FINDS STORED IN NEWCASTLE UNIVERSITY MUSEUM:

Cuirass 1 – Breastplate, collar plate, back plates

Box 1187, Newcastle – Bishop, 1988, fig. 26

Box 1187 contained the breastplate to Cuirass 4 in addition to this right-hand side, breastplate, and fragmented collar plate and back plates assembly of Cuirass 1. The breastplate is 8.8 cm wide, body-shaped and of 2.7 mm average thickness. It is fragmented into three pieces. The lower centre corner has broken off, as has the upper neck part, just below the hinge, this piece being still attached to the collar plate. The plate bears both horizontal hinged copper-alloy buckle and, at right angles to it, a copper-alloy vertical strap hinge, the latter overlapping the former, and being attached by two small dome-headed copper rivets, serving to fix both hinge pieces. It appears that the buckle has at some time been broken off and during conservation has been wrongly glued to the vertical suspension strap.

The breastplate, collar plate and back plates all have a turned neck edge. They are linked by way of two copper-alloy lobate hinges, attached by five small, dome-headed copper rivets to each half. The copper-alloy hinged fastening strap on the back plate still retains traces of its leather strap. The hinge is attached to the plate by two small dome-headed copper rivets, and its corresponding hinged strap plate is similarly attached to the leather strap using two more such rivets.

Cuirass 2 – Breastplate, collar plate, part of back plate

Box 2, Newcastle – Bishop, 1988, fig. 31

Box 2 contained a breastplate, collar plate and part of the top back plate, forming an almost complete Type A, right-hand side, upper-body assembly. The breastplate has now snapped 1.5 cm below the copper-alloy lobate hinge (fixing the shoulder to the collar plate), dividing the assembly into two sections.

The back plate, average thickness 3.4 mm, is similarly attached to the collar plate by a copper-alloy lobate hinge, 2.9 cm wide, fixed by five dome-headed (4.5 to 5 mm), copper rivets. The inner edge of the back plate is missing, snapped vertically at the edge of the lobate hinge. Directly below the hinge, on the lower edge, a 7 mm dome-headed copper rivet can be seen, with traces of internal leathering and squared washer on the inside. On the outer surface at this point, a paler-coloured ring can be seen on the metal, possibly indicating the position of a large decorated boss, 2 cm radius, which is now gone. This may have been missing before deposition and would be indicative of a later repair. The back plate appears to have been forge-shaped to the body. It extends beyond the edge of the collar plate at the arm edge, providing wider protection at this point, and the top corner of the plate has been cut off, presumably to remove the sharp point which could cut the wearer.

The collar plate, average thickness 2.2 mm, is attached to both back and breastplates by copper-alloy lobate hinges, five small dome-headed copper rivets each side. A torn rivet hole can be seen on the top-centre outside edge, slightly towards the front. The neck edge had been turned outwards by 9 mm, with the neck edge rolled outwards by 4 mm, as could also be seen on the small piece of breastplate attached by the hinge. Around this turned neck edge, on the breastplate fragment, a line of in-fill material is visible. This may be residue of a smoothed join, filled perhaps with tin, solder, lead or something similar. Alternatively, it may be residual evidence for the whole plate having once been tinned, or it could even just be residue from whatever material may have been used in antiquity by way of a cleaning paste.

The larger fragment of breastplate identifies this as a Type A assembly, with horizontal, hinged fastening strap and vertical suspension strap attached to the outer surface (the vertical hinge overlapping the horizontal). Within the angle formed by the two copper-alloy hinged straps (1.8 to 1.86 cm wide), a large decorative copper-alloy boss can be seen, 3.4 cm diameter, an inner ring of decoration 2.2 cm diameter, with a domed 8 mm copper rivet inserted through from the front. This then passes through traces of internal leathering, with a large, rectangular copper washer at the back. The average thickness of this plate is 2.6 mm.

Cuirass 3 – Breastplate, collar plate, back plate

Box 2, Newcastle – Bishop, 1988, fig. 34

Box 2 contained a breastplate, collar plate and the top back plate, forming an almost complete left-hand side, upper-body assembly. The breastplate has now snapped into two parts, the lower part being very fragmentary. This plate, at 8.7 cm wide, is wider than that of Cuirass 2. The average plate thickness is 2.7 mm. In the centre of the plate, just below the broken edge, 1.4 cm from the arm edge, a copper-alloy, hinged vertical suspension strap is attached by two small, dome-headed copper rivets, one above the other, identifying the assembly as belonging to Type A. At right angles to this, a horizontal, copper-alloy, hinged buckle is attached by two lop-sided, dome-headed, copper rivets. The upper fragment of the breastplate has a rivet hole at the arm edge, close to the horizontal break, with a trace of leather on the reverse surface. The neck edge has been turned outwards and rolled. The plate is attached to the collar plate by a copper-alloy lobate hinge, fixed by 4.5 mm copper rivets. The hinge is twisted and damaged, torn on the third loop.

The opposite part of the hinge, attaching the breastplate to the collar plate, also exhibits signs of damage and bodged repair. The holes can still be seen where the original small rivets would have gone, but these have now been replaced by four large domed copper rivets (10 mm head). The average plate thickness is 2.5 mm. As with the breastplate, the collar plate neck edge has been turned out and rolled. On the underside, traces of leather can be seen crossing the plate at a slight angle towards the back, fixed at the outside edge, by a round, 8/9 mm flat-headed copper rivet, inserted from the back, through the leather, then the metal, domed/peened on the outer surface. The collar plate has been snapped into two parts, just before the shoulder rivet, the rear part also attached to the back plate using a second copper-alloy lobate hinge, dividing the assembly into three sections.

The back plate, as with the breastplate and collar plate, also has a turned-out and rolled neck edge. Its average thickness is 2.0 mm. At the base of the plate two 8 mm dome-headed copper rivets, with 4 mm shaft, are visible on the outside, which would have served to attach the internal vertical suspension leathers. On the inside surface of the plate, at the rivet closest to the arm edge, a copper-alloy washer roughly 1.2 cm square had been used to anchor the rivet.

Cuirass 3 – Upper shoulder guard and lesser shoulder guards

Box 1217, Newcastle – Bishop, 1988, figs. 33 and 36

This box contained the entire shoulder assembly from Cuirass 3 – upper shoulder guard, two larger shoulder plates and two lesser shoulder plates. The outermost smaller plate is separate. There is no evidence for a turned outer edge. The next two middle plates are fused together, along with a scrap of the first larger plate. The remainder of this larger plate is now missing. On the illustrated diagrams, the lower ends of these plates appear straight across, although they are actually more angled at a slant. All three plates appear now to be the same length, but it is clear that plates 1 and 2 are now broken off and had been longer. The upper shoulder guard bears a decorative boss on its front plate, and the central plate is slightly wider at its centre point. The entire assembly is body-shaped, sloping downwards to the shoulder.

Cuirass 4 – Breastplate

Box 1187, Newcastle – Bishop, 1988, fig. 39

In addition to the complete Cuirass 1 assembly, Box 1187 also contained the left-hand side breastplate of Cuirass 4. The plate is 85.6 mm wide, and of 2.9 mm average thickness. The plate is broken just below the hinge position, just above a rivet hole on the arm edge. A copper-alloy hinged buckle is attached to the plate by two small dome-headed copper rivets, along with a hinged, copper-alloy, vertical strap fastener, set at right angles, also attached by two small dome-headed copper rivets. This method of vertical suspension then identifies this plate as belonging to a Type A cuirass.

Cuirass 5 – Upper shoulder guard (fig. 24)

Box 3, Newcastle – Bishop, 1988, figs. 44 and 45

For comparison purposes to Cuirass 1, the other assembly with a pointed central upper shoulder guard plate, from Cuirass 5, was sought, as it had originally been found complete, and in association with the remainder of its upper body assembly. This was unfortunately not found at Corbridge, other than large and small lesser shoulder plates. It was hoped that the remaining upper body would be found with the Newcastle University part of the collection, but unfortunately it was only possible to locate the upper shoulder guard, and not the front, collar and back plate assembly. In view of the poor state of preservation of this remaining piece, however, it is likely that this piece has now fragmented beyond identification. From examination of this Cuirass 5 upper shoulder guard assembly, it was found to have also been shaped to the body contours, although its shoulder slope, up towards the neck point, is not as extreme as on Cuirass 1. Clearly then, from both reinterpretation of the illustrated patterns and from reassessment of the actual finds, it is apparent that the earlier reconstruction by H. Russell-Robinson is the more accurate, with the point of the central plate of the upper shoulder guard lying towards, and not away from, the neck.

Cuirass 6 – Breastplate, collar plate, back plates (fig. 22)

Box 1218, Newcastle – Bishop, 1988, fig. 49

Box 1218 contained a breastplate, collar plate and the top two back plates, forming an almost complete Type B, right-hand side, upper-body assembly. When tested with a magnet, the plates were found to be still responsive (as indeed were all other plates similarly tested), indicating that they were not entirely mineralised, as had been previously suggested (L. Allason-Jones, pers. comm., February 2003).

The neck edge on breast, collar and back plates had been bent slightly outwards then turned over to form a rolled edge. Average plate thicknesses were 3.7 mm for breastplate, 2.7 mm collar plate and 2.6 mm back plates.

On the top back plate, two domed copper rivets (9 mm head) were visible which would have affixed the internal vertical suspension leathers. These had been inserted from the outside surface, without any form of decorative bosses. Between these, a smaller (8 mm) copper rivet (fixing the horizontal internal leather supporting the shoulder assembly, which overlapped the vertical leathers), had been inserted through a decorative boss, of copper-alloy. This decorative boss was slightly oval in shape, 2.6 to 3.0 cm diameter, with an inner decorative ring 1.8 cm in diameter. Just above these, a copper-alloy, hinged buckle was attached to the outer surface, close to the neck.

On the inside surface, all rivets had been roughly bent over and flattened off, the stems of the rivets appearing to be approximately 3.6 mm wide. Traces of internal leathers were visible, two vertical and one horizontal each averaging 2.5 cm wide. On the lower back plate two sets of two rivets were visible, one set at the top of the plate, the other set below, fixing to the internal vertical leathering, serving to suspend from the plate above and suspending the plate below (not present). Again no decorative bosses had been used, the rivets passing from the front of the plate, through the internal leather, then through roughly square-shaped washers, before being bent over and flattened. At the shoulder, a copper-alloy, lobate hinge served to attach the upper back plate to its collar plate, fixed by five small copper rivets.

The collar plate linked the front breastplate and the back plates by way of two copper-alloy lobate hinges. Each side of these was formed by folding a thin sheet of metal to form a hinge loop, which was then cut or filed in alternating blocks to intersect with its corresponding other half, a copper-alloy rod passing through these, and peened or mushroomed at each end, to act as hinge pin. Each hinge was then attached to the plate, as on the back and front plates, using five small (6 mm diameter), dome-headed, copper rivets, inserted from the outer surface and peened/flattened over on the inside. At the centre point a copper rivet with a large round flat head (12 mm) was inserted from the inside, through the internal leather from which the shoulder assembly was suspended (2.1 cm wide), and peened and flattened on the outside surface.

The front breastplate was attached to the collar plate using a copper-alloy lobate hinge, as described above. An iron vertical fastening loop can be seen on the lower edge, 50 mm from the left-hand edge of the plate, identifying this as a Type B variant (possibly Type C due to its loops being made of iron). In the centre of the plate a hinged copper-alloy buckle (the second hinged plate and buckle loop missing), was attached using two round headed copper rivets (with 6 mm heads, as also used on the hinges), passing from the front surface, through the buckle hinge, then the plate, then through a horizontal internal leather 2.5 cm wide. This internal leather strap was also attached using a wide (9 mm), round, flat-headed, rivet inserted from the rear, 2.4 cm from the arm edge of the plate (which was not shown on the published illustration: Bishop, 1988, fig. 49). This horizontal leather also continues from the buckle attachment point, projecting beyond the front, central edge of the plate, ending in a rough torn edge (again being a feature not shown on the published illustration).

Cuirass i – Girth hoops

Box 3, Newcastle – Bishop, 1988, fig. 54

In addition to the upper shoulder guard from Cuirass 5, Box 3 also contained fragments of girth hoops, fused into two pieces, identifiable as belonging to Cuirass i (Bishop, 1988, fig. 54).

The first fragment consisted of parts of the upper three girdle plates from the right-hand side front section. One buckle was visible, along with traces of mineralised fabric, the presence of the buckle identifying this as part of a Type A cuirass. Because of the poor condition of the plates it was not possible to determine thickness.

The second fragment again consisted of three girth hoops, this time from the bottom of the assembly. Tie loops were visible on two of the plates, and a small scrap of a fourth plate could be seen under the lower plate. It was estimated therefore that the fragment contained parts of plates 5, 6, 7 and a scrap of plate 8.

Cuirass v? – Girth hoops

Box 1210, Newcastle – Bishop, 1988, fig. 67

Box 1210 contained two sets of girdle plates, both in very fragile condition. This set was identifiable as belonging to Cuirass v (Bishop, 1998, fig. 67). It was part flexed and part fused at one end, the fused and corroded end being slightly less fragile. It appeared to belong to the right-hand side of a Type B cuirass, as two hooks could be seen at the back top. In addition, the tie loops appeared to be more 'chunky' than those on plates from cuirasses identified as being Type A. The tie loops were set back from the rear edge, allowing for an overlap of approximately 3 cm with the opposite side. Seven plates were visible, although a corroded mass obscured part of the back above the bottom two plates. A further indeterminate mass obscured part of the front end below the tie loop on plate 4. Internal leather strapping, 3.5 cm wide, was observed at the centre point, secured by paired copper rivets. The top plate dips down towards the centre, at the armhole position, and there is evidence of a turned edge at that point, although not across the entire plate, only starting from just after the second rear suspension loop.

Cuirass iii? – Girth hoops

Box 1210, Newcastle – Bishop, 1988, fig. 60

The second set of girdle plates in Box 1210 bore no traces of either buckles or suspension loops, so it was not possible to state with any certainty that this belonged to a Type A or B cuirass. However, the tie loops were more delicate than those on the other set in Box 1210, bearing more resemblance to other sets belonging to Type A, and for that reason it seemed more probable that these also belonged to a Type A cuirass. Five plates could be seen, with evidence of a turned top edge on the upper plate. Traces of mineralised coarse-weave fabric adhered to the plates, around the bottom part and at one end. At that end three tie loops were visible, although none could be seen at the opposite end. From the shape of the assembly, when viewed from above, it seemed likely that this was a left-hand side and that the end with these tie loops may have been the rear.

BIBLIOGRAPHY

ANCIENT SOURCES

Ammianus Marcellinus, *Histories*, trans. J. C. Rolfe, 3 vols (Loeb Classic Library, 1935–40).

Anonymous, *De Rebus Bellicis*, trans. E. A. Thompson (Oxford, 1952).

Anonymous, *Notitia Dignitatum*, ed. O. Seeck (Berlin, 1876).

Anonymous, *Scriptores Historiae Augustae*, trans. A. Birley, as *Lives of the Later Caesars* (Penguin Classics, 1976).

Apollonius of Rhodes, *Argonautica*, trans. R. C. Seaton (Loeb Classic Library, 1912).

Appian, *Roman History*, trans. H. White, in 4 vols (Loeb Classic Library, 1912–13).

Apuleius, *The Golden Ass*, trans. W. Adlington, 1915, revised S. Gaselee, 1947 (Loeb Classic Library, 1947).

Aristotle, *On Marvellous Things Heard*, trans. W. S. Hett (Loeb Classic Library, 1936).

Arrian, *Ars Tactica*, trans. P. A. Brunt (Loeb Classic Library, 1976–83).

The Bible: Authorized Version, ed. J. Stirling (Oxford University Press, 1966).

Cassius Dio, *Roman History*, trans. I. Scott-Kilvert, as *The Roman History: the Reign of Augustus* (Penguin Classics, 1988).

Claudian, *De Bello Gildonicus*, trans. M. Platnauer, as *The War against Gildonicus*, 2 vols (Loeb Classic Library, 1922).

Columella, *De Rustica*, trans. H. Boyd, E. S. Forster and E. H. Heffner, 4 vols (Loeb Classic Library, 1941–55).

Heliodorus, *Aethiopica*, trans. I. Bekker (1855)

Herodotus, *Histories*, trans. A. D. Godley, vol. IV (Loeb Classic Library, 1957).

Homer, *Iliad*, trans. R. Fitzgerald, (Oxford University Press, 1974).

Hyginus, *Fabulae de Munitionibus Castrorum*, trans. P. K. Marshall (Leipzig, 1993).

Josephus, *Bellum Iudaicum*, trans. H. St. J. Thackerey, R. Marcus, A. Wikgren and L. H. Feldman, as *The Jewish War* (Loeb Classic Library, 1926–65).

Julius Caesar, *Bellum Civile*, trans. J. F. Mitchell, as *The Civil War* (Penguin Classics, 1967).

Julius Caesar, *Bellum Gallium*, trans. S. A. Handford, as *The Conquest of Gaul* (Penguin Classics, 1976).

Juvenal, *Satirae*, trans. E. G. Hardy, as *Satires* (Loeb Classic Library, 1950).

Livy, Books I–V, trans. A. de Selincourt, as *The Early History of Rome from its Foundation* (Penguin Classics, 1969).

Livy, Books VI–X, trans. B. Radice, as *Rome and Italy* (Penguin Classics, 1982)

Livy, Books XXI–XXX, trans. A. de Selincourt, as *The War with Hannibal* (Penguin Classics, 1972).

Livy, Books XXXI–XLV, trans. H. Bettenson, as *Rome and the Mediterranean* (Penguin Classics, 1976).

Maurice, *Strategikon: Handbook of Byzantine Military Strategy*, trans. G. T. Dennis (University of Pennsylvania Press, 1984).

Pausanias, Books I–X, trans. W. H. Jones and H. A. Ormerod, 4 vols (Loeb Classic Library, 1918–35).

Petronius, *Satyricon*, trans. M. Statilii (1669–71)

Pliny the Elder, *Natural History*, trans. H. Rackham et al., 10 vols (Loeb Classic Library, 1938–67).

Plutarch, *Camillus*, vol. II, trans. B. Perrin (Loeb Classic Library, 1914).

Plutarch, *Coriolanus, F. Maximus, Marcellus, Cato the elder, T. and G. Gracchus, Sertorius, Brutus, M. Anthony*, trans. I. Scott-Kilvert, as *The Makers of Rome* (Penguin Classics, 1965).

Plutarch, *Marius, Sulla, Crassus, Pompey, Caesar, Cicero*, trans. R. Warner, as *Fall of the Roman Republic* (Penguin Classics, 1972).

Polybius *Histories*, trans. I. Scott-Kilvert, as *The Rise of the Roman Empire* (Penguin Classics, 1979).

Procopius, *History of the Wars*, trans. H. B. Dewing, 7 vols (Loeb Classic Library, 1914–54).

Sallust, *Bellum Iugurthinum & Catilinae Coniuratio*, trans. S. A. Handford, as *Jugurthine War/ Conspiracy of Catiline* (Penguin Classics, 1970).

Strabo, *Geography*, Books III–V, Vol. II, trans. H. L. Jones, as *The Geography of Strabo* (Loeb Classical Library, 1923)

Tarruntenus Paternus, *Digesta: Corpus Iuris Civilis*, vol. 1, ed. T. Mommsen (Berlin, 1872).

Tacitus, *Annales*, trans. M. Grant, as *The Annals of Imperial Rome* (Penguin Classics, 1973).

Tacitus, *Agricola* and *Germania*, trans. S. A. Handford (Penguin Classics, 1971).

Tacitus, *Historiae*, trans. K. Wellesley, as *The Histories* (Penguin Classics, 1972).

Theophrastus, *De Lapidibus*, ed. D. E. Eichholz (Clarendon Press, 1965).

Theophrastus, *Historia Plantarum*, trans. A. F. Hort, 2 vols (Loeb Classic Library, 1916).

Theophrastus, *De Igne*, ed. V. Coutant (Van Gorcum, 1971).

Theophrastus, *On Mines*, (cf. *De Lapidibus* I and Diogenes Laertius V, 44).

Valerius Maximus, Books I–V, vol. I, trans. D. R. Shackleton (Loeb Classic Library, 2000).

Books VI–IX, vol. II, trans. J. Henderson (Loeb Classic Library, 2000).

Vegetius, *Epitoma Rei Militaris*, trans. N. P. Milner, as *Epitome of Military Science* (Liverpool University Press, 1993).

Virgil, *Georgics*, trans. W. Sotheby (London, 1800).

MODERN SOURCES

Abbott, F. F. 1915. 'The Colonizing Policy of the Romans from 123 to 31 BC', *Classical Philology*, vol. 10, No. 4, pp. 365–380.

Adam, J. P. 2005. *Roman Building Materials and Techniques*, London.

Alfs, J. 1941. 'Der Bewegliche Metalpanzer in Römischen Heer', *Zeitschrift für Historische Waffen und Kostumkunde*, 3–4, pp. 69–126.

Ando, C. 2007. 'The Army and the Urban Elite: A Competition for Power', *A Companion to the Roman Army*, ed. P. Erdkamp, Oxford, pp. 359–378.

Anglim, S. and P. G. Jestice, R. S. Rice, S. M. Rusch, J. Serrati, 2002. *Fighting Techniques of the Ancient World*, Kent.

Armbruster, B. and H. Eilbracht, 2006. 'Technological Aspects of the Viking Age Gold Treasure from Hiddensee, Germany' in 'The Art of the Early Medieval Goldsmith', *Journal of the Historical Metallurgy Society*, vol. 40, part 1, Wakefield, pp. 27–41.

Bain, E. C. 1945. *Functions of the Alloying Elements in Steel*, American Society for Metals, Cleveland, Ohio.

Bergman, F. 1939. 'Archaeological Researches in Sinkiang, Especially the Lop-nor Region', vol. 1, *Reports from the Scientific Expedition to the Northwestern Provinces of China under the Leadership of Dr. Sven Hedin / Scientific Expedition to the North-Western Provinces of China: Publication 7*, Stockholm, pp. 121–124.

Bestwick, J. D. and J. H. Cleland, 1974. 'Metalworking in the North-West', *Roman Manchester*, ed. G. D. B. Jones, Manchester Excavation Committee, Altrincham.

Bidwell, P. 2001. 'A Probable Roman Shipwreck on the Herd Sand at South Shields', *The Arbeia Journal* 6–7, pp. 1997–98, South Shields.

Bidwell, P. 1997. *Roman Forts in Britain*, English Heritage, London.

Biek, L. 1978. 'A First-Century Shield from Doncaster, Yorkshire', Appendix II: 'Examination of the Shield at the Ancient Monuments Laboratory', reprinted from *Britannia*, vol. 9, Society for Promotion of Roman Studies (SPRS), London.

Birley, A. and J. Blake, 2005. *Vindolanda Excavations 2003–2004*, Hexham.

Birley, A. R. 2007. 'Making Emperors. Imperial Instrument or Independent Force?', *A Companion to the Roman Army*, ed. P. Erdkamp, Oxford, pp. 379–394.

Birley, E. 1932. 'Roman Garrisons in the North of Britain', *Journal of Roman Studies*, vol. 22, part 1: 'Papers dedicated to Sir George MacDonald KCB (1932)', pp. 55–59.

Birley, R. 1977. *Vindolanda: A Roman Frontier Post on Hadrian's Wall*, London.

Bishop, M. C. 1989a. *Proceedings of the Fifth Roman Military Equipment Conference*, ed. C. van Driel-Murray, BAR International Series, 476, Oxford.

Bishop, M. C. 1989b. 'The Composition of Some Copper-Alloy Artefacts from Longthorpe', *Arma*, vol. 1.2.

Bishop, M.C. 1998. 'The Development of *Lorica Segmentata*', *Arma*, vol. 10, pp. 10–13.

Bishop, M. C. 1985. *Proceedings of the Second Roman Military Equipment Conference*, ed. M. C. Bishop, BAR International Series, 275, Oxford.

Bishop, M. C. 1987. *Proceedings of the Third Roman Military Equipment Conference*, ed. M. Dawson, BAR International Series, 336, Oxford.

Bishop, M. C. 1988. *Proceedings of the Fourth Roman Military Equipment Conference*, ed. J. C. N. Coulston, BAR International Series, 394, Oxford.

Bishop, M. C. 1989a. 'Belt Fittings in Buxton Museum', *Arma*, vol. 1.1

Bishop, M.C. 2002. '*Lorica Segmentata* Vol. I', *Journal for Roman Military Equipment Studies*, Armatura Press.

Bishop, M. C. and L. Allason-Jones, 1988. *Excavations at Roman Corbridge, The Hoard*, English Heritage, London.

Bishop, M. C. and J. C. N Coulston, 1993. *Roman Military Equipment from the Punic Wars to the Fall of Rome*. London.

Bishop, M. C. and J. C. N. Coulston, 2006. *Roman Military Equipment from the Punic Wars to the Fall of Rome*, 2nd edn, Oxford.

Bishop, M. C. and J. N. Dore, 1988. *Corbridge: Excavations of the Roman Fort and Town 1947–80*, English Heritage, London.

Black, E. W. 1994. 'Villa Owners: Romano-British Gentlemen and Officers', *Britannia*, vol. 25, pp. 99–110.

Boren, H. C. 1956. 'Livius Drusus, t.p. 122, and his Anti-Gracchan Program', *The Classical Journal*, vol. 52, No. 1, pp. 27–36.

Boren, H. C. 1958. 'The Urban Side of the Gracchan Economic Crisis', *The American Historical Review*, vol. 63, No. 4, pp. 890–902.

Boren, H. C. 1961. 'Tiberius Gracchus: The Opposition View', *American Journal of Philology*, vol. 82, No. 4, pp. 358–369.

Brailsford, J. W. 1962. *Antiquities from Hod Hill, in the Durden Collection*, British Museum, London.

Braund, D. 1992. 'A Roman Helmet from Kakheti (Eastern Georgia, Transcaucasia)' *Arma*, vol. 4.1, pp. 9–10.

Bridgewater, N. P. 1965. 'Romano-British Ironworking near Ariconium', *Trans. Woolhope Natur. Field Club* 38, 2, pp. 179-191.

Broadhead, W. 2007. 'Colonization, Land Distribution, and Veteran Settlement', *A Companion to the Roman Army*, ed. P. Erdkamp, Oxford, pp. 148–163.

Bruce-Mitford, R. L. S. 1964. *Antiquities of Roman Britain*, British Museum, London.

Buckland, P. 1978. 'A First-Century Shield from Doncaster, Yorkshire', reprinted from *Britannia*, vol. 9, Society for Promotion of Roman Studies (SPRS), London.

Buckland, P. C. 1986. *Roman South Yorkshire: A Source Book*. Sheffield.

Bunz, K. and W. Spickermann, 2006. *KALKRIESE, Die Örtlichkeit der Varusschlacht, Ein Studentisches Projekt an der Universität Osnabrück*, http://www.geschichte.uni-osnabrueck.de/projekt, 5.12.2006.

Burns, M. 2003. *The Homogenisation of Military Equipment under the Roman Republic*, Institute of Archaeology, University College London, in 'Romanization?', *Digressus* Supplement 1, pp. 60–85, http://www.digressus.org.

Buxton, K. and C. Howard-Davis, J. Huntley, H. Kenward, 2000. 'Phase 4: The Military Fabrica and Extramural Annexe. Bremetenacum', *Excavations at Roman Ribchester, 1980, 1989–1990*, ed. K. Buxton and C. Howard-Davis, Lancaster.

Cagniart, P. 2007. 'The Late Republican Army', *A Companion to the Roman Army*, ed. P. Erdkamp, Oxford, pp. 80–95.

Campbell, B. 2000. *The Roman Army 31BC – AD337: A Source Book*, London.

Caruana, I. 1993. 'A Third-Century *Lorica Segmentata* Back-Plate from Carlisle', *Arma*, vol. 5, pp. 15–18.

Cary, M. and H. Scullard, 1979. *A History of Rome*, 3rd edn, London.

Champion, T. and C. Gamble, S. Shennon, A. Whittle, 1984. *Prehistoric Europe*, London.

Chevallier, R. 1976. *Roman Roads*, London.

Cichorius, C. 1896. *Die Reliefs der Traianssäule*, vol. II (1896), vol. III (1900), Berlin.

Cleere, H. F. 1970. *The Romano-British Industrial Site at Bardown, Wadhurst, Chichester*, Sussex Archaeological Society, Occasional. Paper 1

Cleere, H. F. 1971. 'Ironmaking in a Roman furnace', *Britannia*, vol. 2, pp. 203–217.

Cleere, H. F. 1972. 'The Classification of Early Iron Smelting furnaces', *The Antiquaries Journal*, 52 (1), pp. 8–23.

Cleere, H. F. 1976. 'Operating Parameters for Roman Iron Works', *Bulletin of the Institute of Archaeology*, 13, pp. 233–246.

Cleere, H. F. and D. Crossley, 1985. *The Iron Industry of the Weald*, Leicester.

Clemetson, J. B. 1993. 'Roman Scale Armour', *Arma*, vol. 5.1, pp. 8–10.

Coghlan, H. H. 1977. *Notes on Prehistoric and Early Iron in the Old World*, Oxford, Pitt Rivers Museum, Occasional Papers on Technology, No. 8 (2).

Connolly, P. 1975. *The Roman Army*, London.

Connolly, P. 1977. *The Greek Armies*, London.

Connolly, P. 1978. *Hannibal and the Enemies of Rome*, London.

Connolly, P. 1981. *Greece and Rome at War*, London.

Cornell, T. J. 1997. *The Beginnings of Rome: Italy and Rome from the Bronze Age to the Punic Wars (c. 1000 – 264 BC)*, London.

COTANCE, 2007. 'The Production of Leather', The European Leather Association, http://www.euroleather.com/process.htm 12/06/07.

Cottrell, L. 1992. *Hannibal: Enemy of Rome*, New York.

Couissin, P. 1926. *Les Armes Romaines*, Paris.

Coulston, J. C. N. 1985. 'Roman Archery Equipment', in M. C. Bishop (ed.), *The Production and Distribution of Roman Military Equipment. Proceedings of the Second Roman Military Equipment Seminar*, BAR International Series, 275, Oxford, 1985, pp. 220–366.

Coulston, J. C. N. 1992. 'Preliminary Note on Scale Armour from Carpow, Perthshire', *Arma*, vol. 4.2, pp. 21–22.

Coulston, J. C. N. 1995. 'Sculpture of an Armoured Figure at Alba Iulia, Romania', *Arma*, vol. 7, pp. 13–17.

Crone, P. 2007. 'Quraysh and the Roman army: Making Sense of the Meccan Leather Trade', *Bulletin of SOAS*, 70, 1, pp. 63–88.

Croom, A. T. 2001. 'A Ring Mail Shirt from South Shields Roman Fort', *The Arbeia Journal*, vol. 6–7 1997–98, Tyne and Weir Museums Archaeology Dept, pp. 55–60.

Crow, J. 2004. *Housesteads: A Fort and Garrison on Hadrian's Wall*, Stroud.

Crumlin-Pedersen, O. and A. Trakadas, 2003. *Hjortspring: A Pre-Roman Iron Age Warship in Context*, Copenhagen.

Curle, J. 1911. *A Roman Frontier Post and its People: The Fort at Newstead*, Glasgow.

Cuvigny, H. 1996. 'The Amount of Wages Paid to the Quarry Workers at Mons Claudianus', *The Journal of Roman Studies*, vol. 86, pp. 139–145.

Davies, J. L. 1977. 'Roman Arrowheads from Dinorban and the "Sagittarii" of the Roman Army', *Britannia*, vol. 8, pp. 257–270.

Davies, O. 1935. *Roman Mines in Europe*, Oxford.

Davies, P. J. E. 1997. 'The Politics of Perpetuation: Trajan's Column and the Art of Commemoration', *American Journal of Archaeology*, vol. 101, pp. 41–65.

De Blois, L. 2007. 'Army and General in the Late Roman Republic', *A Companion to the Roman Army*, ed. P. Erdkamp, Oxford, pp. 164–180.

De Ligt, L. 2007. 'Roman Manpower and Recruitment during the Middle Republic', *A Companion to the Roman Army*, ed. P. Erdkamp, Oxford, pp. 114–131.

De Navarro, J. M. 1972. *The Finds From the Site of La Tene, I; Scabbards and the Swords Found in Them*, London.

Dearne, M. J. and K. Branigan, 1993. 'The Use of Coal in Roman Britain', *Antiquaries Journal*, 75, pp. 71–105.

Demetz, S. 1998. *The Guide*, South Tyrol Museum of Archaeology.

Dool, J. 1986. 'Derby Racecourse: Excavations on the Roman Settlement, 1970', *Derbyshire Archaeological Journal* 105, pp. 155–221.

Dore J. N. 2001. *Corbridge Roman Site*, English Heritage, London.

Down, A. 1978. *Chichester Excavations 3*, Chichester.

Down, A. 1981. *Chichester Excavations 5*, Chichester.

Eck, W. 2007. *The Age of Augustus*, 2nd edn, Oxford.

Elton, H. 2007. 'Army and Battle in the Age of Justinian (527–65)', *A Companion to the Roman Army*, ed. P. Erdkamp, Oxford, pp. 532–550.

Erdkamp, P. 2007. *A Companion to the Roman Army*, Oxford.

Erdkamp, P. 2007. 'War and State Formation in the Roman Republic', *A Companion to the Roman Army*, ed. P. Erdkamp, Oxford, pp. 96–113.

Fagan, B. 2004. *The Seventy Great Inventions of the Ancient World*, London.

Fernando, D. 2007. 'Leather Trade', http://www.ferdinando.org.uk/leather.htm 12/06/07.

Feugère, M. 2002. *Weapons of the Romans*, Stroud.

Florescu, F. B. 1965. *Das Siegesdenkmal von Adamklissi: Tropaeum Traiani*, Bucharest-Bonn.

Florescu, F. B. 1969. *Die Traianssäule: Grundfragen und Tafeln*, Bucharest-Bonn.

Forsythe, G. 2007. 'The Army and Centuriate Organization in Early Rome', *A Companion to the Roman Army*, ed. P. Erdkamp, Oxford, pp. 24–42.

Fox, C. 1958. *Pattern and Purpose: A Survey of Early Celtic Art in Britain*, Cardiff.

Franzius, G. 1995. 'Die Romische Funde Aus Kalkriese 1987–95', *Proceedings of the International Roman Military Equipment Conference*, JRMES, vol. 6, pp. 69–88.

Fulford, M. and D. Sim, A. Doig, 2004. 'The Production of Roman Ferrous Armour: A Metallographic Survey of Material from Britain, Denmark, Germany, and its implications', *Journal of Roman Archaeology*, vol. 17, pp. 197–220.

Gawlikowski, M. 1987. 'The Roman Frontier on the Euphrates', *Mesopotamia*, 22, pp. 77–80.

Geer, R. M. 1939. 'III – Notes on the Land Law of Tiberius Gracchus', *Transactions and Proceedings of the American Philological Association*, vol. 70, pp. 30–36.

Gichon, M. 1993. 'Reflections on the *Lorica*, According to Josephus', *Arma*, vol. 5, pp. 10–12.

Gillam, J. 1977. 'The Roman Forts at Corbridge', *Archaeologia Aeliana*, 5th series, vol. 5, Newcastle-upon-Tyne, pp. 47–74.

Gilliam, J. F. 1946. 'XVII Milites Caligati', *Transactions and Proceedings of American Philological Association*, vol. 77, 183–191.

Gilliver, C. M. 1996. 'Mons Graupius and the Role of Auxiliaries in Battle', *Greece and Rome*, 2nd series, vol. 43, No. 1, pp. 54–67.

Gilliver, C. M. 2007. 'The Augustan Reform and the Structure of the Imperial Army', *A Companion to the Roman Army*, ed. P. Erdkamp, Oxford, pp. 180–200.

Gilliver, C. M. 1998. *The Roman Art of War*, Stroud.

Godfrey E. and M. van Nie, 2004. 'Germanic Ultrahigh Carbon Steel Punch of the Late Roman-Iron Age', *Journal of Archaeological Science*, vol. 31, issue 8, pp. 1117–1125.

Goldsworthy, A. 2000. *Roman Warfare*, London.

Goldsworthy, A. 2003. *The Complete Roman Army*, London.

Gryphius, A. 2003. *Varus Kurier*, Kalkriese, vol. 9–1, pp. 4–5.

Gwyn Morgan, M. and J. A. Walsh, 1978. 'Tiberius Gracchus (TR.PL. 133BC), The Numantine Affair, and the Deposition of M. Octavius', *Classical Philosophy*, vol. 73, No. 3, pp. 200–210.

Halpin, A. 1997. 'Military Archery in Medieval Ireland: Archaeology and History', *Military Studies in Medieval Europe – Papers of the 'Medieval Europe Brugge 1997' Conference*, vol 1, Dublin.

Hanel, N. 2007. 'Military Camps, Canabae and Vici. The Archaeological Evidence', *A Companion to the Roman Army*, ed. P. Erdkamp, Oxford, pp. 395–416.

Hannah, I. C. 1932. 'Roman Blast Furnace in Lincolnshire', *The Antiquaries Journal*, vol. 12, pp. 262–268.

Hanson, W. S. and C. M. Daniels, J. N. Dore, J. P. Gillam, 1979. 'The Agricolan Supply Base at Red House, Corbridge', *Archaeologia Aeliana*, 5th Series, vol. 7, Society of Antiquaries, Newcastle-upon-Tyne.

Hardy, R. 1986. *Longbow: A Social and Military History*, 2nd edn, Portsmouth.

Healy, J. F. 1978. *Mining and Metallurgy in the Greek and Roman World*, London.

Hekster, O. 2007. 'The Roman Army and Propaganda', *A Companion to the Roman Army*, ed. P. Erdkamp, Oxford, pp. 339–358.

Herz, P. 2007. 'Finances and Costs of the Roman Army', *A Companion to the Roman Army*, ed. P. Erdkamp, Oxford, pp. 306–322.

Hodges, H. 1976. *Artefacts: An Introduction to Early Materials and Technology*, London.

Hodgson, N. and P. T. Bidwell, 2004. 'Auxiliary Barracks in a New Light: Recent Discoveries on Hadrian's Wall', *Britannia* vol. 35, 121–157.

Holder, P. A. 1982. *The Roman Army in Britain*, London.

Holroyd, M. 1928. 'The Jugurthine War: Was Marius or Metellus the real victor?', *Journal of Roman Studies*, vol. 18, pp. 1–20.

Hölscher, T. 2003. 'Images of War in Greece and Rome: Between Military Practice, Public Memory and Cultural Symbolism', *The Society for the Promotion of Roman Studies*, vol. 93, pp. 1–17, plates 1–7.

Hope, V. M. 2003. 'Trophies and Tombstones Commemorating the Roman Soldier', *World Archaeology*, vol. 35 (1), pp. 79–97.

Howatson, M. C. 1997. *The Oxford Companion to Classical Literature*, Oxford.

Hoyos, D. 2007. 'The Age of Overseas Expansion', *A Companion to the Roman Army*, ed. P. Erdkamp, Oxford, pp. 63–79.

Ilkjaer, J. 2002. *Illerup Adal – Archaeology as a Magic Mirror*, Jutland.

Inker, P. 2008. *Caesar's Gallic Triumph: Alesia 52 BC*, Barnsley.

Izquierdo, P. and J. M. Solias Aris, 2000. *Two Bronze Helmets of Etruscan Typology from a Roman Wreck*, Nordic Underwater Archaeology.

James, S. 1988. 'The *Fabricae*: State Arms Factories of the Later Roman Empire', *Military Equipment and the Identity of Roman Soldiers, Proceedings of 4th Roman Military Equipment Conference* (ROMEC), ed. J.C. Coulston, BAR International Series, 394, Oxford, 257–331.

James, S. 2004. *Excavations at Dura Europos 1928–1937, Final Report VII*, British Museum Press.

Jarrett, M. G. 1994. 'Non-Legionary Troops in Roman Britain: Part One, The Units', *Britannia*, vol. 25, pp. 35–77.

Jenkins, A. S. 1901. 'The "Trajan Reliefs" in the Roman Forum', *American Journal of Archaeology*, 2nd Series, vol. 5, No. 1, pp. 58–82.

Jessop, O. 1996. 'New Artefact Typology for the Study of Medieval Arrowheads', *Medieval Archaeology*, vol. 40, pp. 192–205.

Johnson, A. 1983. *Roman Forts of the 1st and 2nd Centuries AD in Britain and the German Provinces*, London.

Jones G. D. B. and S. Grealey, 1974. *Roman Manchester*, Manchester Excavation Committee, Altrincham.

Jones, B. and D. Mattingly, 1990. *An Atlas of Roman Britain*, London.

Jope, E. M. 1971. *Prehistoric and Roman Studies Commemorating the Opening of the Department of Prehistoric and Romano-British Antiquities*, ed. G. de G. Sieveking, London, pp. 61–69.

Jørgensen, L. and B. Torgaard, L. Gebauer Thomsen, 2003. *The Spoils of Victory – The North in the Shadow of the Roman Empire*, National Museum of Denmark.

Junkelmann, M. 1986. *Die Legionen des Augustus. Der römische Soldat im archäologischen Experiment*, Mainz.

Junkelmann, M. 2000. *Römische Helme*, Band VIII, Axel Guttmann Collection, Mainz.

Kehne, P. 2007. 'War – and Peacetime Logistics: Supplying Imperial Armies in East and West', *A Companion to the Roman Army*, ed. P. Erdkamp, Oxford, pp. 323–338.

Kelly, K. S. 2004. 'Imputrescible Corium: The Production and Structure of Pre-1900 Bookbinding Leather', Conservation Portfolio, Master of Science in Information Studies with Certificate of Advanced Study in Conservation of Library and Archival Materials, Kilgarlin Center for Preservation of the Cultural Record, University of Texas at Austin, www.ischool. utexas.edu/~katkelly/coursework/imputrescible.html, 12/6/07.

Keppie, L. 1998. *The Making of the Roman Army from Republic to Empire*, London.

Kimmig, W. 1940. 'Ein Keltenschild aus Agypten', *Germania*, 24, pp. 106–111.

Kippen, C. 2007. 'The History of Footwear – Sandals', Curtin University of Technology, Dept. of Podiatry, Perth WA, http://podiatry.curtin.edu.au/sandal.html, 18/06/07.

Klindt-Jensen, O. 1949. *Acta Archaeologica*, 20, pp. 1–230, fig. 89.

Klostermann, P. 1997. 'Chainmail Construction Page', http://home.t-online.de/home/Tempora-Nostra/ekeetthm.htm, 25/01/02.

Klumbach, H. 1974. *Römische Helme aus Niedergermanien*, Rheinland, Cologne.

Koninklijke Bibliotheek, 2007. 'Overview of Leather and Parchment Manufacture', National Library of the Netherlands, http://www.kb.nl/cons/leather/chapter1-en.html, 18/06/07.

Lancaster, L. 1998. 'Building Trajan's Markets', *American Journal of Archaeology*, vol. 102, pp. 283–308.

Lancaster, L. 1999. 'Building Trajan's Column', *American Journal of Archaeology*, vol. 103, pp. 419–439.

Lancaster, L. 2000. 'Building Trajan's Markets 2: The Construction Process', *American Journal of Archaeology*, vol. 104, pp. 755–785.

Le Bohec, Y. 2001. *The Imperial Roman Army*, London.

Le Glay, M. and J. L. Voisin, Y. Le Bohec, 2005. *A History of Rome*, 3rd edn, trans. A. Nevill, additional material by D. Cherry and D. G. Kyle, Oxford.

Lendering, J. 2006. 'The Mainz Pedestals', http://www.livius.org/a/germany/mainz, 29/06/06.

Lepper, F. and S. Frere, 1988. *Trajan's Column. A New Edition of the Cichorius Plates*, Gloucester.

Leriche P. and A. Mahmoud, 1994. 'Doura Europos, Bilan des Recherches Recentes', *Comptes Rendues de l'Academie des Inscriptions et Belles-Lettres*, p. 411.

Leriche, P. 1996. 'Dura Europos', *Encyclopaedia Iranica* viii–6.

Levene, D. S. 1992. 'Sallust's Jugurtha: An "Historical Fragment"', *Journal of Roman Studies*, vol. 82, pp. 53–70.

Lewis, M. J. T. 1997. *Millstone and Hammer: The Origins of Water Power*, London.

Liebeschuetz, W. 2007. 'Warlords and Landlords', *A Companion to the Roman Army*, ed. P. Erdkamp, Oxford, pp. 479–494.

Lintott, A. 1994. 'The Gracchi', *The Classical Review*, Oxford University Press, pp. 346–347.

Lucie-Smith, E. 1971. *A Concise History of French Painting*, London.

Lucke, W. 1962. *Die Situla in Providence (Rhode Island): Ein Beitrag zur Situlenkunst des Osthallstattkreises*, ed. O. H. Frey, Berlin.

Luttwark, E. 1999. *The Grand Strategy of the Roman Empire: From the First Century AD to the Third*, London.

MacQueen, J. G. 1986. *The Hittites*, London.

Masson, G. 1973. *A Concise History of Republican Rome*, London.

Mastrotto, G. 2007. 'History – Tanning', http://www.mastrotto.com/jsp/en/tanneryhistory/index.jsp, 12/6/07.

Matyszak, P. 2003. *Chronicle of the Roman Republic: The Rulers of Ancient Rome from Romulus to Augustus*, London.

Matyszak, P. 2004. *The Enemies of Rome, from Hannibal to Attila the Hun*, London.

Maxfield, V.A. 1986. 'Pre-Flavian Forts and their Garrisons', *Britannia*, vol. 17, pp. 59–72.

May, T. 1896. *Transactions on the Altar and Other Relics, Found During Recent Excavations (1895–96) on the Site of the Roman Station at Wilderspool (Veratinum)*, Warrington.

May, T. 1899. *The Roman Fortifications at Wilderspool*, Warrington.

May, T. 1922. *The Roman Forts at Templeborough near Rotherham*, Rotherham.

McDermott, W. C. 1970. 'Milites Gregarii', *Greece and Rome*, 2nd series, vol. 17, No. 2, pp. 185–196.

Morris, P. 1979. *Agricultural Buildings in Roman Britain*, BAR, British series 70, Oxford.

Negin, A. E. 1998. 'Sarmatian Cataphracts as prototypes for Roman *Equites Cataphractarii*', *Journal for Roman Military Equipment Studies* (JRMES) 9, pp. 71–74.

Osborne, H. 1970. *Oxford Companion to Art*, ed. H. Osborne, Oxford.

Packer, J. and K. L. Sarring, R. M. Sheldon, 1988. 'A New Excavation in Trajan's Forum', *American Journal of Archaeology*, vol. 87, No. 2, pp. 165–172, plates 21–23.

Paddock, J. 1985. 'Some Changes in the Manufacture and Supply of Roman Bronze Helmets Under the Late Republic and Early Empire', *The Production and Distribution of Roman Military Equipment, Proceedings of 2nd Roman Military Equipment Conference* (ROMEC), ed. M. C. Bishop, BAR International Series, 275, Oxford.

Paterson, T. 2007. 'Glue Used by the Romans Has Stuck Around for 2,000 Years', *The Independent*, http://news.independent.co.uk/europe/article3226417.ece, 08/12/07.

Pearlman, M. 1966. *The Zealots of Masada: Story of a Dig*, Israel.

Phang, S. E. 2007. 'Military Documents, Language and Literacy', *A Companion to the Roman Army*, ed. P. Erdkamp, Oxford, pp. 286–305.

Piggott, S. 1965. *Ancient Europe, From the Beginnings of Agriculture to Classical Antiquity*, Chicago.

Poulter, A. G. 1988. 'Certain Doubts and Doubtful Conclusions: the *Lorica Segmentata* from Newstead and the Antonine garrison', *Military Equipment and the Identity of Roman Soldiers: Proceedings of the Fourth Military Equipment Conference*, ed. J. C. Coulston. BAR International Series, 394, Oxford.

Quesada Sanz, F. 1997. 'Montefortino-Type and Related Helmets in the Iberian Peninsula', *Journal of Roman Military Equipment Studies*, 8, pp. 151–166.

Radice, B. 1973. *Who's Who in the Ancient World*, London.

Radley, J. and M. Plant, 1969a. 'Roman Remains from South Yorkshire and North-East Derbyshire', *Transactions of the Hunter Archaeological Society*, 9, pp. 158–169.

Radley, J. and M. Plant, 1969b. 'An Extension to the Roman Site at Kiveton', *Transactions of the Hunter Archaeological Society*, 9, pp. 229–251.

Radley, J. and M. Plant, 1969c. 'A Romano-British Field System and Other Finds at South Anston', *Transactions of the Hunter Archaeological Society*, 9, pp. 252–264.

Rawes, B. 1991. 'A Prehistoric and Romano-British settlement at Vineyards Farm, Charlton Kings, Gloucestershire', *Transactions of the Bristol and Gloucestershire Archaeological Society*, 109, pp. 25–90.

Rawlings, L. 2007. 'Army and Battle during the Conquest of Italy (350–264 BC)', *A Companion to the Roman Army*, ed. P. Erdkamp, Oxford, pp. 45–62.

Rees, W. G. 1995. 'The Physics of Medieval Archery', *Physics Review* 4 (3), pp. 2–5.

Rich, J. 2007. 'Warfare and the Army in Early Rome', *A Companion to the Roman Army*, ed. P. Erdkamp, Oxford, pp. 7–23.

Richmond, I. A. 1967. 'Adamklissi', *Papers of the British School at Rome*, vol. 35, pp. 34–35.

Richmond, I. A. 1982. *Trajan's Army on Trajan's Column*, London.

Robinson, C. E. 1971. *A History of Rome, from 753 BC to AD 410*, London.

Rosenstein, N. 2007. 'Military Command, Political Power and the Republican Elite', *A Companion to the Roman Army*, ed. P. Erdkamp, Oxford, pp. 132–147.

Rossi, L. 1971. *Trajan's Column and the Dacian Wars*, trans. J. M. C. Toynbee, New York.

Rostovtzeff, M. 1938. *Dura Europos and its Art*, Oxford.

Rostovtzeff, M. 1959. *Social and Economic History of the Roman Empire*, 2nd edn, Oxford.

Russell-Robinson, H. 1975. *The Armour of Imperial Rome*, London.

Saddington, D. B. 2007. 'Classes: The Evolution of the Roman Imperial Fleets', *A Companion to the Roman Army*, ed. P. Erdkamp, Oxford, pp. 201–217.

Salway, P. 1980. *Roman Britain*, Oxford.

Sampson, G. C. 2008. *The Defeat of Rome: Crassus, Carrhae and the Invasion of the East*, Barnsley.

Sanders, N. K. 1987. *The Sea Peoples*, London.

Scheidel, W. 2007. 'Marriage, Families and Survival: Demographic Aspects', *A Companion to the Roman Army*, ed. P. Erdkamp, Oxford, pp. 417–434.

Schoppa, H. 1961. *Die Funde aus dem Vicus des Steinkastells Hofheim*, Wiesbaden.

Scullard, H. H. 1980. *A History of the Roman World 753 to 146 BC*, 4th edn, London.

Scullard, H. H. 1970. *From the Gracchi to Nero, A History of Rome from 133BC to AD68*, London.

Sekunda, N. and S. Northwood, R. Hook, 1999. *Early Roman Armies*, Osprey – Men at Arms series, 283, London.

Sherwin-White, A. N. 1982. 'The Lex Repetundarum and the Political ideas of Gaius Gracchus', *Journal of Roman Studies*, vol. 72, pp. 18–31.

Shotter, D. 1996. *The Roman Frontier in Britain: Hadrian's Wall, The Antonine Wall and the Roman Policy in the North*, Carnegie Publications.

Sim, D. 1998. *Beyond the Bloom: Bloom Refining and Iron Artefact Production in the Roman World*, ed. Isabel Ridge, BAR International Series, 725, Oxford.

Sim, D. 1998. 'Report on 2 Sections of *Lorica Segmentata* found at Vindolanda', *Arma*, vol. 10, p. 9.

Sim, D. 2005. Presentation at the Carlisle Millennium Conference.

Sim, D. and I. Ridge, 2002. *Iron for the Eagles*, Stroud.

Simkins, M. 1990. '*Lorica Segmentata*', *Arma*, vol. 2, p. 11.

Snodgrass, A. M. 1967. *Arms and Armour of the Greeks*, London.

Sommer, C. S. 1989. 'The Inner and Outer Relations of the Military Fort to its Vicus', *Proceedings of the Fifth Roman Military Equipment Conference*, ed. C. van Driel-Murray, BAR International Series, 476, Oxford.

Sommer, C. S. 1984. *The Military Vici in Roman Britain*, BAR British Series, 129.

Southern, P. 1988. 'The Numeri of the Roman Imperial Army', *Britannia*, vol. 10, pp. 81–140.

Sparkes, I. G. 1991. *Woodland Craftsmen*, Shire Album, 25, Princes Risborough.

Starley, D. 2005. '*De Re Metallica*. The Uses of Metal in the Middle Ages', *AVISTA Studies in the History of Medieval Technology, Science and Art*, ed. Robert Bork, vol. 4, Ashgate.

Stephenson I. P. and K. R. Dixon, 2003. *Roman Cavalry Equipment*, Stroud.

Stephenson, I. P. 2001. *Roman Infantry Equipment: The Later Empire*, Stroud.

Stickler, T. 2007. 'The Foederati', *A Companion to the Roman Army*, ed. P. Erdkamp, Oxford, pp. 495–514.

Stiebel, G. D. and J. Magness, 2007. 'The Military Equipment from Masada', *Masada VIII: The Yigael Yadin Excavations 1963–1965, Final Reports*, Jerusalem, pp. 1–94.

Stjernquist, B. 1955. 'Simris – "On Cultural Connections of Scania in the Roman Iron Age"', *Acta Archaeologia Lundensia*, 2.

Stoll, O. 2007. 'The Religions of the Armies', *A Companion to the Roman Army*, ed. P. Erdkamp, Oxford, pp. 451–476.

Strobel, K. 2007. 'Strategy and Army Structure between Septimus Severus and Constantine the Great', *A Companion to the Roman Army*, ed. P. Erdkamp, Oxford, pp. 267–285.

Sulimirski, T. 1954. 'Scythian Antiquities in Western Asia', *Artibus Asiae*, vol. 17, No 3/4, pp. 282–318.

Taylor, L. R. 1962. 'Forerunners of the Gracchi', *Journal of Roman Studies*, vol. 52, parts 1 and 2, pp. 19–27.

Teixidor, J. 1987. 'Parthian officials in Lower Mesopotamia', *Mesopotamia*, 22, pp. 187–188.

Thayer, W. 2001. 'The Romano-British Settlements', in Bill Thayer's *Roman Gazetteer*, http://www.roman-britain.org/places/_sin.htm, 02/02/01.

Thomas, M. 2001. 'Roman Military Headgear', www.hmforum/articles/mikethomas/romanheadgear/romanheadgear.htm, 02/02/01.

Thomas, M. 2003. *Lorica Segmentata*, vol. II, JRMES, Armatura Press.

Thorne, J. 2007. 'Battle, Tactics and the emergence of the *Limites* in the West', *A Companion to the Roman Army*, ed. P. Erdkamp, Oxford, pp. 218–234.

Trachsel, M. 1997. 'Ein tragbarer Giesserofen aus dem Legionslager von Vindonissa – Beschreibung, Rekonstruktion und Experiment', *Experimentelle Archaeologie Bilanz 1997*, Symposium in Bad Buchau Federsee Museum, October 1996, pp. 141–155.

Travis, J. R. 2008. *Coal in Roman Britain*, Bar British Series, 468.

Tylecote, R. F. 1976. *A History of Metallurgy in the British Isles*, The Metals Society, London.

Tylecote, R. F. 1986. *The Prehistory of Metallurgy in the British Isles*, The Institute of Metals. London.

Tylecote, R. F. 1987. *The Early History of Metallurgy in Europe*, London.

Ulrich, R. B. 2007. *Roman Woodworking*, Michigan.

Van Driel-Murray, C. 1985. 'The Production and Supply of Military Leatherwork in the First and Second Centuries AD: A Review of the Archaeological Evidence', *The Production and Distribution of Roman Military Equipment, Proceedings of 2nd Roman Military Equipment Conference* (ROMEC), ed. M. C. Bishop, BAR International Series, 275, pp. 43–48.

Van Driel-Murray, C. 1989. 'A Circular Shield Cover', *Arma*, vol. 1.2, pp. 18–19.

Van Driel-Murray, C. 1999. 'A Rectangular Shield Cover of the Coh. XV Voluntariorum C.R.', *Journal of Roman Military Equipment Studies*, vol. 10, pp. 45–54.

Von Fritz, K. 1943. 'XI – Sallust and the Attitude of the Roman Nobility at the Time of the Wars against Jugurtha (112–105 BC)', *Transactions and Proceedings of the American Philological Association*, vol. 74, pp. 134–168.

Von Groller, M. 1901a. 'Das Lager von Carnuntum', *Der Romische Limes in Osterreich* vol. I, Vienna.

Von Groller, M. 1901b. 'Romische Waffen', *Der Romische Limes in Osterreich* vol. II, Vienna.

Walthew, C. V. 1981. 'Possible Standard Units of Measurement in Roman Military Planning', *Britannia*, vol. 12, pp. 15–35.

Wamser, L. 2000. *Die Römer Zwischen Alpen und Nordmeer*, Mainz.

Warde Fowler, W. 1905. 'Notes on Gaius Gracchus', *The English Historical Review*, vol. 20 No. 77, pp. 209–227.

Warry, J. 1980. *Warfare in the Classical World*, London.

Webster, G. 1956. *The Roman Army*, Grosvenor Museum Publication, Chester.

Webster, G. 1964. 'Further Investigations on the Roman Fort at Waddon Hill', *Proceedings of the Dorset Natural History and Archaeological Society*, 86, pp. 135–49.

Webster, G. 1998. *The Roman Imperial Army of the First and Second centuries AD*, 3rd edn, London.

Wesch-Klein, G. 2007. 'Recruits and Veterans', *A Companion to the Roman Army*, ed. P. Erdkamp, Oxford, pp. 435–450.

Wheeler, E. L. 2007. 'The Army and the *Limes* in the East', *A Companion to the Roman Army*, ed. P. Erdkamp, Oxford, pp. 235–266.

Wheeler, H. 1986a. 'North-West Sector Excavations 1979–1980', *Derbyshire Archaeological Journal*, 105, pp. 38–153.

Wheeler, H. 1986b. 'The Racecourse Industrial Area 1969 and 1973', *Derbyshire Archaeological Journal*, vol. 105, p. 154.

Wheeler, H. 1986c. 'Conclusion: The Development of Roman Derby', *Derbyshire Archaeological Journal*, Vol. 105, pp. 300–304.

Wheeler, M. 1971. *Roman Art and Architecture*, London.

Wheeler, R. E. M. 1939. 'Report on the Excavations at Lydney Park', *Society of Antiquaries of London*, Report 9.

Whitby, M. 2007. 'Army and Society in the Late Roman World: A Context for Decline?', *A Companion to the Roman Army*, ed. P. Erdkamp, Oxford, pp. 515–531.

Wilbers-Rost, S. and H. P. Uerpmann, M. Uerpmann, B. Grosskopf, E. Tolksdorf-Lienemann, 2007. *Kalkriese 3. Interdisziplinäre Untersuchungen auf dem Oberesch in Kalkriese*, Mainz.

Wise, T. 1987. *Ancient Armies of the Middle East*, Osprey – Men at Arms series, 109, London.

Wood, M. 1981. *In Search of the Dark Ages*, London.

Yadin, Y. 1966. *Masada: Herod's Fortress and the Zealot's Last Stand*, Jerusalem.

Zant, J. 2005. Presentation at the Carlisle Millennium Conference.

Zotti, N. 2006. *La Situla della Certosa*, www.warfare.it/tattiche/situla_certosa.html, 10/12/06.

INDEX